Praise for *The Closing of the Muslim Mind*

"Bob Reilly's analysis provides a new starting point for American engagement with the Muslim world—one in which the true enemy is recognized as being not a religion, a social class, or a single terrorist group, but rather a misguided interpretation of an ancient belief system."
—**Edwin Feulner, Ph.D., president of the Heritage Foundation**

"This meticulously researched book provides the historical context that has given rise to violent Islamism, and explains why the ethos of multiculturalism in the West is a largely misguided response to this violence. A must-read for today's national security leaders."
—**John M. Poindexter, Vice Admiral, U.S. Navy, National Security Advisor to President Reagan**

"Reilly's scholarly work is timely and relevant. The battle within Islam between reason and revelation is an old one, yet it continues with potentially appalling consequences. This book is a masterpiece—a must-read for those who want to understand the struggles within the Islamic world today and why the Muslim mind is closed."
—**Patrick Sookhdeo, director of the Institute for the Study of Islam and Christianity**

"Somewhere, the Jewish sages said monotheism can become a form of idolatry. This has happened to Islam. But as Reilly says lucidly and persuasively in *The Closing of the Muslim Mind*, the most serious flaw in Sunni Islam is its erroneous conception of God. I urge especially every Jewish scholar—rabbis, theologians, philosophers, and political scientists—to place Reilly's book on his or her must-read list. You will not only be enlightened, but you may also see how the West might prevent a new Dark Ages."
—**Paul Eidelberg, president of the Foundation for Constitutional Democracy (Jerusalem)**

"Wars, terror, and expansion are caused and explained primarily by ideas. Economic or political explanations are only secondary. When religions rapidly expand by the success of arms, eventually they must explain themselves. Robert Reilly's book grasps the connection between the political forms and actions of Islam over against its own ideas developed to justify what Islam invariably does when it obtains political power. This book is a major, much-needed philosophical explication of what is the present Muslim mind, where it came from, and where it leads."
—**James V. Schall, S.J. Georgetown University, author of *The Life of the Mind***

"For some fourteen hundred years, Islam has been both intent on making the West Islamic and also in deep turmoil about its own identity and incapacity to govern itself. In this short book, Reilly offers an intelligent person's guide to both of these longtime struggles."

—**Michael Novak, American Enterprise Institute**

"A penetrating and sympathetic exploration of how minds closed for centuries might be reopened—and thus recivilized. Required reading for anyone who wants to understand the gravity of the jihadist threat and the imperative of meeting it by deepening the West's civilizational self-awareness."

—**George Weigel, Ethics and Public Policy Center, biographer of Pope John Paul II**

"Reilly explains how Islam's mainstream rejected reason and shows what happens to a civilization when it fails to give reason its due. Reilly's point, like Pope Benedict XVI's at Regensburg, applies to us as well as to Muslims: shortcutting reason for the sake of politically preferred conclusions closes minds and makes for lives nasty, brutish, and short. This book teaches and warns. Read it."

—**Angelo Codevilla, author of *Advice for War Presidents***

"I strongly recommend this book to anyone who wants to deeply understand the different ways of thinking within Islam and the phenomenon of radical Islam."

—**Tawfik Hamid, chair for the Study of Islamic Radicalism at the Potomac Institute for Policy Studies**

"Robert Reilly has done everyone—students of civilization, researchers into contemporary Islamist ideology, the general reader—a massive service by compiling an authoritative account of the troubling trajectory that Islamic thought has taken in history, and the inevitable political and ideological implications of this course. His work is not only comprehensive in its vision but also succinct, well-written, and eminently readable, and it will do much to project the study and analysis of the rise of Islamist extremism onto its more deeply rooted causes. *The Closing of the Muslim Mind* should become a work of reference not only for students of philosophy and comparative theology but also required reading for all who seek answers to the conundrum of violence that claims religious faith for its motivation and support."

—**Stephen Ulph, senior fellow at the Jamestown Foundation**

THE CLOSING OF THE MUSLIM MIND

How Intellectual Suicide Created the Modern Islamist Crisis

ROBERT R. REILLY

WILMINGTON, DELAWARE

Reilly, Robert R.
     The closing of the Muslim mind : how intellectual suicide created
     the modern Islamist crisis / Robert R. Reilly.

     p. cm.
     ISBN 1-933859-91-1

      1. Islamic countries—Intellectual life. 2. Islamic civilization—
History. 3. Islamic fundamentalism. 4. Islam—Doctrines—History. I. Title.

DS36.8.R45 2010
 320.5'57—dc22   2009052660

ISI Books
Intercollegiate Studies Institute
3901 Centerville Road
Wilmington, DE 19807-1938
www.isibooks.org

Manufactured in the United States of America

To the courageous men and women throughout the Islamic world, here nameless for reasons of their own security, who are struggling for a reopening of the Muslim mind.

Contents

CONTENTS

Foreword

by Roger Scruton

The roots of Western civilization lie in the religion of Israel, the culture of Greece, and the law of Rome, and the resulting synthesis has flourished and decayed in a thousand ways during the two millennia that have followed the death of Christ. Whether expanding into new territories or retreating into cities, Western civilization has continually experimented with new institutions, new laws, new forms of political order, new scientific beliefs, and new practices in the arts. And this tradition of experiment led, in time, to the Enlightenment, to democracy, and to forms of social order in which free opinion and freedom of religion are guaranteed by the state.

Why did not something similar happen in the Islamic world? Why is it that this civilization, which sprang up with such an abundance of energy in the seventh century of our era, and which spread across North Africa and the Middle East to produce cities, universities, libraries, and a flourishing courtly culture which has left a permanent mark on the world, is now in so many places mute, violent, and resentful? Why does Islam today seem not merely to tolerate the violence of its fiercest advocates, but to condone and preach it? Why is it that Muslim minorities in Europe, who migrate in order to enjoy the benefits of a secular jurisdiction, call for another kind of law altogether, even though so few of them seem able to agree what that law says or who is entitled to pronounce it?

In this lucid and fascinating book, Robert Reilly sets out to answer those questions. His purpose is to show that Islamic civilization, which led to the urbane princedoms of Andalusia in the West, and to the mystical laughter of the Sufis in the East, underwent a moral and intellectual crisis in the ninth to the eleventh century of our era, when it turned its back on philosophy and took refuge in dogma. Several factors are responsible for this sudden ossification, but the principal one, in Reilly's view, was the rise of the Ash'arite sect in the tenth century and the defeat of the rival sect of the Mu'tazalites. The Ash'arites found a potent voice in the Imam al-Ghazali (d. 1111), a brilliant philosopher and theologian whose tormented spirit found refuge at the last in a mystical oneness with Allah. Human reason teaches us to question things, to discover things, and to make new laws for our better governance. Hence reason was— for al-Ghazali—the enemy of Islam, which requires absolute and unquestioning submission to the will of Allah. In his celebrated treatise *The Incoherence of the Philosophers*, al-Ghazali set out to show that reason, as enshrined in the writings of Plato, Aristotle, and their followers, leads to nothing save darkness and contradiction, and that the only light that shines in the mind of man is the light of revelation. Although al-Ghazali's arguments are soundly refuted by Averroes (Ibn Rushd) in his *The Incoherence of the Incoherence*, Islam rushed to embrace the Ash'arite doctrine, which made so much better sense of the ruling idea of submission. Averroes was sent from Andalusia into exile, and the voice of reason was heard no more in the courts of Sunni Muslim princes.

The assault on philosophy went hand-in-hand with an equally determined assault on law and jurisprudence (*fiqh*). The early Islamic jurists had sought to reconcile the Qur'an and the traditions with the demands of ordinary justice, and had developed a system of law which could be applied in the developing circumstances of social and commercial life. The interpretation of the law was subject to study and amendment by the individual effort (*ijtihad*) of the jurists, who were thereby able to adapt the brittle injunctions of the Holy Book to the reality of Muslim societies. In the tenth or eleventh century of our era it became accepted that "the gate of ijtihad is closed"—as al-Ghazali himself declared. Since then Sunni Islam has adopted the official position that no new interpretations of the law can be entertained, and that what seemed right in twelfth-century Cairo or Baghdad must seem right today. Should we be surprised, therefore, if nobody can find a clear way of reconciling the *Shari'a* with the facts of modern life and government, or that a leading jurist from al-Azhar, the ancient university of Cairo, can rule that it is okay for a man and a woman who do not know each other to be alone together, provided he sucks her breasts?

Philosophy and dogma, civil law and divine law, are always hard to reconcile. But in the Islamic world the tension between them has taken on a special character, since it involves a conflict between two rival interpretations of the Qur'an. On one interpretation, that of the Mu'tazalites, the Qur'an was created by God at the moment of its revelation. It therefore stands to be interpreted in terms of the circumstances in which it was revealed, and of God's purpose in revealing it. On the Ash'arite interpretation, the Qur'an is uncreated, being coeval with the Almighty, his eternal word that owes nothing to the contingencies of life in Muhammad's war-torn Arabia. Reilly's account of this dispute is particularly illuminating, since it suggests how very difficult it will be to secure, in our dealings with the self-appointed leaders of the Sunni community, the kind of flexible interpretations of the faith that would permit the growth of a real and lasting tolerance towards those who reject it.

Reilly's brilliant account of the long-term effect of the "closing of the Muslim mind" makes sobering reading. Muslim societies, as he shows, have rarely adapted to the forms of modern politics, to the outlook of modern science, or to the demands of global migration. If Reilly is right—as he surely is—then the resentment that animates the Islamist terrorist is to be blamed not on our success, but rather on Muslim failure. This failure is not the inevitable result of Islam; rather, it is the effect of an act of cultural and intellectual suicide, which occurred eight centuries ago.

Reilly offers a cogent explanation not of *what* went wrong but of *why* it went wrong. He locates the source in a deformed theology gestated in the ninth and tenth centuries and in the dysfunctional culture that emerged from it. The Ash'arite orthodoxy, he argues, has bequeathed to modern Islam *the wrong concept of God.*

Policy makers beware: unless you are ready to admit that you are facing an essentially theological problem in the Middle East, do not go about prescribing solutions, for you may actually make matters worse—particularly by creating the false impression that economic, sociological, or political programs can fix what is, in fact, a delusion of faith. They cannot. As Reilly persuasively argues, the problem has to be addressed at the level at which it exists. The great merit of this book is in clearly stating the terms of this profound theological problem, the crisis to which it has led, and, finally, the choices which are now starkly laid out before contemporary Muslims. As Reilly shows, there are Muslims who know the way out of the morass, but seldom are they able to find audiences or regimes that are willing to listen to and to protect them.

The outcome of the struggle within Islam today will have major consequences for all of us. In helping us to understand that struggle, this book serves a purpose for which we should all be profoundly grateful.

Introduction
INTELLECTUAL SUICIDE

Dost thou not know that God has the power to will anything?
—*Qur'an 2:106*

Philosophy is a lie.[1]
—*Abu Sa'id ibn-Dust (d. 1040)*

Wherever I go in the Islamic world, it's the same problem: cause and effect; cause and effect.[2]
—*Fouad Ajami, 2005*

This book is about one of the greatest intellectual dramas in human history. Its landscape is the Muslim mind. How man regards his powers of reason has been a decisive influence on the shape and destiny of civilizations, including the Islamic one. How could it be otherwise, when these rational powers affect how reality is perceived, how revelation is received, what can be known, and how to discern the meaning of the known? This is the story of how Islam grappled with the role of reason after its conquests exposed it to Hellenic thought and how the side of reason ultimately lost in the ensuing, deadly struggle.

It may seem outrageous to say in the title of this book that the Muslim mind has closed—that a whole civilization has mentally shut down and abandoned reason and philosophy. I do not mean that the minds of every individual Muslim are closed, or that there are not varieties of Islam in which the Muslim mind is still open. I do mean, however, that a large portion of mainstream Sunni Islam, the majority expression of the faith, has shut the door to reality in a profound way.[*] The evidence attesting to this embrace of unreality is unfortunately abundant and has been offered by Muslims themselves. This closure is especially true of, and due to, a particular current of Muslim theology, the Ash'arite school of Islam, which predominates in the Arab Middle East (and is heavily present in other areas such as Pakistan and south Asia). As it has in the past, this part of the world plays the leading role in Islam today.

The great twentieth-century Muslim scholar Fazlur Rahman said, "A people that deprives itself of philosophy necessarily exposes itself to starvation in terms of fresh ideas—in fact, it commits intellectual suicide."[3] In his September 2006 Regensburg address, Pope Benedict XVI said something similar. He spoke of dehellenization—meaning the loss of reason, the gift of the Greeks—as one of the West's main problems. Less well known is the dehellenization that has afflicted Islam—its denigration of and divorce from reason. (The pope alluded to this only briefly, though it became a source of major controversy.) The dehellenization of Islam is less well known because it was so thorough and effective that few are aware that there was a process of hellenization preceding it—especially during the ninth and tenth centuries. It was a pivotal period for Islam and

---

[*] I do not include Shi'a Islam in this book except tangentially, because it is different enough from Sunni Islam as to require a separate work. Also, my general theme would have to be treated in a very different manner, if at all, for the simple reason that Shi'a Islam's relationship to philosophy was and is entirely different, for reasons that will be alluded to in Chapter 2.

the world. As the late King Hussein of Jordan said in his last interview, it was then, toward the end of this period, that the Muslim world took a decisive turn in the wrong direction.

This is an account of Sunni Islam's intellectual suicide—in Fazlur Rahman's meaning of the term—and the reasons for it. This book will relate not so much *how* it happened, but *why* it happened; not so much *what* went wrong, but *why* it went wrong. This book will detail the devastating consequences of Islam's intellectual suicide, and how the Muslim mind might possibly be reopened (as suggested by Muslims themselves), an endeavor fraught with repercussions for the West, as well as for the Islamic world.

The dehellenization of Islam had its roots in a particular idea of God that took definitive shape in the ninth century, though a large portion of Islam had embraced a version of it far earlier. The struggle over reason involved a profound disagreement about who God is. Each side in the dispute had certain prerequisites for who God *must* be, originating in or confirmed by their distinct readings of the Qur'an. On one side was God's will and power, and on the other his justice and rationality. The argument, precipitated and exacerbated by the encounter with Greek philosophy, took place over the status of reason in relation to God's revelation and omnipotence. The questions involved: What has reason to do with man's encounter with God? Is there any relationship between reason and revelation? Does reason have any standing to address God's revelation, or must reason remain outside of it? And perhaps most importantly, can reason know the truth?

It is on account of certain theological notions that philosophy was ultimately found to be incompatible with Ash'arite Islam (and that Islamic jurisprudence rose to be by far the most important discipline). How did such a conception of God develop, and why did it prevail? Muhammad was not a theologian. It was up to his followers to develop the notions of God contained both explicitly and implicitly in the Qur'an. They did so according to the needs that arose from various disputes within Islam and, also, as Islam encountered the ideas and religions of the civilizations it conquered.

The issues dealt with here are among the most difficult and profound with which the followers of any religion have had to wrestle. *Every* monotheistic religion has had to consider the same theological, philosophical, metaphysical, and epistemological problems that Islam has faced. This book shows how these perennial challenges were raised and treated in Sunni Islam, and how the outcomes of these considerations decisively influenced the shape of the Muslim world today. This may make for heavy slogging in places. However, the reader who does not make the effort to understand the struggle at the level at which it took place—and is still taking place—will be unable to grasp why the Sunni Islamic world has found itself in such a predicament, and whether it has the means within itself to find an opening back to reality.

There are two fundamental ways to close the mind. One is to deny reason's capability of knowing anything. The other is to dismiss reality as unknowable. Reason cannot know, or there is nothing to be known. Either approach suffices in making reality irrelevant. In Sunni Islam, elements of both were employed in the Ash'arite school. As a consequence, a fissure opened between man's reason and reality—and, most importantly, between man's reason and God. The fatal disconnect between the Creator and the mind of his creature is the source of Sunni Islam's most profound woes. This bifurcation, located not in the Qur'an but in early Islamic theology, ultimately led to the closing of the Muslim mind.

The key contemporary question may be this: If one's theological assumptions about reality are incorrect, can one recover from them if these assumptions have been dogmatized and made pillars of one's faith? If one wishes, for instance, to admit to the reality of "cause and effect" in the natural order, there does not seem to be any obstacle in the Qur'an to doing so, even though the Qur'an explains events almost exclusively as the direct product of God's actions. After all, the Old Testament tells much of its story with the same kind of emphasis on God acting directly on humanity and the world, but this did not prevent Jews, or the Christians after them, from embracing causality. It is Ash'arite theology, as it developed in the ninth to twelfth centuries, which makes this a problem in Islam today, because its denial of causality became, broadly speaking, Sunni orthodoxy and a part of Arab culture. This is what led to Lebanese-American intellectual Fouad Ajami's observation that "wherever I go in the Islamic world, it's the same problem: cause and effect; cause and effect." Is this dysfunctional view now sanctioned by consensus or *ijma* making it hard if not impossible to reverse? Muhammad proclaimed that "my community will never agree upon an error," meaning that something confirmed by that community, or *umma,* is taken to be infallible.

Much of this subject matter may seem remote from day-to-day concerns, and therefore easily dismissible. No doubt, the average Muslim may be as unaware of the teachings of medieval-era Islamic thinkers like al-Ashari and al-Ghazali as the average Christian is of the teachings of Augustine and Aquinas. If asked which Islamic theological school he belongs to, the Muslim man in the street may not know whether he is an Ash'arite or a Maturidite, any more than the Christian would know if he is an Augustinian or a Thomist. This, however, does not mean that the respective Muslim and Christian are any less under the influence of the ideas of these thinkers. Despite such lack of awareness, philosophical, metaphysical, and theological issues ultimately determine how daily concerns are addressed; indeed, they even determine what these concerns are. What may seem abstruse theological points can have the most practical and devastating consequences.

The closure of the Muslim mind has created the crisis of which modern Islamist terrorism is only one manifestation. The problem is much broader and deeper. It enfolds Islam's loss of science and of the prospect of indigenously developing democratic constitutional government. It is the key to unlocking such puzzles as why the Arab world stands near the bottom of every measure of human development; why scientific inquiry is nearly moribund in the Islamic world; why Spain translates more books in a single year than the entire Arab world has in the past *thousand* years; why some people in Saudi Arabia still refuse to believe man has been to the moon; and why some Muslim media present natural disasters like Hurricane Katrina as God's direct retribution. Without understanding this story, we cannot grasp what is taking place in the Islamic world today, or the potential paths to recovery—paths many Muslims are pointing to with their rejection of the idea of God that produced this crisis in the first place.

The closing of the Muslim mind is the direct if somewhat distant antecedent of today's radical Islamist ideology, and this ideology cannot be understood without divining its roots in that closing. The ideas animating terrorist acts from September 11, to the bombings in London, Madrid, and Mumbai, to the attempted airline bombing in Detroit on Christmas 2009, and beyond have been loudly proclaimed by their perpetrators and their many sympathizers in every form of media. We know what they think; they tell us every day. But questions arise concerning the provenance of their ideas, which they claim are Islamic. Are they something new or a resurgence of something from the past? How much of this is Islam and how much is Islamism? Is Islamism a deformation of Islam? If so, in what way and from where has it come? And why is Islam susceptible to this kind of deformation? The latter part of the book will address these questions.

The book's approach will be to cite translated primary sources wherever possible and, within the necessary context, to let the texts speak for themselves. For those unfamiliar with the material, the quotations from some of the key Muslim theologians from the ninth to twelfth centuries will be surprising, even shocking. The radical voluntarism (God as pure will) and occasionalism (no cause and effect in the natural order) found in them were not seen to any significant extent in the West until Scottish philosopher David Hume began writing in the eighteenth century. By that time the recognition of reality had become firmly enough established to withstand the assault (until fairly recently, that is, when a form of voluntarism has also undermined reason in the West). Unfortunately, this was not true in Sunni Islam, where these views arrived so much earlier.

The voluntaristic and occasionalist character of Sunni Islam is hardly a recent discovery. St. John of Damascus, Maimonides, Hegel, and many others amply noted it. However, the reason many Westerners today remain perplexed by Muslim behavior is that they are unaware of the fundamental theological doctrines that animate it. I abundantly cite twentieth-century scholarship on these theological issues, both Western and Islamic, to affirm their essential importance as the formative influence on Sunni character. The abiding influence of these doctrines will be, for some, hard to believe or accept because they are so remote from the modern Western world. But they are largely responsible for the situation today and present a profound obstacle to the reform that many Muslims, as well as those in West, hope to see in a reopening of the Muslim mind. To many in the Sunni Muslim world, reality has become inaccessible because the views of certain theologians of the ninth to twelfth centuries prevailed. The reasons for this must be understood, so that hopes are not misplaced and the path to recovery runs true.

Many Muslims recognize this. In "Reinventing the Muslim Mind," a contemporary Indian leader of reformist thought, Rashid Shaz, states: "Those eager to make a new beginning must accept beforehand that the traditional mind will lead them to nowhere. A new Muslim mind is the minimum to start with. Without reactivating our brains we would even fall short of realising in full the nature and magnitude of our malaise."[4]

This book, then, is an effort to understand the journey that Sunni Islam took to "nowhere." It may be the only way to make the journey back.

Overview and Apologia

I propose to sketch briefly the early Muslim world and its first theological controversy, then to introduce the first fully developed school of theology, the Mu'tazilites, then their opponents, the Ash'arites, and then the pivotal figure of Abu Hamid al-Ghazali (d. 1111). In the latter part of the book, I will suggest the profound consequences of the triumph of al-Ghazali and the Ash'arites, including the extirpation of philosophy, and then trace the effects of this to modern-day behavior. This will include an examination of the susceptibility of Islam today to Islamism, which is driving Sunni Muslims back to nowhere. Throughout, I try to keep the crucial issue of the status of reason—and the effects of its decline—in the forefront.

Also, the purpose here is not to explicate the works of the great thinkers in Islamic philosophy. It would be an enormous task even to survey this subject matter, which has been well enough done in other places. Rather, I intend to suggest why these works, despite their brilliance, gained little if any purchase on the Sunni Muslim mind, then or now. We restrict ourselves to a broad outline of the major intellectual events in Sunni Muslim history that decisively formed today's world. Some of the figures with whom we deal, such as Abu Hamid al-Ghazali, are still subjects of controversy as to what their real thinking might have been. Did they have esoteric teachings? The goal here is not to resolve such disputes but to point out the primary influence of their thinking as it has been generally felt and understood within Islam.

On a personal note, I would like to say that I am fully aware that I have embarked upon a difficult and sensitive subject. I will not be surprised by strong reactions to what is said here. I should like to be dissuaded of this book's thesis, and to be convinced that the obstacles to reform are not as great as they seem. However, I am trying to understand the situation as it is and the reasons for it. I am simply offering the conclusions to which I have come after searching for years to make sense of what I have seen, experienced, and read. If there is a thesis that explains more of it than I have here, I welcome it. I reserve the right to learn more.

Chapter 1

THE OPENING:

ISLAM DISCOVERS HELLENIC THOUGHT

One cannot address the closing of the Muslim mind unless one is aware of its opening. And concomitantly, one must know what it initially opened *from* and on *to*.

The opening should be seen against the background of pre-Islamic Arabia, a typical tribal society, immersed in polytheism (though a supreme deity, Allah, was vaguely acknowledged), pantheism, animism, fetishism, and superstition. The Ka'ba in Mecca contained a pantheon of some 360 tribal gods and goddesses in its precincts. Trading and raiding (*razzias*) were the principal livelihoods. As is typical of tribal societies, conflict was the norm—within certain traditional limits, such as the prohibition against fighting during the four "sacred months." Force defined the status of relations between tribes, which were themselves defined by family or blood. Strength ruled with the sanction of custom. Arabia had some familiarity with Judaism (with a few resident Jewish tribes) and Christianity, but was thoroughly pagan.

Philosophy in the form of Greek thought had not penetrated the peninsula. At least, there seems to be no evidence of its having done so. Under this multiplicity of gods and without philosophy, it would not naturally have occurred to the warring tribes that they had something in common that was more important than themselves—that the differences among them, defined by bloodlines and different gods, could be superseded by a higher good. Monotheism was that higher good, as propounded by Muhammad starting around A.D. 610. The unity of Islam, based upon *tawhid*—the unity or unicity of Allah—stopped the near-constant tribal raiding through its teaching of profound equality among Muslims. Fellow Muslims became sacrosanct. As the Qur'an enjoined, "Hold fast, all of you together, to Allah's rope, and do not separate. Remember Allah's beneficence to you, for you were enemies but He composed your hearts so that by His favour you have become brothers" (3:103).

At the same time, Islam divinely sanctioned a kind of mega-tribal raiding of the rest of the non-Muslim world. "Allah has promised you much booty that you will take [in the future] . . . and other booty, over which ye have not yet had power: but God compassed them for you" (Qur'an 48:20–21). According to this new revelation, it was now only right and just that non-Muslims should be subdued and ruled by the true followers of God. How to conduct these raids and divide the booty from them is an important part of the Qur'an (Qur'an 8: The Spoils; 59:6 The Mustering). The first biographies of Muhammad were titled *kitab al-meghazi*, the Book of Raids.[1]

The early conquests were staggeringly successful and seemed to confirm the Qur'an's claims. By A.D. 650, Muslims ruled Arabia, Iraq, Syria, Lebanon, Palestine, and Egypt. Less than a century later, Islam spread from the fringes of China and India in the East to North Africa and Spain in the West. Early Islam's energies were spent in absorbing its mandated conquests and in defining its creed, which was held to be superior to any earlier revelation of any other religion (Qur'an 9:33). Thus Islam was naturally suspicious of anything outside of itself. The Qur'an, it was thought, contained everything needed, and non-Qur'anic things were either against it or superfluous. The great fourteenth-century historian Ibn Khaldun wrote that, when the Muslims conquered Persia, general Sa'd bin Abi Waqqas petitioned Caliph Omar for permission to distribute the huge quantity of captured books and scientific papers as booty. Caliph Omar wrote back: "Throw them in the water. If what they contain is right guidance, God has given us better guidance. If it is error, God has protected us against it."[2]

This intellectual quarantine could not, however, be maintained outside of Islam's peninsular homeland. In the conquered Sassanid and Byzantine territories, Islam encountered civilizations superior to itself by any measure. When the capital of the Islamic empire moved from Medina to Damascus under the Umayyad dynasty (660–750), the Muslim rulers were surrounded by an alien culture. How should Islam react to what it now ruled? How much could it absorb and what should it reject, and why? What should its attitude be toward the beliefs and teachings of those whom it had conquered?

The First Encounter

Islam encountered Greek thought in its new Byzantine and Sassanid possessions. Exactly how these early Hellenic influences reached into Islam is a matter of some conjecture. What is clear is that huge areas of what had been the Byzantine Empire were largely Christian, and in them Greek philosophical notions had long been employed in Christian apologetics. There were also centers of Hellenistic learning in Alexandria (which moved to Antioch, Syria, around A.D. 718) and Gondeshakpur, northeast of Basra, Iraq. The latter had been maintained by the Sassanids, who had employed mainly Christian (Nestorian) teachers. The body of what were called "the intellectual sciences" included logic and philosophy, as well as the natural, medical, engineering, and mathematical sciences. A good deal of Greek philosophical and scientific treatises had been translated into Syriac by Christian scholars. As these subjects were not familiar to Arab culture, the Arabs dubbed them "intruding sciences."[3]

The initial Muslim interest in the Greek sciences was in practical matters such as medicine, mathematics, natural science, alchemy, and astrology.

Most learned men in these sciences, however, were also schooled in philosophy and theology, which meant that Muslim interest began to spill over into philosophical and theological issues. Muslims were also called upon to defend and advance their faith against Christians and others who used philosophical methods in their apologetics. Some Muslim converts in these new territories were already versed in Greek learning and prepared to deploy it on behalf of their new faith. Thus, by the late eighth and early ninth centuries, a new kind of discourse began to affect Islamic thought that had hitherto been largely doctrinal and jurisprudential. New words were created in Arabic to take in Greek concepts. Philosophy opened the Muslim mind in a way in which it had never been before in the spirit of free inquiry and speculative thought. It is at this juncture that the greatest intellectual drama of Islam took place.

After Islam encountered Hellenic thought, the most challenging issue it faced involved the status of reason. What is reason's ability to apprehend reality? Can God be known rationally? How does the voice of reason comport with the claims of revelation as contained in the Qur'an? Does reason precede faith? Is revelation addressed to reason? Can reason comprehend moral principles outside of the Qur'an? What if something in the Qur'an appears to be unreasonable? Is it legitimate even to ask these questions? Is Islam compatible with anything other than itself? Was it capable of assimilating philosophy? If so, on what grounds?

A pitched battle took place over the answers to these questions, most particularly during the ninth and tenth centuries of the Abbasid caliphate. At stake were man's free will, his ability to know through his reason, and the very nature of reality and of God. At the conclusion of this battle, the triumphant side gradually extirpated philosophy and dehellenized the Muslim world. This did not take place without a fight from those Muslim thinkers and their followers who precipitated the opening. In many ways, the struggle continues today.

The First Struggle: *Qadar* (Man's Power to Act) versus *Jabr* (Fate/Compulsion)

The side in this emerging debate most easily recognizable to a Westerner was the Mu'tazilite school, composed of the Muslim rationalist theologians who fought for the primacy of reason. Their appearance in the late eighth and early ninth centuries should be seen in the context of a preceding dispute within Islam about predestination and free will. This issue was, in fact, the source of the earliest theological debate in Islam. Some scholars say this dispute was completely native to Islam, while others, such as Duncan Macdonald, aver that "it is impossible to mistake the workings of the dialectic refinements of Greek theology as developed in the Byzantine and Syrian schools."[4] The pre-Mu'tazilites were called Qadarites, or Qadariyya, after the Arabic word *qadar*, which can mean divine decree or predestination, or power. They stood for the opposite of predestination: man's free will and consequent responsibility for his actions. Man has power (*qadar*) over his own actions. If men were not able to control their behavior, said the Qadarites, the moral obligation to do good and avoid evil, enjoined by the Qur'an, would be meaningless.

Contrary to this view, the Jabariyya (determinists; from *jabr*, meaning blind compulsion) embraced the doctrine that divine omnipotence requires the absolute determination of man's actions by God. One of the names of God in the Qur'an is al-Jabbar, the Compeller (59:23), whose power cannot be resisted. God alone authors man's every movement. To say otherwise ties God's hands and limits his absolute freedom. One of the exponents of this view, Jahm bin Safwan (d. 745), argued that man's actions are imputed to him only in the same way as one imputes "the bearing of fruit to the tree, flowing to the stream, motion to the stone, rising or setting to the sun—blooming and vegetating to the earth."[5] As Fazlur Rahman summed up the dispute, "In the eyes of the orthodox, this freedom for man was bondage for God."[6]

As in the case of other theological issues within Islam, the Qur'an offers support for both positions. The disputants could each quote verses supporting their respective sides. British Islamic historian Alfred Guillaume claims, however, that things appear to favor the Jabariyya side, especially when the Hadith are considered. (The Hadith are the "traditions" that report various sayings and actions of Muhammad, which were first passed on orally before being written down in collections, six of which are accepted as genuine sources of revelation.) Guillaume states that "the orthodox party had the Qur'an on their side when they asserted that God's predestination was absolute. This view is borne out by the chapter on predestination in the books of canonical tradition which do not contain a single saying of Muhammad's which leaves freedom of action to man. Everything is predestined from the first and a man's fate is fixed before he is born."[7]

Here are several examples of such Hadith:

Hudhayfa bin Asid reported that the Prophet said, "Two angels visit every foetus in the womb upon the completion of forty or forty-five nights and say, 'O Lord! Is it misguided or righteous?' Then they write [the answer]. Then they ask, 'O lord! Is it male or female?' Then they write [the answer]. They also write its deed, wealth and means of livelihood, and death. Then they roll off the parchment to which nothing is added nor detracted afterwards."[8]

Abu Huraira reported Muhammad as saying: "Verily Allah has fixed the very portion of adultery which a man will indulge in and which he of necessity must commit."[9]

A Hadith found in both Muslim and al-Bukhari (the two most authoritative sources of Hadith) has Moses, upon meeting Adam, asking him: "Are you the Adam, the father of all humanity, whom He created with His own hand. . . . Why did you get us and yourself expelled from the garden?" To this Adam replies, "Are you the Moses whom God chose for His messengership, distinguished him by speaking to him and wrote the Torah for him with His own hand? How long before my creation did you find the words pre-written: 'Adam disobeyed His order and went astray (Qu'ran 20:121)?'" Moses then answers: "This was [pre-written] so much time before [your creation]."[10] Thus does Adam confound Moses.

A Qur'anic verse supporting this orientation says: "So whoever Allah wants to guide—He expands his breast to [contain] Islam; and whoever He wants to misguide—He makes his breast tight and constricted as though he were climbing into the sky" (6:125). And "When you shot it was not you who shot but God" (8:17).

Counterpoised to these are other citations from the Qur'an that seem to confirm the Qadarite position and make clear that man can choose freely and will be held accountable on judgment day. For example, the Qadarites could quote: "Whosoever does an evil deed shall be recompensed only with the like of it, but whosoever does a righteous deed, be it male or female, believing shall enter Paradise, therein provided without reckoning" (40:40). Or, "Say, 'The Truth is from your Lord.' Let him who will, believe; and let him who will reject [it]" (18:29). Or, "Each soul earns but its own due" (6:164). Also: "And Allah created the heavens and the earth with truth, so that each soul might be recompensed according to what it has earned, with no one wronged" (45:22). There are many such verses that refer to man's responsibility and accountability for his actions.

The conundrum created by these two conflicting positions seems to be contained within the same Qur'anic citation: "If Allah so willed, he could make you all one people. But He leaves straying whom He pleases, and He guides whom He pleases and you shall certainly be called to account for all your actions" (16:93).

The Qur'an's ambiguity allowed room for this dispute and for political maneuver and advantage from it. Both the Qadarite and the Jabrite views had profound political implications. The Umayyad caliphs ruling in Damascus enjoyed the sanction provided by the Jabariyya doctrine because it excused them from responsibility for any unjust acts. How could they be blamed for their foreordained brutality? As such, out of piety, their subjects should accept, or at least ignore, their misdeeds (which included an attack on the Ka'ba). In order to secure his power, Umayyad Caliph 'Abd al-Malik brought one of his rivals, 'Amr ibn Sa'id, into the palace under false pretenses, beheaded him, and then had his head tossed to his awaiting crowd of supporters with the announcement that "the Commander of the Faithful has killed your leader, as it was foreordained in God's inalterable decree."[11] The erstwhile supporters of Ibn Sa'id then paid obeisance to the caliph.

Not all, however, were willing to abide by this interpretation. Hassan al-Basri (d. 728) was asked his opinion of "those kings [the Umayyad caliphs] who spill the blood of Muslims, appropriate their possessions, do what they please and say, 'Our actions are indeed part of God's fore-ordination.'" Al-Basri, whose student, Wasil ibn 'Ata (d. 748), founded the Mu'tazilite school, answered: "The enemies of God lie."[12] Allah, he said, quoting the Qur'an, was "no unjust dealer with His servants." Allah is not the source of evil; men are—in their evil actions. This theological position was taken as a political attack. Two Qadarite theologians, Ma'bad al-Juhani (d. 699) and Ghailan al-Dimashqi (d. before 743), were executed by the Umayyads for their defense of free will, which was considered subversive and a direct challenge to the Umayyad theological rationalization of its atrocities.

In 750, the Abbasids overthrew the Umayyads, along with their doctrine of predestination. The Abbasids had cause to embrace the Mu'tazilites, who succeeded to the Qadariyya position. The Mu'tazilites agreed with the Qadariyya that, without man's freedom, God's justice is unintelligible. To be held justly accountable for his acts, man must be free. The political implications of this position favored the Abbasid attempt to rein in the power of the *ulema* (Islamic jurisprudential scholars), whose monopoly on the interpretation of the Qur'an gave them great influence. When he acceded to the throne, al-Ma'mun took the title of imam, and chose a Shi'a as his successor. These actions clearly implied a claim on his part that he also had the authority to interpret Islamic scripture, and perhaps even to amend it. The Mu'tazilite teaching that the freedom of man also meant the freedom to interpret sacred texts reinforced this claim from another direction.

The freedom to interpret revelation was based upon the Mu'tazilite teaching, shocking to the traditionalists, that the Qur'an was created in time. The standard orthodox belief was that the Qur'an is uncreated and exits coeternally with Allah. If the Qur'an was created, it is subject to rational criteria. If it is subject to rational criteria, it is not the exclusive domain of the *ulema*. An uncreated Qur'an would not allow for this interpretive freedom. Caliph al-Ma'mun knew that the teaching of a created Qur'an and of man's free will would enhance his authority and undermine that of the traditionalist *ulema*. Therefore, he sponsored the Mu'tazilites. He also genuinely embraced their views because he was fascinated by philosophy.

The Second Struggle: *'Aql* (Reason) versus *Naql* (Traditional Faith)

The Mu'tazilites, who created the first fully developed theological school in Islam, championed the primary role of reason; reason's ability to know morality; the goodness and justice of God as required by reason; the unity of God; and the necessity of man's free will. They represented the beginning of the hellenization of Islamic thought insofar as they employed Greek philosophical concepts and logic in their consideration of theological questions. They were rationalist theologians.

Their new discipline became known as *kalam*, and its practitioners as *mutakallimun* (though this term is sometimes used to signify the opponents of the Mu'tazilites). At a very basic Socratic and Aristotelian level, they embraced the propositions that the mind can know things, as distinct from having opinions about them; that objective reality exists; that there is some purpose implied in its construction; that this purpose has to do with what man calls "the good"; and that man's soul is ordered to this "good," which is universal.

One problem in accurately ascertaining the thought of the losing side in Muslim theological debates is that the losers' books were usually burnt. What information we have is from the heresiographies of the winning side, which state the positions of opponents only for the purposes of refutation (although this was often done with scrupulous fairness, as in the case of al-Ghazali's writings). In the early 1950s, however, Egyptian scholars discovered a large amount of texts by the last great Mu'tazilite theologian, 'Abd al-Jabbar (c. 935–1025), in a mosque in Yemen. Thus, there is now a reliable reference by which to come to know the core Mu'tazilite teachings: 'Abd al-Jabbar's *Book of the Five Fundamentals.*

In general, members of the school adhered to five principles, which were clearly enunciated for the first time by Abu al-Hudhayl (d. 849), who helped to formalize Mu'tazilite teachings in Basra, Iraq. These were: (1) *tawhid*, the unity of God; (2) divine justice; (3) the promise and the threat; (4) the intermediate position; and (5) the commanding of good and forbidding of evil. The first three principles are the most relevant to a consideration of the role of reason in respect to God. They are particularly significant in their differences with the staunch traditionalist positions of what were called *ahl al-Hadith*, the people of tradition. They also generated vehement opposition from the Ash'arites, a school of theology developed in direct opposition to the Mu'tazilites, which used the Mu'tazilites' own tools of Greek philosophy to try to destroy them.

The Mu'tazilite concern with *tawhid*, or God's unity, had to do with the multitude of attributes given to Allah by the traditionalists and the ontological status of those attributes. The Mu'tazilites thought that these compromised God's indivisible unity. The traditionalist insistence on the uncreatedness of the Qur'an, which made the Qur'an eternally coexistent with God, was another infraction of God's unity from the Mu'tazilite perspective.

The matter of divine justice goes to the heart of who God is and the nature of his relationship to man. It involves the very order and nature of creation as based on reason. The Mu'tazilites held that man's freedom is a matter of God's justice, as is reason's ability to apprehend an objective moral order. The "promise and the threat" is an extension of the issue of divine justice in that the Mu'tazilites held that God is reasonably *required* to keep his word and reward good and punish evil, an obligation which their opponents insisted was an infringement of God's freedom and omnipotence.

The Primacy of Reason

The Mu'tazilites differed from their opponents in their teaching that God has endowed man with reason specifically so that he can come to know the moral order in creation and its Creator; that is what reason is for. Reason is central to man's relationship to God. In the *Fundamentals*, 'Abd al-Jabbar begins by positing the *primary* duty to reason: "If it is asked: What is the first duty that God imposes upon you? Say to him: Speculative reasoning which leads to knowledge of God, because He is not known intuitively or by the senses. Thus, He must be known by reflection and speculation."[13]

Therefore, reason logically precedes revelation. Reason first needs to establish the existence of God before undertaking the question as to whether God has spoken to man. Natural theology must be antecedent to theology. Al-Jabbar says, "The stipulates of revelation concerning what [we should] say and do are no good until after there is knowledge of God," which knowledge comes from reason. "Therefore," he concludes, "it is incumbent on me to establish His existence and to know Him so that I can worship Him, give Him thanks and do what satisfies Him and avoid disobedience toward Him."[14]

How does reason lead man to the conclusion of God's existence? It is through his observation of the ordered universe that man first comes to know that God exists, says 'Abd al-Jabbar. As he sees that nothing in the world is its own cause, but is caused by something else, man arrives at the contingent nature of creation. From there, man reasons to the necessity of a Creator, an uncaused cause; otherwise one is caught in an infinite regress of contingent things, a logical impossibility. (This was a familiar argument from both Greek philosophy and Christian apologetics.) It is through the observation of nature—the ways in which the world seems to move according to certain laws—that man comes to know God. God's laws are the laws of nature (*tab'*), which are also manifested in divine law, the *shari'a*.

The concept of an inherent nature in things (*tab'*) means that God, though he is the First Cause, acts indirectly through secondary causes, such as the physical law of gravity. In other words, God does not immediately and directly do everything. He does not make the rock fall; gravity does. God allows some autonomy in His creation, which has its own set of rules, according to how it was made. As Mu'tazilite writer and theologian 'Uthman al-Jahiz (776–869) stated, every material element has its own nature.[15] God created each thing with a nature according to which it consistently behaves. The unsupported rock will *always* fall where there is gravitational pull. These laws of nature, then, are not an imposition of order from without by a commander-in-chief, but an expression of it from within the very essence of things, which have their own integrity. Creation is possessed of an intrinsic rationality from the Creator. That is why and how man is able to understand God's reason as manifested in his creation. (This does not discount God's ability to supersede natural laws in the case of a miracle.)

For scriptural support, the Mu'tazilites could point to multiple invitations to natural theology in the Qur'an. For example, in Surah 15, "The Bee," verses remarking upon natural wonders frequently end with, "Indeed in that is a sign for a people who give thought," or "Indeed in that are signs for a people who reason." Other Surahs further support the Mu'tazilite position: "Then do they not look at the camels—how they are created? And at the sky—how it is raised? And at the mountains—how they are erected? And at the earth—how it is spread out?" (88:17–20). Also: "And it is He who gives life and causes death, and His is the alternation of the night and the day. Then will you not reason?" (23:80). Finally, and perhaps most famously, there is Surah 2, "The Cow," 164: "Indeed, in the creation of the heavens and the earth, and the alternation of the night and the day, and the [great] ships which sail through the sea with that which benefits people, and what Allah has sent down from the heavens of rain, giving life thereby to the earth after its lifelessness and dispersing therein every [kind of] moving creature, and [His] directing of the winds and the clouds controlled between the heaven and the earth are signs for a people who use reason."

Reason and Reflection

It is, therefore, the exercise of reason that creates the opening to the possibility of revelation. In fact, man's reason comprehends the *need* for such revelation when it sees that revelation is required by God's justice to guide man rightly. For confirmation, the Mu'tazilites could point to the Qur'an: "It is incumbent upon Allah to give right guidance" (16:9).

After determining that God exists, one can then reasonably ask whether God has spoken to man. Has revelation occurred? How would one know if it is genuine? Here, 'Abd al-Jabbar goes even further in his claims for reason by stating that it is reason that authenticates revelation. 'Abd al-Jabbar contends that "knowledge of God can only be gained by speculation with rational argument, because if we do not [first] know that He is truthful we will not know the authenticity of the Book, the Sunna and the communal consensus."[16] It is only logical then, since God is reason and reason comes from Him, that His revealed words in the Qur'an would be decipherable by man's reason and congruent with what man knows through His creation.

What is more, revelation only *reveals*; it does not *make* things good or bad by decree. God forbids murder because it is evil; it is not evil because He forbids it. Even if reason could not independently arrive at the content of revelation, it finds nothing in it that is not reasonable, and reason can nonetheless confirm the good in it. 'Abd al-Jabbar states:

> Revelation only uncovers about the character of these acts aspects whose evilness or goodness we should recognize if we knew them by reason; for if we had known by reason that prayer is of great benefit to us, leading us to choose our duty and to earn Reward thereby, we should have known its obligatory character [also] by reason. Therefore we say that revelation does not necessitate the evilness or goodness of anything, it only uncovers the character of the act by way of indication, just as reason does, and distinguishes between the command of the Exalted and that of another being by His Wisdom.[17]

It is only logical from this general orientation that the Mu'tazilites would find the Qur'an open to rational interpretation. It must be, since the Qur'an itself admits to verses that are "univocal" and others that are "equivocal" (3:7). How is one to understand which are which, without reasoned interpretation? Revealed truths, according to 'Abd al-Jabbar, cannot be in contradiction to the truths of reason. As the philosopher Averroes would later say, "The right does not contradict the right, but agrees with it and confirms it."[18] Therefore, says 'Abd al-Jabbar, "It is obligatory for you to carry out what accords with reason.... Thus, judge that which accords with rational proof to be true, and bring that which contradicts [reason] into accord with it."[19] By this principle, advises 'Abd al-Jabbar, "That which is transmitted in conflict with the Book and rational evidence we will interpret metaphorically in a sound manner, just as we interpret the Book of God in accord with rational proof, not with that which is in conflict with it."[20] By this means, the Mu'tazilites overcame such obstacles as the anthropomorphisms in the Qur'an, which speaks of God's "hands" (38:75), "eyes" (54:14), and "face" (55:27). The traditionalists were forced into a conundrum by their literal reading of these passages, which confounded the doctrine that God was an incorporeal spirit. In particular, they bitterly contested the Mu'tazilite spiritual interpretation of the text in verse 75:23 that those in paradise will actually "see" God.[21]

According to the traditionalists, whatever inconsistencies may appear in the Qur'an must simply be accepted without questioning. Malik ibn Anas (715–795), founder of one of the four schools of Islamic jurisprudence, addressed the anthropomorphisms, which include Allah "sitting upon the throne" (7:54; 20:5), by purportedly saying: "The sitting is known, its modality is unknown. Belief in it is an obligation and raising questions regarding it is a heresy [*bid'ah*]."[22] This is the classic Hanbalite-Ash'arite formula of *bila kayfa wala tashbih* (without inquiring how and without making comparison).

To the contrary, the Mu'tazilites thought that the grand harmonization of man's reason with the order in the world and with divine revelation must obtain because God is not only power; He *is* reason. Reason in man, says 'Abd al-Jabbar, was the product of God's "grace." The Mu'tazilites would have been in accord with Thomas Aquinas's proposition that man can apprehend created things with his mind because they were first *thought* by God. God's intelligibility is the cause of the intelligibility of creation. Averroes held this as well: "If we have knowledge of these possibles, then there is a condition in the possible existens [existing things] to which our knowledge pertains . . . and this is what the philosophers designate as nature. Likewise, the knowledge of God is through the existens, although [God's knowledge] is their cause . . . and therefore it is necessary that the existens come about in accordance with His knowledge."[23] The Mu'tazilites trusted that God is guided by the rationality of the universe He created. Their cosmology rested upon the trinity of God as reason, creation as a manifestation of that reason, and man's gift of reason as the means by which to apprehend God through His creation and, then, through His revelation.

Thus for the Mu'tazilites, as Richard Martin states in *Defenders of Reason in Islam,* "confidence in the rational and knowable nature of physical reality is based on theodicy: God would not deceive His creatures by creating an irrational universe."[24] In other words, not acting reasonably is contrary to God's *nature.* (When Benedict XVI cited the Byzantine emperor Manuel II Paleologus as saying this very thing to a Persian in the late fourteenth century, many Muslims vehemently protested—it seems without realizing that this was once a respectable theological position within Islam.) If God is reason, then there exist standards of reasonableness. The Mu'tazilites believed that God acts with purpose and his purposes are intelligible and benign. There certainly exist divine mysteries beyond man's comprehension, but God would not go against reason in His revelation in such a way as to require man to deny His reason. His revelation is addressed to, and does not supplant, man's reason. For the Mu'tazilites, faith required an intellectual assent; as Ignaz Goldziher, author of *Introduction to Islamic Theology and Law,* put it, "there could be no belief without the exercise of reason."[25]

Father James Schall has pointed out the deep significance of this view in general:

> The rational creature can only "participate" in the eternal law of God if that law is itself founded in *Logos*, in Word [or Reason]. If it is grounded merely in will, even if it is God's will, as various theologies and philosophies are tempted to maintain, there can be no real "participation" in the eternal law by the human being. Why? Essentially, because there is nothing to participate in if what is grounded in and known only by will can, at any time, be the opposite of what it is at first thought to be.[26]

From al-Jabbar's writings, it is clear that the Mu'tazilites saw man as a full participant in the eternal law in this very way, just as their opponents explicitly did not.

The Objectivity of Morality: Knowing the Good

Man as a participant in the eternal law means that, quite apart from revelation, man has the ability to make moral discernments concerning good and evil, justice and injustice. Reason can distinguish between good and evil because the standard of good and evil exists objectively. The moral character of acts is intrinsic to them. Al-Shahrastani, an Ash'arite opponent of the Mu'tazilites, fairly characterized the Mu'tazilite position regarding the imperatives issuing from moral reasoning as follows: "The adherents of justice [as the Mu'tazilites were known] say: All objects of knowledge fall under the supervision of reason and receive their obligatory power from rational insight. Consequently, obligatory gratitude for divine bounty precedes the orders given by [divine] Law; and beauty and ugliness are qualities belonging intrinsically to what is beautiful and ugly."[27] Because good and evil are intrinsic to the nature of acts themselves, man can know their moral character through his reason alone. For the Mu'tazilites, a purely rational ethics is possible, just as it was for the Greeks and for Aristotle in *The Ethics*.

It is precisely man's ability to discern these things that makes a morally good life obligatory. The status of reason was the key to Mu'tazilite support of free will, which makes no sense unless man can know the difference between good and evil, justice and injustice. In turn, man's freedom, said the Mu'tazilites (like their Qadarite predecessors), was necessary to vindicate God's justice. Man is responsible *because* he is free. Otherwise, God would not be justified in rewarding or condemning man for his actions. In answering the claim that God creates man's acts, 'Abd al-Jabbar responds, "If they were done by God then what good would there be in His commanding those that are ethically good and prohibiting those that are ethically bad, and praising and rewarding obedience but blaming and punishing disobedience?" What is more, says 'Abd al-Jabbar, "How can it be possible for God to create erroneous behaviour in them and then punish them, thus saying: 'Why do you disbelieve?' Isn't that the same as someone commanding his slave to do something, then punishing him for it? And that would clearly be corrupt."[28]

The Goodness and Justice of God

Implicit in the last sentence is the Mu'tazilite belief that God is subject to His own justice and that He cannot act outside of it. He cannot be corrupt. In other words, God can be held to account. Certain things are incumbent upon Him. The Mu'tazilites were the only theological school to use the term *wajib* (obligatory) in reference to God. The notion that God *had* to do something was anathema to the traditionalists and to the Ash'arites. For them, Allah is not bound by anything. Nothing is obligatory for Him. If it were, His omnipotence would be compromised. The Mu'tazilite response to this was that God must be consistent with Himself, and that in no way compromises His omnipotence. It simply defines who He is.

For the Mu'tazilites, God is good and cannot do evil. The Mu'tazilite al-Nazzam (d. 848) claimed that it is impossible for

God to act unjustly.[29] Neo-Mu'tazilite Harun Nasution (1919–1998) stated that "because He is completely perfect, God *cannot* do that which is not good."[30] Though like other Muslims, the Mu'tazilites had no notion of "original sin," they firmly held that evil is a consequence of man's actions, and that God does not will evil, even if He allows it. "Thus every immoral thing that happens in the world," says 'Abd al-Jabbar, "must be a human act, for God transcends doing immoral acts. Indeed, God has distanced Himself from that with His saying: 'But Allah wills no injustice to His servants' (40:31) and His saying: 'Verily Allah will not deal unjustly with humankind in anything' (10:44)."[31]

What then of disease and sickness? 'Abd al-Jabbar answers with a notion of providence: "Verily, if He caused sickness, He would turn it into greater advantage in the hereafter. If that were not so then it would not be ethically good for Him to cause animals and children to be sick, just as it would not be ethically good for us to hire somebody and work him to exhaustion without paying him his wage."[32] 'Abd al-Jabbar makes it clear that God is not outside the idea of justice with which He has endowed man. "Thus, if God committed injustice He would be unjust, just as if He acted justly He would be just, and whoever says [otherwise] is an unbeliever."[33]

By His justice, according to al-Jabbar, God is also obliged to keep His word to man and to let man know what His word is. "We do not believe that His word was a lie and an order that could be nullified, for that then would necessitate that we [could] not trust in His Promise and threat. And we do not believe that He sends prophets to the Hellfire and enemies and unbelievers to Paradise. Anyone who did such things would not command our obedience to Him because we could not be safe from His evil, and by obeying Him we would create the utmost havoc."[34] Therefore, "He will not go back on His word, nor can he act contrary to His promise and threat nor lie in what He reports."[35]

As Majid Fakhry summarizes in *A History of Islamic Philosophy*: "God cannot enjoin what is contrary to reason or act with total disregard for the welfare of His creatures, in so far as this would compromise His justice and His wisdom. Unlike the Traditionalists, those ethical rationalists could not reconcile themselves to the concept of an omnipotent Deity who could act in total violation of all the precepts of justice and righteousness, torture the innocent, and demand the impossible simply because He was God."[36]

As 'Abd al-Jabbar says, "God is removed from all that is morally wrong and all His acts are morally good."[37] And "He does not transgress His rule. . . . He does the best for all of His creatures."[38] By His nature, God must do what is best for man. It is not possible for God to be unfaithful to man. These views were anathema to the traditionalists and the Ash'arites, who saw them as an impermissible imposition of obligations on an omnipotent God that compromised His total freedom.

The Unity of God

The Mu'tazilites called themselves the upholders of "divine unity and justice." We have seen what they meant by God's justice. The unity refers to *tawhid*, the unity of God, the central doctrine of Islam. As noted, Mu'tazilite monotheism was a challenge to the orthodox, who held that God's qualities, such as those mentioned in the famous ninety-nine names, are possessed by Allah as attributes, the chief seven of which are: living, knowing, omnipotence, willing, seeing, hearing, and speaking.* They include others as well, such as compassion, mercy (invoked at the beginning of all but one of the 114 Surahs in the Qur'an), forgiveness, and wisdom. The dispute concerned the ontological status of these attributes. The traditionalists held

---

* According to a famous Hadith (Sahih Muslim), Muhammad said, "Verily, there are ninety-nine names of God, one hundred minus one. He who enumerates them will get into Paradise." These names are said to be in the Qur'an and the Hadith, though there is no agreed list of them.

that the attributes were distinct from God's essence, but some-how existed coeternally with Him.

The Mu'tazilites objected that, if God is one, how could He have these numerous attributes somehow coexisting sepa-rately with Him? In what way do they coexist? If they are not part of God's essence, what are they? They were, suspected the Mu'tazilites, personifications become other gods exist-ing coeternally with Allah; in other words, a form of poly-theism, the worst offense to Islam. Wasil ibn 'Ata, one of the first Mu'tazilites, declared: "He who affirms an eternal qual-ity beside God, affirms two gods."[39] So the Mu'tazilites insisted that a greatly reduced number of attributes were, in fact, God's essence. Duncan Macdonald writes that Abu Hudhayl "taught that the qualities were not in His essence, and thus separable from, thinkable apart from it, but that they were His essence."[40] Therefore, for instance, God knows through His essence, which is omniscience, and not through an attribute separable from Him. Likewise, God is powerful by His essence, and so forth. Because of this position, the opponents of the Mu'tazilites called them al-mu'atilah—those who deny God's attributes.

The orthodox and the Ash'arites, who followed them, had no answer to the dilemma of God's unity and His attributes. Yet they insisted that God's attributes were not His essence, but still not completely separate from it. In response to the question as to how this could be, they simply said it had to be accepted, bila kayfa (without saying how). "Secondly," as M. M. Sharif observed, "they argued that if all the attributes of God are identical with His essence, the divine essence must be a homogeneous combination of contradictory qualities. For instance, God is merciful (rahim) and also revengeful (qahhar); both the contradictory attributes would constitute the essence of God, which is one, unique, and indivisible (ahad), and that is absurd."[41]

This was a hugely significant dispute, as one would expect when it comes to an understanding of who God is. For the

Mu'tazilites, God must be who He is and no other. As odd as it may sound to express it in this way, He is *bound* to be who He is. He cannot act against or deny His own nature. For instance, God does not have reason; He *is* reason. Therefore, He cannot do anything unreasonable. This is not a constraint; it is freedom. The ability to negate who and what you are is not freedom; it is nihilism. For the Ash'arites, however, God, as pure will, is not *bound* by anything, including Himself. His freedom of will is absolute. He has no "nature" to deny. He *has* reason, but is not reason. Therefore, by removing God's attributes from His essence, the Ash'arites made these attributes products of His will. In other words, God was not mercy, but merciful when He wished to be. Likewise, there was no impediment to His acting unreasonably when He wished to do so.

The stripping down of God's essence to His will and making His attributes products of His will guaranteed His absolute freedom and power.[42] Thus, He did not by any necessity of His nature need to be merciful (indeed, another of His attributes was "vengeful"). He could choose to be unmerciful, as well, without contradicting Himself. Pure will cannot contradict itself. The Mu'tazilites found this abhorrent. God must do what is good because it would be against His nature, which is goodness itself, to do otherwise.

In the Fifth Surah, the Qur'an inveighs against the Jews for having said, "The hand of Allah is chained." In response, the Qur'an states: "Chained are their hands, and cursed are they for what they say" (5:64). Nothing constrains Allah or chains His hand. Al Fakhr al-Razi, an Ash'arite of the late twelfth century, used this same verse from the Fifth Surah against the Mu'tazilites for their having chained God's hand by saying that Allah *must* act in certain ways and not in others. Nothing could impute a lower regard for, or express a greater outrage at, the Mu'tazilites than comparing them with the Jews, who are accused in the same Surah of having changed God's words and broken their covenant.

The Created Qur'an and Man's Free Will

The dispute about free will involved the debate about the nature of the Qur'an. Was it created in time, or has it coexisted with Allah in eternity? Doctrinally, the traditionalist school held that the Qur'an was not created in time; the Qur'an has forever coexisted with Allah on a tablet in heaven in Arabic, as it exists today. The Qur'an is outside the scope of history. Al-Ash'ari, who supported the traditionalist position, stated clearly:

> The Qur'an is on the preserved (heavenly) tablet.... It is written down in books in reality; it is recited by our tongues in reality; it is heard by us in reality. . . . All of these are essentially identical with the uncreated divine word, which has been on the heavenly tablet from all eternity, in reality, and not in some figurative sense, not in the sense that all these are copies, citations, or communications of a heavenly original. No; all these are identical with the heavily original; what is true of the original is true of those spatial and temporal manifestations that ostensibly come into being through a human agency.[43]

Although coeternal with God, the Qur'an is somehow, like His attributes, distinct from God's essence. The profound problem with this position, which the Mu'tazilites pointed out, was dismissed by Hadith collector al-Bukhari (d. 933), who said, "The Qur'an is the speech of God uncreated, the acts of men are created, and inquiry into the matter is heresy."[44]

Nevertheless, to the utter dismay of the traditionalists, the Mu'tazilites did inquire into the matter, and this difference between them became the most bitter and costly of their disputes. The Mu'tazilites held that the Qur'an had to have been created; otherwise, the historical events it relates would have necessarily been predetermined. The doctrine of *Khalq al-Qur'an,* the createdness of the Qur'an, according to Joseph Kenny in *Theological Themes Common to Islam and Christianity,* means that "the historical events mentioned in the Qur'an would not have been determined from eternity and room would be left for free human choice."[45] Also, as Islamic scholar Neal Robinson points out, for the Mu'tazilites it made no sense "to think of his commandments as existing before the creation of the beings to whom they are addressed."[46]

The Mu'tazilites were correct in detecting the profound theological problem presented by the doctrine of an uncreated Qur'an, the logic of which brought the Qur'an uncomfortably close to the conception of the Christian Word. As Thomas Aquinas would later teach in *Reasons for the Faith against Muslim Objections,* "The Word of God ... is co-eternal with God."[47] The force of Aquinas's argument in developing the implications of this position reveals exactly why the Mu'tazilites objected to the Christ-like status of the uncreated Qur'an; it led ineluctably to another Person in the Godhead, a conclusion inimical to *tawhid.*

Like the Mu'tazilites, Aquinas held that "in God understanding is not different from his being." In other words, His understanding is not an attribute separable from His essence. Therefore, an uncreated Word had to be in His essence and equal to Him. As Aquinas said:

> The divine Word measures up to the power of God, because by his essence He understands himself and everything else. So the Word He conceives by his essence, when He understands himself and everything else, is as great as his essence. It is therefore perfect, simple and equal to God. We call this Word of God a Son, as said above, because He is of the same nature with the Father, and we profess that he is co-eternal with the Father, only begotten and perfect.[48]

The Mu'tazilites, sensing the inexorable force of the logic of this position (well before it was elaborated by Aquinas), equated the doctrine of the uncreated Qur'an with polytheism, a grave violation of the doctrine of *tawhid*. "If the Qur'an was uncreated then it must be another God, and therefore the unity of God would be violated."[49]

The Temporary Triumph of the Mu'tazilites

In 827, the Mu'tazilites succeeded in this dispute to the extent of having the teaching of a created Qur'an (*Khalq al-Qu'ran*) enshrined as a state doctrine by Caliph al-Ma'mun. Al-Ma'mun was the greatest supporter of Greek thought in Islamic history and the creator of the famous Bait al-Hikmah, the House of Wisdom, a great library and translation center, which opened in 830. According to Arab historian Ibn al-Nadim, Aristotle was supposed to have appeared to al-Ma'mun in a dream. When asked about the nature of the good, Aristotle is reported to have replied that, in the first instance, it is "what is rationally good."[50] That answer was embraced by the Mu'tazilites, as well as by the first Arab philosopher, al-Kindi, who was also sponsored by al-Ma'mun. One of the shining stars of al-Ma'mun's reign was the Nestorian Hunayn ibn Ishaq (d. 873), who hailed from al-Hirah in Iraq. Hunayn's son Ishaq (d. 911) was responsible for translating Aristotle's *Nicomachean Ethics* into Arabic.

In al-Ma'mun's court, Christians such as Theodore Abu Qurrah, bishop of Harran and a disciple of St. John of Damascus, could appear before the caliph to debate Muslim theologians over the truth of their respective religions. There are even extant accounts of some of the dialogue from this debate. There took place another very interesting encounter between two of al-Ma'mun's courtiers, one a Muslim, who was a cousin to the caliph, and the other a learned Arab Christian named al-Kindi (not to be confused with the Arab philosopher of that name). This debate, conducted in letters, is still available in a book, *The Apology of Al Kindi*, or "The Epistle of Abdallah ibn Ismaîl the Hâshimite to Abd al Masîh ibn Ishâc al Kindy, inviting him to embrace Islam; and the reply of Abd al Masîh, refuting the same, and inviting the Hâshimite to embrace the Christian Faith." Al-Ma'mun was said to have been so interested in this exchange that he had the letters read to him without stopping.

Addressed to his Christian adversary, Ibn Ismaîl's preamble to the debate is worth quoting at length for what it reveals about the spirit of free inquiry at al-Ma'mun's court and the esteem in which reason was held at the time. It also contains clear references to Mu'tazilite teachings of free will and responsibility.

> Therefore bring forward all the arguments you wish and say whatever you please and speak your mind freely. Now that you are safe and free to say whatever you please, appoint some arbitrator who will impartially judge between us and lean only towards the truth and be free from the empery of passion: and that arbitrator shall be reason, whereby God makes us responsible for our own rewards and punishments. Hereby I have dealt justly with you and have given you full security and am ready to accept whatever decision reason may give for me or against me.[51]

While any Muslim convert to Christianity would have been executed for apostasy, the fact that discussions of this kind could be openly held in the court of the caliph is highly remarkable, all the more so since after the Mu'tazilite caliphs this kind of thing rarely if ever happened. Al-Kindi's letters were subsequently banned. In fact, the extent of al-Ma'mun's liberality in allowing the exchange should be appreciated in light of the lengths to which subsequent authorities went to suppress it. At one time, the law of Egypt required that any house in which *The Apology of Al Kindi* might be found was liable to be razed to the ground, along with forty houses around it.

The period of al-Ma'mun's reign (813–833) is often referred

to as the golden age of Islam for its extraordinary intellectual openness and richness. Science writer Frances Luttikhuizen states in *Christianity and Science* that "al-Ma'mun, strongly influenced by the Mutazilite movement, was the greatest patron of philosophy and science in the history of Islam."[52] By any standard, the person of al-Ma'mun and his court in Baghdad are among the most notable in history.

It was also under al-Ma'mun's patronage that the first Muslim Arab philosopher, Abu Ya'qub al-Kindi (801–873), appeared. Al-Kindi's views reflected the same rational orientation: "Nothing should be dearer to the seeker after truth than truth itself."[53] Regarding sources of learning outside of Islam, he declared, "We ought not to be ashamed of appreciating the truth and of acquiring it wherever it comes from, even if it comes from races distant and nations different from us. For the seeker of truth nothing takes precedence over the truth, and there is no disparagement of the truth, nor belittling either of him who speaks it or of him who conveys it. [The status of] no one is diminished by the truth; rather does the truth ennoble all."[54] The caliph appointed al-Kindi to the House of Wisdom, and made him tutor to the prince, his brother, who followed al-Ma'mun on the throne as al-Mu'tasim. Al-Mu'tasim, in turn, appointed al-Kindi as a tutor to his son.

In *On First Philosophy*, al-Kindi wrote, "Philosophy is the knowledge of the reality of things within people's possibility, because the philosopher's end in theoretical knowledge is to gain truth and in practical knowledge to behave in accordance with truth." To his traditionalist religious opponents, al-Kindi responded: "So anyone who makes business out of religion has no religion, and should rightly be deprived of [the offices] of religion for having opposed the desire to know the truth of things and for calling this desire disbelief."[55] In the philosophical twilight of the Islamic world, Averroes, or Ibn Rushd, (1126–1198) echoed al-Kindi's position in his *Book of the Decisive Treatise*. He wrote that, since "their [the Ancients'] aim and intention in their books is the very intention to which the Law urges us. . . . Whoever forbids reflection upon them by anyone suited to reflect upon them . . . surely bars people from the door through which the Law calls them to cognizance of God."[56] And in his *Exposition of Religious Arguments*, he wrote that "religion commands the study of philosophy."[57]

Al-Kindi assimilated what he could from Aristotle, while rejecting the positions inimical to his Islamic faith. W. Montgomery Watt, author of *A Study of Al-Ghazali*, wrote, "What is remarkable in al-Kindi is the absence of any sense of conflict or tension between philosophy and the Islamic sciences [meaning jurisprudence]."[58] In fact, al-Kindi held that, although prophecy is superior in some ways to philosophy, the content of both is the same. Like the Muʻtazilites, al-Kindi achieved a harmony between reason and revelation by giving an allegorical interpretation to any passage from Qur'an that seemed to contradict reason. At the same time, he defended the Islamic doctrines of the creation of the world ex nihilo and of the resurrection of the body. Most Muslim philosophers who came after him did neither, and were not accepted as a result. Almost without exception, they were supporters of neo-Platonic notions of emanationism, materialistic pantheism, the eternity of the universe, and the immortality of the soul, but not of the body. When dealing with al-Ghazali, we shall see more specifically what was objected to in philosophy and why it was rejected.

Al-Ma'mun's pronouncement of a created Qur'an as state doctrine did not go unopposed. The caliph required religious judges to swear an oath that the Qur'an had been created. A kind of inquisition, the *mihnah* (the testing), was instituted to enforce this (from 833–848). The most severe penalty was death for unbelief for those who refused to take the test. Only those who would testify that the Qur'an was created could be legal witnesses. Those who believed in the uncreated Qur'an could be and were punished and imprisoned for abandoning the doctrine of *tawhid*. The *mihnah* was later extended to include the doctrine of free will and other matters.

One of the most famous prisoners was Ahmad ibn Hanbal (d. 855), the founder of the most literalist school of Islamic jurisprudence. He was flogged, but his life spared. During his inquisition, he answered all questions by quoting from either the Qur'an or the Hadith. If a question could not be answered in this way, he remained silent. Ibn Hanbal became the hero of the traditionalists. The slogan of his supporters was: "nothing which is of God is created and the Qur'an is of God." (The force employed on behalf of the Mu'tazilites is sometimes used to discredit them. But an argument can be made that the use of force to defend rationality is in itself reasonable—in fact required under certain circumstances. Obviously, the enemies of reason cannot be opposed by reason alone.)

After al-Ma'mun, Mu'tazilite doctrine was upheld by the next two caliphs, al-Mu'tasim (833–842) and Harun al-Wathiq (842–847), although without al-Ma'mun's enthusiasm.

Chapter 2

THE OVERTHROW OF THE
MU'TAZILITES:
THE CLOSING COMMENCES

Although the Mu'tazilites enjoyed supremacy under several caliphs, it was not to last.

In the second year of the reign of Caliph Ja'afar al-Mutawakkil (847–861), the tables were turned. The *mihnah* was shut down and the Mu'tazilite judges responsible for the inquisition were cursed from the pulpits by name.[1] Holding the Mu'tazilite doctrine became a crime punishable by death. The Mu'tazilites were expelled from court, removed from all government positions, and their works were largely destroyed. Al-Mutawakkil released the aged Ibn Hanbal from prison and prohibited "discussing the intricacies of what is created and what is uncreated in a copy or vocal recitation of the Qur'an."[2] He also closed down al-Ma'mun's House of Wisdom (though he is credited by some with reopening it and supporting scientific research and translation activity). Despite his religious orthodoxy, al-Kindi was persecuted and driven from Baghdad.[3] Al-Mutawakkil confiscated al-Kindi's library, and the sixty-year-old philosopher was administered sixty lashes before an approving crowd.[4]

Things were to get even worse. Historian Abu Jafar Muhammad ibn Jarir al-Tabari (838–923) relates that in the year from April 892 to March 893, "the booksellers were sworn not to trade in books of theology (*kalam*), dialectical disputation (*gadal*) or philosophy (*falsafa*)."[5] And "In 885, all professional copyists in Baghdad were required to promise under oath to exclude from their professional activities the copying of books of philosophy."[6] Also, "the traditionists' [*sic*] opposition to Mu'tazilism and to these subjects [philosophical theology and dialectical disputation] had consequences in later educational policy because it was the traditionists [*sic*] who eventually formed the curriculum of formal legal education in Islamic societies. In this curriculum they did not include, as was to be expected, these subjects, but neither did they include any of the other translated sciences."[7] *Kalam* (theology) was banned from the curriculum of colleges of law and generally from any institutions of learning based on the charitable trust, know as *waqf.*

The persecution did not immediately end the Mu'tazilite school of thought. Nor did the Mu'tazilite suppression prevent the flourishing of the Greek-influenced *faylasuf* (philosophers) who followed them, such as Alfarabi, Avicenna, and Averroes. Some Mu'tazilites fled to the more hospitable Shi'a areas under the Buwayhid rulers in eastern Persia. As Wadi Kayani remarks, "The Buwayhid period clearly gave room for the Mu'tazilite school to develop much further, to spread and refine itself which is shown by the work of Qadi 'Abd al-Jabbar, secondly this period was also when the 12th Imam of the Shi'ah Imamis went into major occultation and thus for the Shi'ah an infallible guide to develop their doctrine was no longer available; this established a great intellectual bond between the Shi'a and the Mu'tazilite mutakallimun."[8] In the absence of an imam to guide them infallibly, the Shi'a had to think for themselves. The Mu'tazilites could show them how to do this. Eventually, wrote historian Albert Hourani, "the most widely accepted Shi'i teaching contained elements derived from the Mu'tazili school."[9]

However, the long process of dehellenization and ossification had begun. British-Lebanese scholar George Hourani claimed that "the turning point in the suppression of Muʿtazilism occurred in the eleventh century with credal proclamations of the caliph Qadir beginning 1017, followed by Hanbalite demonstrations in Baghdad in the 1060s and the favour shown to the Ashʿarites by the Seljuq sultans and their *wazir* Nizam al-Mulk."[10] "Thus ended," writes Pakistani physicist Pervez Hoodbhoy, "the most serious attempt to combine reason with revelation in Islam."[11] "By the 12th century," he concludes, "the conservative, antirationalist schools of thought had almost completely destroyed the Muʿtazila influence. So hard was this reaction, that al-Ashʿari is considered to be relatively moderate as compared with Ibn Hanbal, and later the Wahhabis, who did not allow any form of speculation."[12] Islamic studies scholar Richard Martin adds this provisional obituary: "Muʿtazilism, by the end of the Abbasid Age in the thirteenth century, was no longer an intellectual force in Dar al-Islam [the abode of Islam]. It existed only in small, remote outposts in the Caspian region and in the madrasas [schools] and libraries of Zaydi in northern Yemen."[13]

By the fourteenth century, these antirationalist tendencies had reached a stage that led Arnold Toynbee to say of the greatest Islamic thinker at that time that "the loneliness of Ibn Khaldun's star is as striking as its brilliance."[14] Ironically, Ibn Khaldun was an Ashʿarite. Even in his superb work the *Muqaddimah* ("Introduction"), the damage is evident in his dismissal of physics: "We must refrain from studying these things [general classes] since such restraint falls under the duty of the Muslim not to do what does not concern him. The problems of physics are of no importance for us in our religious affairs or our livelihoods. Therefore we must leave them alone."[15]

An apt symbol of the tension between reason and revelation in Islam was the famous library of Cordoba. It was one of the glories of Moorish civilization. In the tenth century, the library contained some 400,000 manuscripts—more books than were in France and quite possibly all of western Europe at that time—with some five hundred attendants. However, Muslims not only built it, they also destroyed it, although, according to Arab historian Ibn Sa'id (1214–1286), this was done by Berbers, not Arabs, in 1013. A much earlier apocryphal story, which Hegel related in his *Philosophy of History*, holds that Caliph Omar ordered the destruction of what was left of the library of Alexandria in 638. The story is spurious (as the library did not exist at that time), but Omar is supposed to have said, "These books either contain what is in the Qur'an or something else. In either case, they are superfluous."[16] This, of course, sounds very much like a paraphrase of what, according to Ibn Khaldun, Omar wrote to his victorious general in Persia ordering the destruction of captured books. More recently, the Taliban followed a similar injunction and ordered the destruction of all books in Afghanistan except the Qur'an.

The Opposition of the Traditionalists

Those most offended by the Mu'tazilites were the traditional religious scholars and the followers of Ahmad ibn Hanbal who had been imprisoned and flogged for refusing to consent to the doctrine of a created Qur'an. Hanbalism is the most literalist school of *fiqh*, or Islamic jurisprudence. It continues to be followed today, most notably in Saudi Arabia.

Here one should briefly point out the role of the four Sunni legal schools and the role they play. Al-Shafi'i (767–820), Abu Hanifa (c. 699–767), Ahmad ibn Hanbal (780–855), and Malik ibn Anas (c. 715–796) founded the four Sunni legal schools, or *madhabs*, from which Sunni Muslims could choose with an assurance of orthodoxy. Interpretation (*ijtihad*) of the Qur'an and the Sunnah, insofar as it was needed, was accomplished by these four imams by the early ninth century. By the twelfth century, it was thought that there was no need for further interpretation or elaboration, just application; the door to *ijtihad* (the authorization for scholars individually to interpret the sacred texts through *ra'y*, personal judgment) closed. After the fixation of the law, *taqlid* (the opposite of *ijtihad*), or imitation of the recognized rulings, became the norm. This is why, according to British scholar W. Montgomery Watt, "the central discipline in Islamic education was not theology but jurisprudence."[17] The right path had been set. Within it, all human actions were categorized as: obligatory, "duty" (*fard*); "recommended" (*mandub*); legitimate or indifferent, "permitted" (*mubah*); discouraged, "reprehensible" (*makruh*); and "forbidden" (*haram*). There was nothing one could do for which guidance was not available and necessary. One needed only to follow the prescriptions as instructed by the *ulema* (Islamic jurisprudential scholars). There was no need to look beyond sacred scripture. This was obviously not an orientation conducive to philosophy, ethics, or natural theology. In fact, the subject of philosophy was removed from the curriculum of the famous al-Azhar university in Cairo and was not reinstated until late in the nineteenth century at the insistence of the Egyptian reformer Muhammad 'Abduh.[18]

The door to *ijtihad* was shut so decisively that even efforts to open it in the early nineteenth century were rebuked. When Muhammad Ali as-Sanusi (1787–1859), known as the Grand Sanusi, attempted to reopen the gates to *ijtihad*, he was rebuked in a typical *fatwa* by the mufti of Cairo, who said, "For no one denies the fact that the dignity of *ijtihad* has long disappeared and that at the present time no man has attained this degree of learning. He who believed himself to be a *mujtahid* [a scholar qualified to exercise *ijtihad*] would be under the influence of his hallucinations and of the devil."[19]

Although all four legal schools were highly critical of *kalam* (speculative theology), it was the Hanbali that totally rejected the application of philosophical thought to the Qur'an and even protested against the Ash'arites when they used Aristotelian logic to attack the Mu'tazilites, their common adversary. According to the Hanbalites, one should not be contaminated by employing the weapons of the enemy. In *Istihsan al-Khaud* (*The Vindication of the Science of Kalam*), al-Ash'ari described the objections raised by the orthodox school against the use of reason in matters of faith:

> A section of the people [i.e., the Zahirites and other orthodox people] . . . became inclined to blind faith and blind following (*taqlid*). They condemned those who tried to rationalize the principles of religion as "innovators." . . . They said that had such discussions been the right thing, the Prophet and his Companions would have definitely done so; they further pointed out that the Prophet, before his death, discussed and fully explained all those matters which were necessary from the religious point of view, leaving none of them to be discussed by his followers; and since he did not discuss the problems mentioned above, it was evident that to discuss them must be regarded as an innovation.[20]

Innovation (*bid'ah* or *bida'ah*) is a high offense in Islam. In a Hadith, Muhammad had warned, "Every innovation is *Bida'ah* and every *Bida'ah* is a misguidance (*Dalalah*) and every misguidance is in hell fire."[21]

Ibn Hanbal thought that religion was better off without theology. Since God has spoken to man, man no longer needs to think in any critical fashion. Revelation replaces reason. In the Qur'an and the Sunnah (practices of the Prophet, or his way and deeds), Allah provided all that men needed to know; it was unnecessary to consider anything else. Ibn Hanbal stated:

> Religion is only the book of God, the *athar* [sayings or acts of pious men], the *sunan* [standard practices], and sound narratives from reliable men about recognized sound valid Traditions [*akhbar*] confirming one another . . . until that ends with the Messenger of God and his Companions and the Followers and the

Followers of the Followers, and after them the recognized imams who are taken as exemplars, who hold to the Sunna and keep to the *athar*, who do not recognize heresy and are not accused of falsehood or of divergence [from one another]. They are not upholders of *qiyas* [analogical reasoning] and *raʾy* [personal opinion], for *qiyas* in religion is worthless, and *raʾy* is the same and worse. The upholders of *raʾy* and *qiyas* in religion are heretical and in error.[22]

Since the Qurʾan did not authorize the use of *kalam*, there is no need for it. Ibn Hanbal stated, "Whoever involves themselves in any theological rhetoric is not counted amongst the Ahl us-Sunnah, even if by that he arrives at the Sunnah, until he abandons debating and surrenders to the texts."[23] The use of rational arguments violated faith. Faith is not addressed to reason. Simply accept—*bila kayfa* (without saying how). As Ibn Hanbal declared, "Every discussion about a thing which the Prophet did not discuss is an error."[24] Ibn Hanbal was said to have never eaten watermelon because there was no known instance of Muhammad having done so.[25]

Imitation (*taqlid*) is the way and is above criticism. Ibn Hanbal instructed: "He who supposes that *taqlid* [following an authority without criticism] is not approved and that his religion is not thus following anyone . . . only wants to invalidate the *athar* and to weaken knowledge and the Sunna, and to stand isolated in *raʾy* and Kalam and heresy and divergence [from others]."[26] Ibn Hanbal's teaching resonated with the Muslim man in the street. He became so popular that 150,000 people are said to have flooded the streets of Baghdad for his funeral.[27]

The traditionalists were known as *ahl al-Hadith*, those committed to defending tradition, the authority of the Hadith. (The Hadith are the "traditions" which report various sayings and actions of Muhammad that were first passed on orally before being written down in collections, six of which are accepted as genuine sources of revelation.) A contemporary expression of Hanbali sentiment from Saudi Arabia, which continues to follow this school of *fiqh*, is: "Abandon debate and surrender to the text."[28] If what is revealed in the text demands the denial of the intellect, so be it, *bila kayfa*.

The Demotion of Reason

As the theological school most opposed to the Mu'tazilites, the Ash'arites supported Hanbalite doctrine, though they employed philosophical tools to do so. They abjured reason as comprising man's first duty or as exercising the leading role in validating revelation. The autonomy of reason was anathema to them. Revelation was primary and supreme. In Ash'arism, as we shall see, the primacy of revelation over reason rises from the very nature of what is revealed: God as pure will and power. The response to this God is submission, not interrogation.

It was only within revelation's strictures that reason could legitimately operate in a limited way. According to Pakistani Muslim scholar M. Abdul Hye, "[Reason's] function was to rationalize faith in the basic principles of Islam and not to question the validity or truth of the principles established on the basis of revelation as embodied in the Qur'an and the Sunnah."[29] Logic and even metaphysics could be used to explain and defend the truth of revelation, but not as independent sources of religious or moral knowledge.[30] As the renowned Algerian-French philosopher Muhammad Arkoun characterizes it, the faculty of reason had to accept "the role of handmaid to the revealed Text; its sole function is to shape, bend and systemize reality in accordance with the ideal meanings it recognizes in God's 'signs.'" On this basis, the role of the mind is to "reflect"—in the literal sense—truths that are already given or revealed, "not those that might be found at the end of a gradual search, let alone a speculative quest."[31] Certainly, nothing outside of the Qur'an and the Hadith could be brought to bear upon its interpretation. Otherwise, reason must remain silent before what it might find contradictory and could not understand (*bila kayfa*).

The Ash'arites were particularly offended by the Mu'tazilite claim that unaided reason could discern good and evil. They vehemently denied this, and said that the Mu'tazilites were undermining the need for scripture by saying all men had access to this knowledge. If this were so, what would be the need for the Qur'an (even though the Mu'tazilites held that revelation was necessary for God to make His way clear to man)? Together with the Hanbalites, the Ash'arites, as sarcastically characterized by British missionary scholar W. H. T. Gairdner, "cursed the men who thought that God's concern for His creatures' good might be looked for as the motive for His actions towards them; and who asserted that man was responsible to seek for the will of God, and to perform it if he knew it."[32]

The name of the Ash'arite school came from its founder, Abu Hasan al-Ash'ari (873–935). Al-Ash'ari had been a Mu'tazilite until the age of forty. He then announced: "He who knows me, knows who I am, and he who does not know me, let him know that I am abu al-Hasan 'Ali al-Ash'ari, that I used to maintain that the Qur'an is created, that eyes of men shall not see God, and that the creatures create their actions. Lo! I repent that I have been a Mu'tazilite. I renounce these opinions and I take the engagement to refute the Mu'tazilites and expose their infamy and turpitude."[33]

There are two stories as to why al-Ash'ari renounced and then tried to destroy the Mu'tazilite school. One is that he had three dreams in which Muhammad came to him to tell him to defend the Hadith. As a consequence of the first two dreams, al-Ash'ari abandoned rational methods and devoted himself to the study of the Qur'an and the Hadith. In the third dream, according to W. Montgomery Watt, Muhammad "angrily said that he had commanded him to defend the doctrines related from himself, but had not commanded him to give up rational methods."[34] Therefore, al-Ash'ari returned to *kalam* (rational or speculative theology), but as an anti-Mu'tazilite to defend the traditional doctrines of Ibn Hanbal.

The other story is that his disillusionment apparently came about through an unsatisfactory answer to a case he had put to his old Mu'tazilite teacher, al-Jubba'i. In order to challenge the Mu'tazilite concepts of God's providence and justice, al-Ash'ari posed to his teacher the case of three brothers. The first brother lived as a faithful Muslim and went to paradise when he died. The second brother lived as an infidel, performed evil deeds, and went to hell when he died. The third brother died in infancy, and ended up somewhere between paradise and hell because he did not have time to become a believer but was not an infidel either.

Why, asked al-Ash'ari, did God not allow the infant to grow up? Because, al-Jubba'i purportedly responded, God knows best and the child might have grown up to be an infidel like his older brother.

But why then, retorted al-Ash'ari, did God prolong the life of the second brother if He knew he was going to become an infidel? Is not God obliged to do the best for man? In which case, He must make all men believers so they would go to paradise. This is clearly not the case, as most men in the world are infidels. Therefore, concluded al-Ash'ari, the Mu'tazilite theory that God must do the best for man is false.

The interesting thing about al-Ash'ari's argument is its presumption that the existence of man's free will is incompatible with God's justice and providence. Unless people are compelled to be good, God cannot be just. It is as if to say that, if man is free, there cannot be a God. Al-Ash'ari resolved the dilemma, as we shall see, by denying both man's free will and God's justice as implying anything God is required to do. Underlying the Ash'arite view is a conception of God as pure will, without or above reason.

It is extremely important to spell out the theology, epistemology, and metaphysics involved in this position because of its formative impact on subsequent Sunni Islamic culture. Also, the extremity of its views must be appreciated within the perspective of its having been seen as a "middle way" between the literalism of the traditionalists and what was considered the radical rationalism of the Muʻtazilites.

The Primacy of the Will

The Ashʻarite view developed a theological basis for the primacy of will by claiming that the revelation of Muhammad emphasizes most particularly, and above all, two attributes of God: His uncompromising omnipotence and will. "Allah does what He wills" (Quʼran 14:27). God's nature *is* His will. He is "the great Doer of what He wills" and "Effecter of what He intends" (Qurʼan 85:15). All monotheistic religions hold that, in order to be one, God must be omnipotent. But the Ashʻarite argument reduced God to His omnipotence by concentrating exclusively on His unlimited power, as against His reason. God's "reasons" are unknowable by man. God rules as He pleases. Allah had only to say "be" in order to bring the world into existence, but He may also say "not be" to bring about its end—without a reason for doing either. His word is sufficient for creation or annihilation, though His word is His will, rather than an expression of His reason (*Logos*). Therefore, creation is not imprinted with reason. It cannot reflect what is not there. As a result, there is no rational order invested in the universe upon which one can rely, only the second-to-second manifestation of God's will.

God is so powerful that every instant is the equivalent of a miracle. Nothing intervenes or has independent or even semi-autonomous existence. The universe is in no way self-subsistent. In philosophical language, this view, called "voluntarism," holds that God is the primary cause of everything and there are no secondary causes. There is no causal mediation. Therefore, what may seem to be "natural laws," such as the laws of gravity, physics, etc., are really nothing more than God's customs or habits, which He is at complete liberty to break or change at any moment.

More than 150 years after al-Ash'ari's death, one of his successors, Abu Hamid al-Ghazali (1058–1111), wrote in *Deliverance from Error*: "Nature is entirely subject to God; incapable of acting by itself, it is an instrument in the hand of the Creator; sun, moon, stars, and elements are subject to God and can produce nothing of themselves. In a word, nothing in nature can act spontaneously and apart from God."[35]

One could say that everything that happens is the result of supernatural causes, though the word *supernatural* becomes meaningless in the absence of the word *natural* from which to distinguish it. As Duncan Macdonald observed, "Miracles and what we regard as the ordinary operations of nature are on the same level."[36] In the introduction to his translation of Averroes's *The Incoherence of the Incoherence*, Simon Van Den Bergh quipped: "One might say that, for the [Muslim] theologian, all nature is miraculous and all miracles are natural."[37] In other words, every "natural" event is the result of a particular *divine* act. If this is true, if divine intervention is used to explain natural phenomena, then rational explanations for them or inquiries into them become forms of impiety, if not blasphemy.

The consequences of this voluntaristic view are momentous. If creation exists simply as a succession of miraculous moments, it cannot be apprehended by reason. Other religions, including Christianity, recognize miracles. But they recognize them precisely as temporary and extraordinary suspensions of the natural law. In fact, that is what defines them as miracles. One admits to the possibility of a miracle only after discounting every possible explanation of its occurrence by natural causes. In voluntaristic Islamic thought, however, there are no natural causes to discount. As a result, reality becomes incomprehensible and the purpose of things in themselves indiscernible because they have no inner logic. If unlimited will is the exclusive constituent of reality, there is really nothing left to reason about. The primacy of will has no boundaries in reason.

Macdonald wrote that, for al-Ghazali, "the fundamental thing in the world and the starting point of all speculation is will."[38] Whereas the philosophers and the Muʿtazilites shared the view that things exist because God has first *thought* them, al-Ghazali reversed this relationship by stating that "God has cognizance of the world because He wills it and in His willing it."[39] In other words, God knows *because* He wills; will precedes knowledge. For al-Ghazali, thought or knowledge does not come before act; it is the act that produces knowledge. Though written more than half a millennium before Goethe's *Faust*, al-Ghazali's statement neatly presages Faust's substitution of the "Deed" for the "Word" (*Logos*) at the beginning of the Gospel of St. John. "In the beginning was the Word" is transformed into "In the beginning was the Deed." This contrast captures the two radically different theologies of the Muʿtazilites and the Ashʿarites. Fazlur Rahman summed up the differences by saying that Ashʿarism "had rendered God a concentrate of power and will, just as the Muʿtazila had made Him a concentrate of justice and rationality."[40]

According to the M. Abdul Hye, the Ashʿarites held that "God, being absolutely free in His action, is not bound to act on rational purpose. He does not act teleologically for, otherwise, His actions would be determined by something external to and other than Himself and He would not remain absolutely free. External purpose would put a limit to God's omnipotence. Like Spinoza, al-Ashʿari held that there is no purpose in the mind of God which would determine His activity. From this anti-teleological view it follows that as God's action is not teleological, He is not bound to do what is best for His creatures. He does whatever He wills."[41] Pure will has no purpose other than the indiscriminate exercise of itself. In and of itself, it is directionless and therefore arbitrary.

The Unknowable God

If God is pure will, then He is incomprehensible. There are two reasons for this. One is the doctrine of *tanzih*, which refers to God's absolute transcendence and utter incomparability. There is no correspondence at all between God and His creation. The distance between the infinite and the finite is immeasurable. This is the meaning of the second half of the Hanbalite-Ash'arite formula, *bila kayfa wala tashbih* (without inquiring how and without making comparison). Comparison between God and man cannot be made because man is not made in His image or likeness. "Nothing is like Him" (Surah 42:11). While there are numerous statements in the Qur'an as to God's closeness or nearness to man, this is necessarily on account of the complete contingency of creation; it is the closeness of the Willer to the willed.

The other reason follows as a simple conclusion from the incomprehensibility of the world as the direct and instantaneous product of the will of God. If the world cannot be understood by reason, how possibly could its Creator? What would be the point of access? God is incomprehensible *in Himself* because pure will has no reason. God is unknown because He is unknowable. What Allah reveals in the Qur'an is not Himself, but His rules for man. The result is what Duncan Macdonald called "the awful impassability of the logically unified absolute."[42]

As a consequence of Ash'arite views, Fazlur Rahman said, the endeavor "to search for ends and purposes in His laws is not only meaningless, but also grave disobedience to Him."[43] The theology of pure will anathematizes the search for rational meaning. "Theology thus monopolized the whole field of metaphysics and would not allow pure *thought* any claim to investigate rationally the nature of the universe and the nature of man."[44]

We can see how this idea of God influenced Muslim thinkers up to the present day, including those most known for reform in the late nineteenth and early twentieth centuries.

The famous Egyptian reformer Muhammad ʿAbduh (1849–1905), who hoped to reconcile Islam with modernity, said: "But reason quite lacks the competence to penetrate to the essence of things. For the attempt to discern the nature of things, which necessarily belongs with their essential complexity, would have to lead to the pure essence and to this, necessarily, there is no rational access." Of course, if one cannot know a thing's essence, one cannot know what it is. ʿAbduh appears to be saying that an attempt to apprehend a thing's essence would lead ineluctably to God's essence, the pure essence, and this is a forbidden pursuit. He continues:

> Thought on the essence of the creator, or the demand to know the essence—these are interdicted to human reason. For there is, as we know, a complete otherness between the two existences, and the Divine Being is immune from all compositeness. To ask to know it is totally to overextend the power man possesses and is a vain and dangerous enterprise. It is in fact a delusion because it essays the inconceivable and a danger because it conduces to an offence against faith, involving a will to definition of the indefinable and the limitation of the illimitable.[45]

In a similar vein, renowned Palestinian-American philosopher and professor of Islamic studies Ismaʿil Al-Faruqi (1921–1986) wrote:

> The will of God is God *in percipe*—the nature of God in so far as I can know anything about Him. This is God's will and that is all we have—and we have it in perfection in the Qurʾan. But Islam does not equate the Qurʾan with the nature or essence of God. It is the "Word of God, the Commandment of God, the Will of God." But God does not reveal Himself to

anyone. Christians talk about the revelation of God Himself—by God of God—but this is the great difference between Christianity and Islam. God is transcendent, and once you talk about hierophancy and immanence, then the transcendence of God is compromised. You may not have complete transcendence and self-revelation at the same time.[46]

The Implications from Christianity

To understand the ultimate significance of the Ash'arite teaching of an unreasoning God, contrast it to the Christian teaching that was similarly tempted to such extremes, but resisted them. Why, for instance, did this exclusive preoccupation with God's omnipotence not afflict Christianity, which is, after all, also monotheistic? Christianity holds that God is omnipotent and the primary cause of all things, as well. In fact, there were strong tendencies within Christianity to move in the very same direction as the Ash'arites.

The early Christian thinker Tertullian questioned what possible relevance reason could have to Christian revelation in his famous remark: "What has Athens to do with Jerusalem?" The antirational view was apparent in Duns Scotus's and Nicholas of Autrecourt's advocacy of voluntarism.[47] It was violently manifested in the millenarian movements of the Middle Ages, and somewhat within the movement that was known as fideism—faith alone, *sola scriptura*. In its most radical form, this school held that the scriptures are enough. Forget reason, Greek philosophy, and Thomas Aquinas.

Yet the antirationalist view in its more extreme forms has never predominated in Christianity, and was considered broadly heretical. The reason Christianity was insulated from an obsession with God's omnipotence was the revelation of Christ as *Logos* in the Gospel of St. John. If Christ is *Logos*, if God introduces himself as *ratio*, then God is not only all-powerful, He *is* reason. While the Mu'tazilites claimed something similar, they did not have a scriptural authority of similar significance to confirm their position in an unassailable way, while their opponents had ample scriptural material to oppose them.

Also, Christian revelation claims that everything was created through Christ as *Logos*. Since it was through *Logos* that all things were created, creation carries the imprint of its Creator as reason. Nature bespeaks an intelligibility that derives from a transcendent source. Benedict XVI often speaks to this point. He has referred to the "world as a product of creative reason" and said that "at the origin of everything is the creative reason of God."[48] What is more, Christ, as *Logos*, is He "who sustains all things by his mighty *word*" [my emphasis]" (Hebrews 1:3). Because it is primarily His Word upon which creation rests—rather than solely His will—creation has a steady, rational foundation upon which man can rely. This view constitutes an open invitation to examine the rules and laws of creation in order to know the Creator, an invitation very familiar from the Old Testament (Wisdom 13:1–6). In Romans 1, St. Paul reiterated it by saying, "Ever since the creation of the world, the invisible existence of God and His everlasting power have been clearly seen by the mind's understanding of created things." The laws of nature are not a challenge to God's authority but an expression of it, as seen in Thomas Aquinas's statement that we are able to apprehend created things with our minds because they were first "thought" by God. Reason and revelation are compatible. The tension between Athens and Jerusalem was reconciled in Rome.

As the then Cardinal Ratzinger said in his 2005 Subiaco address, "From the beginning, Christianity has understood itself as the religion of the 'Logos,' as the religion according to reason. In the first place, it has not identified its precursors in the other religions, but in the philosophical enlightenment which has cleared the path of tradition to turn to the search of the truth and toward the good, toward the one God who is above all gods."[49]

Ultimately, this theological view developed into the realist metaphysics of Aquinas, which then became the foundation for modern science, as Father Stanley Jaki, a Hungarian theologian and physicist, explained in his voluminous writings on the origins of modern science. Jaki laid out, as well, the reasons modern science was stillborn in the Muslim world after what seemed to be its real start.[50] No one offers a more profound understanding of the consequences of the view of God as pure will than Jaki has. The metaphysical support for natural law not only laid the foundations for modern science but also provided the basis for the gradual development of constitutional government.

Islam, in contrast, lost its balance in its Ash'arite form. The Ash'arites feared *Logos* would somehow compromise the omnipotence that God must have in order to be one. Ash'arite theologians then deduced from their voluntaristic view of God, in an a priori way, one of the strangest, most extreme metaphysical constructs ever conceived. If this is *who* God is, they seemed to think, then this is the *way* things must be metaphysically.

Chapter 3
THE METAPHYSICS OF THE WILL

A l-Ash'ari elaborated a metaphysics to support his volunta-ristic theology. This metaphysics had profound implications for causality, epistemology, and human freedom.

Al-Ash'ari used early Greek atomistic philosophy to assert that reality is composed of atoms. Whereas the ancient Greeks and Romans (Lucretius) used atomism as the foundation for a materialistic philosophy, al-Ash'ari put it to opposite use. Through atomism, Lucretius wished to demonstrate that there is no divine intervention in the world and that things do not move in "furtherance of some divine plan,"[1] but randomly. Al-Ash'ari wished to show the reverse: that everything depends directly on God's intervention. He was able to employ atomism in this way because, unlike Lucretius, who believed matter was eternal, al-Ash'ari, like all orthodox Muslims, believed matter was created ex nihilo. God's configuration of these atoms at any given moment makes things what they are. In *Islam in the World*, British analyst Malise Ruthven explains, "The Ash'aris rationalized God's omnipotence within an atomistic theory of creation, according to which the world was made up of the discrete points in space and time whose only connection was the will of God, which created them anew at every moment."[2] For example, there is a collection of atoms which is a plant. Does the plant remain a plant as you are reading this line because it has the nature of a plant, or because Allah wishes it to be a plant from this moment to the next? The Ash'arites held that it is a plant only for the moment. For the plant to remain a plant depends on the will of Allah, and if one contends that it has to remain a plant because it has the nature of plant, this is *shirk*—blasphemy (in the form of polytheism, or "the association of others with Allah").

In order to realize exactly how radical Ash'arite metaphysics is, consider the following examples that make the instability of the Ash'arite metaphysical scheme startlingly clear:

In *Islam and Science,* Pervez Hoodbhoy, a physicist at Islamabad University, writes of Ash'arites, "Even a speeding arrow may or may not reach its destination, they said, because at each moment along its path God destroys the world and then creates it afresh at the next moment. Where the arrow will be at the next moment, given that it was at a particular spot at an earlier moment, cannot be predicted because it is God alone who knows how the world is to be recreated."[3]

Movement is actually illusory. Things do not change in themselves. A body only seems to be moving. What is really happening is that the atoms of the body in one position are annihilated, and the object is then completely reconstituted by new or similar atoms in a second location minutely removed from the first, and so on until the appearance of motion is made by a series of successive annihilations and recreations. Things actually have no past or future. They exist only in the now.

However, this sequence of near instantaneous annihilation and creation is also true of stationary objects, as well as of their properties, such as color. As Canadian philosopher Floy E. Doull describes it in "Peace with Islam," "For example, we have not really dyed the dress red when we believe we've coloured it with red dye; rather, at that instant God has made the red colour the property of the dress, and continuously recreates the red colour instant by instant."[4]

Duncan Macdonald summarizes:

> The time-atoms, if the expression may be permitted, are equally unextended and have also absolute void—of time—between them. Just as space is only in a series of atoms, so time is only in a succession of untouching moments and leaps across the void from one to the other with the jerk of the hand of a clock. Time, in this view, is in grains and can exist only in connection with change. The monads differ from those of Leibniz in having no nature in themselves, no possibility of development along certain lines. The Muslim monads are, and again are not, all change and action in the world are produced by their entering into existence and dropping out again, not by any change in themselves.[5]

Majid Fakhry explains further:

> The world, which they defined as everything other than God, was composed of atoms and accidents. Now the accidents (singular 'arad) they argued, cannot endure for two instants of time, but are continually created by God who creates or annihilates them at will. Al-Baqilani (d. 1013) who appears to follow the lead of Al-Ash'ari in this respect, actually defines the accident as entities "the duration of which is impossible . . . and which cease to exist in the second instant of their coming to be." Similarly, the atoms (sing. al-juz') in which the accidents inhere are continually created by God and endure simply by reason of the accident of duration (baqa') which God creates in them. But insofar as this accident of duration, like the other accidents, is itself perishable, the whole world of atoms and accidents is in a state of continuous generation and corruption.[6]

For al-Ash'ari's disciple, Abu Bakr al-Baqilani (d. 1013), the atomistic discontinuity of created things itself proves the absolute transcendence and omnipotence of Allah as the sole agent. If creation is a group of free-floating atoms in space and time, then ipso facto *only* Allah can make them what they are at any given time in any given way.[7] Al-Baqilani went so far as to say that this concept of atomism was "co-essential" with the text of the Qur'an. So consequential was his thought that Ibn Taymiyya, the thirteenth-century Muslim thinker revered by today's Islamists, saluted al-Baqilani as "the best of the Ash'ari mutakallimun, unrivalled by any predecessor or successor."[8]

The Loss of Causality

The catastrophic result of this view was the denial of the relationship between cause and effect in the natural order. In *The Incoherence of the Philosophers*, al-Ghazali, who vehemently rejected Plato and Aristotle, insisted that God is not bound by any order and that there is, therefore, no "natural" sequence of cause and effect, as in fire burning cotton or, more colorfully, as in "the purging of the bowels and the using of a purgative."[9] Rather than a clear and binding relationship between cause and effect, there are merely juxtapositions of discrete events that make it appear that the fire is burning the cotton, but God could just as well do otherwise. (This doctrine is known as occasionalism.) In other words, there is no continuous narrative of cause and effect tying these moments together in a comprehensible way.

Al-Ghazali's refutation of causality must be quoted at length to appreciate its radical and comprehensive nature. In *The Incoherence of the Philosophers*, he stated:

> The connection between what is habitually believed to be a cause and what is habitually believed to be an effect is not necessary, according to us. For example, there is no causal connection between the quenching

of thirst and drinking, satiety and eating, burning and contact with fire. Light and the appearance of the sun, death and decapitation, healing and the drinking of medicine, the purging of the bowels and the using of a purgative, and so on to [include] all [that is] observable among connected things in medicine, astronomy, arts, and crafts. Their connection is due to the prior decree of God, who creates them side by side, not to it being necessary in itself, incapable of separation. On the contrary, it is within [divine] power to create satiety without eating, to create death without decapitation, to continue life after decapitation, and so on to all connected things. . . .

Our opponent claims that the agent of the burning is the fire exclusively; this is a natural, not a voluntary agent, and cannot abstain from what is in its nature when it is brought into contact with a receptive substratum. This we deny, saying: The agent of the burning is God, through His creating the black in the cotton and the disconnection of its parts, and it is God who made the cotton burn and made it ashes either through the intermediation of angels or without intermediation. For fire is a dead body which has no action, and what is the proof that it is the agent? Indeed, the philosophers have no other proof than the observation of the occurrence of the burning, when there is contact with fire, but observation proves only simultaneity, not causation, and, in reality, there is no other cause . . . but God.[10]

It is interesting to contrast this view with that of Thomas Aquinas in the *Summa Contra Gentiles*, where he states that "whoever answers the question, why wood got hot, because God has willed it so, answers appropriately if he intends to carry back the question to the prime cause; but inappropriately, if he intends to exclude all other causes." Aquinas said that the latter position "is the mistake of those who believe that all things follow, without any rational plan, from God's pure will. This is the error of the exponents of the Law of the Moors, as Rabbi Moses [Maimonides] says; according to them, it makes no difference whether fire heats or cools, unless God [directly] wills it so."[11]

Without causality in the natural order, anything can come of anything, and nothing necessarily follows. How, in such circumstances, can man live in any practical, daily sense without knowing what will follow what? As al-Ghazali says (in mimicking the objections of his opponents), "For God is capable of everything, and it is not necessary for the horse to be created from the sperm nor the tree to be created from the seed—indeed it is not necessary for either of the two to be created from anything."[12] How then does the horse breeder or the horticulturalist proceed with his work? If fire does not burn cotton, how does the cook start a fire to cook a meal? Al-Ghazali answers that "God has created within us knowledge that He will not bring about everything that is possible."[13] God, apparently, sticks to his habits—the doctrine of 'ada (God's "habit"). "They are possibilities that may or may not occur. But the continuous habit of their occurrence repeatedly, one time after another, fixes unshakably in our minds the belief in their occurrence according to past habit."[14] But it is *only* that—a belief in a habit, nothing more.

The ultimate meaning of this is that "there is no unity in the world, moral or physical or metaphysical; all hangs from the individual will of Allah."[15] Averroes expressed the inescapable consequence of this position by saying that "once it is held that there are no intermediates between the beginnings and the ends of products, on which the existence of these ends depends, there will be no order or organization [in this world]. And if there is no order or organization, then there would be no indication that these existing entities have a willing and knowing agent. For order, organization, and the founding of effects upon cause are the indicators that [existing entities] were produced through knowledge and wisdom."[16] This is exactly the disputed point: for Averroes and Aquinas the source of creation is knowledge and wisdom; for al-Ghazali it is will and power. Knowledge and wisdom have an inherent order; will and power do not.

Al-Ghazali seems to have been impelled to embrace this view because he, like al-Ash'ari, thought that the acceptance of cause and effect in the natural order would mean that God acted out of necessity rather than free will. This would mean a world created necessarily, rather than freely ex nihilo. If "x causes y" in the natural order in such a way that "y *must* follow x," then a deterministic sequence of necessary causality could be retrofitted up the chain of being all the way to Allah Himself. God would then be incapable of miracles, the defense of which seems to concern al-Ghazali foremost. Also, the suggestion of the autonomous or semiautonomous operation of natural cause and effect would vitiate God's omnipotence and implies polytheism, as it allows for a cause other than God. If He is not the only cause, then He is not God, who will have no other causes before Him.

Such was the influence of the Ash'arite school and of al-Ghazali in particular that the denial of secondary causality became embedded in Sunni orthodoxy. It was repeated by the Egyptian Hanafi jurist Ahmad ibn Naqib al-Misri (d. 1368) in *Reliance of the Traveller: A Classic Manual of Sacred Islamic Law*. Al-Misri wrote that "the science of the materialists" is based on the "conviction of materialists that things in themselves or by their own nature have a causal influence independent of the will of Allah. To believe this is unbelief that puts one beyond the pale of Islam."[17]

Carrying this teaching into the fifteenth century, Muhammad Yusuf as-Sanusi, using some of al-Ghazali's examples, wrote: "You become aware of the impossibility of anything in the world producing any effect whatsoever, because that entails the removal of that effect from the power and will of our majestic and mighty Protector. . . . For that matter, food has no effect on satiety, nor water on moistening the land . . . nor fire on burning. . . . Know that it is from God from the start, without the other accompanying things having any intermediacy or effect on it, neither by their nature, nor by a power or peculiarity placed in it by God, as many ignorant people think. . . . Whoever holds that those things produce an effect by their nature is an unbeliever." As for the appearance of causes, "God has created them as signs and indications of the things he wishes to create without any logical connection between them and that of which they are the indications. Thus God can break the accustomed order of things whenever he wishes and for whomsoever he wishes."[18]

This teaching and its profound effects are the reason why, even in the twenty-first century, Fouad Ajami would report, "Wherever I go in the Islamic world, it's the same problem: cause and effect; cause and effect."[19] The following is an example of this problem from the late twentieth century. In *Islam and Science*, Pakistani physicist Pervez Hoodbhoy writes about the attempt by the Institute of Policy Studies, an offshoot of the Islamist group Jamaat-e-Islami, to ensure that Pakistan's science textbooks were sufficiently Islamized. The institute's guidelines directed that "in writing a science book for Class 3 children, one should *not* ask, 'What will happen if an animal does not take any food?' Instead, the following question should be asked: 'What will happen if Allah does not give the animal food.'"[20] Also, states Hoodbhoy, "Effect must not be related to physical cause. To do so leads towards atheism. For example, says the IPS recommendation, 'there is latent poison present in the subheading *Energy Causes Changes* because it gives the impression that energy is the true cause rather than Allah.'" Hoodbhoy concludes, "The basic assumption of science—that each physical effect has a corresponding physical cause—is being specifically refuted. Instead of physical forces, it is continuous divine intervention which moves matter."[21]

The elimination of cause and effect makes prediction epistemologically impossible and theologically undesirable. This can result in some unusual behavior affecting everyday matters. Thus, points out Hoodbhoy, "Many, if not most, orthodox *ulema* contend that prediction of rain lies outside of what can be lawfully known to man, and infringes on the supernatural domain. Consequently, between 1983 and 1984, weather forecasts were quietly suspended by the Pakistani media, although they were later reinstated."[22] If an incalculable God directly creates the weather, then the weather cannot be calculable.

The Loss of Epistemology

The weather report was not the only epistemological casualty of Ash'arism. In his rebuttal to al-Ghazali in *The Incoherence of the Incoherence*, Averroes said that the activity of reason is "nothing more than its knowledge of existing entities through the knowledge of their causes." Therefore, "whoever repudiates causes actually repudiates reason."[23] The denial of causality makes "genuine knowledge impossible [and] will only leave us with opinion (*doxa*)."[24] Or from the same work, "To deny the existence of efficient causes which are observed in sensible things is sophistry. . . . Denial of cause implies the denial of knowledge, and denial of knowledge implies that nothing in the world can really be known."[25] Again, he points out that if causality is denied, "there is no fixed knowledge of anything," because "true knowledge is the knowledge of the thing according to what it is in itself."[26] In this way, Ash'arite metaphysics makes epistemology impossible and closes off its adherents from knowledge of reality.

Certainly, one cannot know ethics. As British-Lebanese scholar George Hourani pointed out, the main objection al-Ash'ari raised against rationalistic ethics was that "independent human reason implies a limit on the power of God; for if man could judge what is right and wrong he could rule on what God could rightly prescribe for man, and this would be presumptuous and blasphemous." The Ash'arites also objected that the Mu'tazilites "arrogated the function of revelation and rendered it useless."[27] In their metaphysics, the Ash'arites made sure that such ethical knowledge is unobtainable independent of revelation.

Morality, or what is just, cannot be known rationally for two reasons. One is practical: reason is too corrupted by man's self-interest. As Muslim scholar Fazlur Rahman characterizes the Ash'arite view, "In a natural state the only law was self-interest. And, because human beings will deem all such things that promote their self-interest to be good, and those that thwart their self-interest as bad, therefore God has to declare, through revelation, what is good and what is evil."[28] This derogation of the status of reason in respect to its corruption is repeated in al-Ghazali's *Moderation in Belief*, where he writes that reason is so infected by man's self-interest that it cannot know moral principles; they can be known only through revelation. This was the typical Ash'arite view that man calls "good' whatever advances his self-interests, and "bad" whatever subverts them. Therefore, man's laws are only expressions of his corrupted will.

The Mu'tazilites objected to al-Ghazali's position that each person will simply create his own "good" in conformity with his desires, saying:

> Your discourse comes to this: that (rational) "good" and "bad" are reducible to being conducive to and thwarting desires. But we see that a rational being regards as good that wherein he does not (necessarily) see any benefit and (sometimes) regards as bad that wherein he may find benefit. ... If someone sees a man or an animal on the verge of perishing, he regards it as good to save him ... although not believing in the Shari'a and even when he does not expect any benefit from this in this world, and even though this may occur in a place where there is nobody to see him and

praise him for doing so. We may indeed suppose the
absence of every (selfish) motive. . . . It is clear then
that "good" and "bad" have a meaning other than what
you have described.[29]

Al-Ghazali responded to this objection with an approach
that is so reductionist it is almost proto-Marxian in defining
reason as an excrescence of self-interest, if not of material forces
themselves. As paraphrased by Fazlur Rahman, al-Ghazali
claimed that "the rescuer is primarily led to save a living being
in danger, because if he does not do so this would hurt his own
natural strong feelings of compassion: he is thus satisfying himself by rescuing the person in danger."[30]

The other reason man cannot independently know right
from wrong, which really makes the first reason close to dis-
ingenuous, is epistemological: man *cannot* know what does not
exist to be known (whether he is self-interested or not). Since
nothing is right or wrong intrinsically, there is nothing to be
known in this respect. As a consequence, the Ash'arite theologian Abu'l el-Ma'ali al-Juwayni (1028–1085), al-Ghazali's
teacher, concluded "that there is nothing obligatory by reason
for the servant or for God."[31] This important statement means
that nothing that man knows or can learn by his reason can
possibly carry any moral weight concerning what he must do
or not do. It also means that the "moral" obligations that God
sets upon man do not originate in reason, nor is there anything
that God is obligated to do by reason. God can command what
is evil to be good, or good to be evil. Reason has nothing to do
with justice or morality. Only absolute divine will does.

The Loss of Objective Morality

Since reason is not a source of moral truth, al-Ghazali reaches
the same conclusion as al-Juwayni: "No obligations flow from
reason but from the *Shari'a*."[32] The metaphysical reason for the
exclusive authority of revelation in moral matters is that things

or acts are not good or bad in themselves, according to their nature or essence. They have no nature or essence. All acts are in themselves morally neutral. As al-Juwayni taught, "The intellect does not indicate either that a thing is noble or that it is vile in a judgment that obliges (*hukm al-takif*). It is informed about what it must consider as noble and as vile only by the resources of the law (*shar*') and by what tradition renders necessary. The principle of what must be said [on a subject] is that a thing is not noble by itself, by its genre, or by an attribute that belongs to it."[33]

This version of Islam decisively answers Socrates' famous question from the *Euthyphro*: "Is the pious or holy loved by the gods because it is pious? Or is it pious because it is loved by the gods?"[34] The Ash'arite answer is that it is the latter. Allah does not command certain behavior because it is good; it is good because He commands it. Likewise, He does not forbid murder because it is bad; it is bad because He forbids it.

If Allah is pure will, good and evil are only conventions of Allah's—some things are *halal* (permitted/lawful) and others are *haram* (forbidden/unlawful), simply because He says so and for no reasons in themselves. Evil is simply what is forbidden. What is forbidden today could be permitted tomorrow without inconsistency. God, in short, is a legal positivist.

Al-Ash'ari expressed this view in a question and answer dialogue:

> Since the Creator is subject to no one and bound by no command, nothing can be evil on His part.
>
> *Objection*: Then lying is evil only because God has declared it to be evil.
>
> *Answer*: Certainly. And if He declared it to be good, it would be good; and if He commanded it, no one could gainsay Him.[35]

Thus, al-Ash'ari excluded anything objective in the character of acts themselves. Evil is only a rule, or rather it is not obeying the rule. For al-Ash'ari, a thing is evil only because it is proclaimed as such by God. We know the limits and boundaries because they have been revealed. Al-Juwayni stated: "Thus the meaning of 'good' is that for which scripture reveals praise for its agent, and the intention of 'evil' is that for which scripture reveals blame for its agent."[36]

No one, however, is in authority over God to set limits or boundaries for Him. Al-Ash'ari wrote: "The proof that He is free to do whatever He does is that He is the Supreme Monarch, subject to no one, with no superior over Him who can permit, or command, or chide, or forbid, or prescribe what He shall do and fix bounds for Him. This being so, nothing can be evil on the part of God. For a thing is evil on our part only because we transgress the limit and bound set for us and do what we have no right to do. But since the Creator is subject to no one and bound by no command, nothing can be evil on His part."[37]

Therefore, God is not subject to justice and injustice. There is no standard by which He can be questioned. If Allah is pure will, one act of His pure will cannot be morally differentiated from another act of His pure will. There are no standards outside of Him by which to do so; in fact, there are no standards within Him, either, or at least He is not subject to them. He is beyond good and evil. In this sense, God is a Nietzschean. The Ash'arite view of God is a vindication, or theological expression, of Thrasymachus's famous assertion in *The Republic* that right is the rule of the stronger. Ash'arism is the theology of "might makes right" in that it asserts that might *should* make right. As God is the strongest, His rule is right, by definition. Allah, then, is not only a Nietzschean; He is also a sophist, like Thrasymachus. George Hourani calls this "theistic subjectivism." He states: "It is subjectivist because it relates values to the view of a judge who *decides* them, denying anything objective in the character of acts themselves, that would make them right or wrong independently of anyone's decision or opinion. And theistic because the decider of value is taken to be God. A more usual name is 'ethical voluntarism.'"[38] Iranian philosopher Abdulkarim Soroush calls the Ash'arites the "nominalists" of Islam.[39]

What kind of society does the embrace of this Nietzschean God produce? This will be discussed later in the book. For now, one may wonder if there is any connection between it and the situation observed in Jerusalem by French author Chateaubriand in his *Itinéraire de Paris à Jérusalem* (1811), which comes uncannily close to what one might imagine a society organized around Thrasymachus's dictum would look like: "Accustomed to follow the fortunes of a master, they have no law that connects them to ideas of order and political moderation: to kill, when one is the stronger, seems to them a legitimate right; they exercise that right or submit to it with the same indifference. . . . They don't know liberty; they have no property rights; force is their God."[40]

In any case, it would appear that this extraordinary conception of a God without morals is the solution to the problem of theodicy that Ash'arism created by denying man's free will, but at the same time still being left with the existence of evil. While the Mu'tazilites could claim that the origin of evil was in man's free but disordered will, the Ash'arites did not have recourse to this explanation because of their denial of that freedom. If God is the sole cause of everything, is He not also the cause of evil? In order to absolve God of this charge, they made Him above or without morality. Al-Juwayni dismissed the Mu'tazilites' explanation for suffering, which justified God by saying that He would use suffering as the requital for sins or as the basis for some greater future good. To al-Juwayni, such justification was unnecessary and presumptuous; George Hourani paraphrases al-Juwayni as saying of the "pains inflicted by God on men and animals" that "it is enough to know that they are created by God, and everything created by God is good for that reason alone."[41] With this bit of positivistic legerdemain, the problem of evil disappears.

Though not an Ash'arite, Ahmad ibn Hazm, a follower of the Zahiri sect (interpreting the Qur'an according to its literal meaning and without the use of *qiyas* or analogies), clearly articulated the same view in eleventh-century Spain, which shows how widespread the rebuttal to the Mu'tazilites had become. He proclaimed: "Anyone that says that God would do nothing save what is good according to our understanding and would create nothing that our understanding classes as evil, must be told that he has . . . perversely applied human argument to God. Nothing is good but Allah has made it so, and nothing is evil, but by his doing. Nothing in the world, indeed, is good or bad in its own essence; but what God has called good is good, and the doer is virtuous; and similarly, what God has called evil is evil and the doer is a sinner. All depends on God's decree, for an act that may at one time be good may be bad at another time."[42] In his Regensburg address, Pope Benedict XVI was referring to this aspect of Islam when he quoted Ibn Hazm as saying, "Were it God's will, we would even have to practise idolatry."[43] Thus, moral "obligation is intelligible only in terms of the commands of revelation," and certainly not from reason. Ibn Hazm said, "It belongs to the intellect only to understand the command of God the Exalted and [to understand] the obligation [or necessity] (*wujub*) of avoiding transgression in cases where eternal punishment is to be feared."[44]

In the fourteenth century, al-Misri reiterated the Ash'arite teachings on reason's inability to know ethics and revelation's monopoly on this knowledge: "The basic premise of this school of thought is that the good of the acts of those morally responsible is what the Lawgiver (Allah or His messenger) has indicated is good by permitting it or asking it be done. And the bad is what the Lawgiver has indicated is bad by asking it not be done. The good is not what reason considers good, nor the bad what reason considers bad. The measure of good and bad, according to this school of thought, is the sacred Law, not reason."[45]

Muhammad Yusuf as-Sanusi showed how consistently this view was held when he restated it in the early fifteenth century: "It is impossible for the Most High to determine an act as obligatory or forbidden . . . for the sake of any objective, since all acts are equal in that they are his creation and production. Therefore the specification of certain acts as obligatory and others as forbidden or with any other determination takes place by his pure choice, which has no cause. Intelligibility has no place at all in it rather it can be known only by revealed law (*shari'a*)."[46]

This view remains relevant today. As Ed Husain, a British Muslim, recounts in *The Islamist*, "Sheikh Nabhani [the founder of Hizb ut-Tahrir, a group dedicated to the restoration of the caliphate] always taught that there was no such thing as morality in Islam; it was simply what God taught. If Allah allowed it, it was moral. If He forbade it, it was immoral."[47]

The consequences of this ethical orientation were captured in the great Hungarian Jewish scholar of Islam Ignaz Goldziher's descriptions of Arab behavior after Muhammad: "People did not so much ask what was, in a given situation, good or proper in itself, as what the Prophet and his Companions had said about the matter, how they had acted, and what had accordingly been passed down as the proper view and the proper action."[48] Since nothing is good or proper in itself, this was the only alternative—a kind of complete legal positivism, rooted in scriptural texts and reports of Muhammad's sayings and doings. Instead of engaging in moral philosophy, one had to discern the *isnad*, or chain of transmission, to authenticate a saying of Muhammad in the Hadith that might apply to a certain situation for moral guidance—in case there was not a clear directive from the Qur'an itself. The saying or Hadith could be judged not on the basis of any intrinsic merit or moral worth, but *only* on its genealogy and the credibility of the witnesses to it. For instance, here is an example of the use of *isnad* to give validity to a Hadith used by Osama bin Laden's deputy, Ayman al-Zawahiri: "We heard from Harun bin Ma'ruf, citing Abu Wahab, who quoted Amru bin al-Harith citing Abu Ali Tamamah bin Shafi that he heard Uqbah bin Amir saying, 'I heard the Prophet say from the pulpit: "Against them make ready your strength.""[49]

The significance of the Ash'arite position can hardly be overstated. It makes moral philosophy, as in Aristotle's *Ethics*, impossible. There is no sense in this form of Islam of man fulfilling his nature, or of the "good" as that which aids him in doing so, or of the fulfillment of man's nature as defining his "good." Rather, the good is understood only as a matter of obedience to the external commandments of God—whatever they may be—unrelated to any internal logic in man himself or in creation. As the Qur'an states: "It may be that you dislike a thing that is good for you and like a thing that is bad for you. Allah knows but you do not know" (2:216). Not only do you not know, but you *cannot* know. Therefore, one can perceive what is good or bad only through the Qur'an or the *Shari'a*. This means that, in this form of Islam, there can be no distinction between law and morality. Law *is* morality. There is no morality outside of the revealed law. As a consequence, wrote Fazlur Rahman, the teaching that "pure reason yields no obligations or 'reason is not a Legislator' (*inna l-aql laysa bi-shari*) became the juristic axiom of all Muslim jurists."[50] One can see this pervasive view well into the nineteenth century. 'Abd al-Ali Muhammad al Ansari stated, "No one who professes Islam would be so brazen as to regard the human reason as law-giver."[51]

This accounts for the overwhelming prominence of jurisprudence in Sunni Islam. Its dominance is the direct result of the occasionalist metaphysics, the consequent collapse of epistemology, and the voluntaristic ethics proffered by the Ash'arites. Its prominence comes from a process of elimination. *Fiq*, or jurisprudence, is all that is left. This had significant, long-range consequences for the Muslim world. As contemporary Muslim scholar Bassam Tibi explains, "The *fiqh*-orthodoxy had the power to determine the curriculum of Islamic education. Thus, the distinction between *fiqh* and *falsafa* [philosophy] was lost. In Islam '*ilm*/science' was identified with *fiqh*. No debate was allowed and this mindset led to the decline of Islamic civilization."[52] He adds, "The control of the educational system allowed the *fiqh*-orthodoxy to prevent the spread of the Islamic rationalists' attempt to break out of the inherited religious concept of the world's natural order."[53] This resulted in the displacement of critical thinking by rote learning. The most prominent feature of Muslim education became memorization.

The delegitimization of ethics as a field of rational inquiry has also led, quite logically, to the moral infantilization of many Muslims, who are not allowed to think for themselves as to whether an act is good or evil, lawful or forbidden. If one is without the required knowledge of the law regarding a specific act, one must consult jurisprudential authority. In contemporary Islam, this has resulted in such things as dial-a-*fatwa* programs in places like Cairo, where a mufti stands by on the phone lines, at an extra charge, to meet the moral quandaries of the day. TV, radio, and newspapers also offer streams of *fatwas*. The *reductio ad absurdum* to which this has gone was illustrated by Father Samir Khalil Samir, an Egyptian Jesuit, with the following examples from Cairo in 2006:

"Should or should not a launderer (laundry shops are everywhere in Egypt) handle the clothes of a woman who normally does not wear an Islamic veil?" "If a woman gets out of the bath naked and there is a dog in the apartment, has she done something forbidden?" Answer: "It depends on the dog. If the dog is male, the woman has done something which is forbidden."

Another *fatwa*, reported by newspapers: "While I pray a woman goes by. Is my prayer valid or not?" Answer: "If a donkey, a woman, or a black dog goes by, the prayer must be repeated." The explanation: "The donkey is an impure animal;

the black dog could be Satan in disguise; women are impure regardless."[54]

Rather than accepting morality as within the reach of reason, the Ash'arites seemed to suffer from an underlying fear that if man could autonomously reach an understanding of good and evil, perhaps he might become autonomous, as well. This possibility could not be allowed, as it would directly challenge the radically contingent status of man as totally reliant on an all-powerful God. God is not "like" anything, or comparable to anything. If man could ascertain morality through his reason, he would be, in a way, God-like or in His likeness. Such a proposition was sheer *shirk.*

Those searching for the reason why freedom of conscience is not acknowledged in Sunni Islam's four legal schools may dwell on this teaching for a possible explanation. The underlying premise of freedom of conscience is that man is capable of grasping moral truth and that all men are endowed with the means for reaching it through their reason. This is true even in light of man's corruption by self-interest. As St. Augustine wrote, "There is no soul, albeit corrupted, as long as it can reason, in whose conscience God does not speak. For who wrote natural law in the hearts of men, if not God?"[55]

Undermine the integrity of reason and you subvert the foundation for freedom of conscience. Since reason is without integrity in Ash'arite Islam, there is no basis for freedom of conscience. In fact, there is not an Arabic word for conscience.[56] This, of course, does not mean that Islam is without a moral sense. It simply means that its moral sense is not the product of conscience. In fact, this form of Islam does not allow for the possibility of there being any rational grounds on which to reject Islam, because it provides no grounds for reason at all. Islam is called the *din al-fitra,* the religion that is "natural" to man, since it is directly revealed by the first and only cause, Allah. Therefore, deviation from it must be seen as a form of willful perversity. The Qur'an warns, "If anyone desires a religion other than

Islam, never will it be accepted of him; and in the hereafter he will be in the ranks of those who have lost" (3:85).

This is why every Sunni legal school prescribes death for apostasy.

Loss of Justice

Law is all that is left in the ruins—law as a willful, external imposition by God. What is more, it is law unrelated to justice in the classical meaning of the term. It is hollow law, purely juridical, without foundation in natural law. If justice is giving to things what is their due according to what they are, then one must know what things are in order to act justly. Since things in the Ash'arite view have no nature, however, one cannot apprehend them in this way; they are only momentary assemblages of atoms.

What, then, is justice, and how can it be discussed? Only, it seems, by saying that Allah says to do certain things and not to do certain other things—the exclusive realm of revelation. As al-Shafi'i, the founder of the Shafi'i legal school, defined it, "Justice is that one should act in obedience to God."[57] Whatever the law ordains is just, and there is no way to think of justice outside of this definition. In *Al-Mustasfa fi 'Ilm al-Usul* (the best [or choicest] on the subject of [Islamic] theology), al-Ghazali made this explicit: "*Wajib* [what is obligatory or necessary] has no meaning (*ma'na*) but what God the Exalted has made necessary (*awjaba*) and commanded, with threat of punishment for omission; so if there is no revelation, what is the meaning of *wajib*?"[58]

The answer to this rhetorical question, obviously, is that there is none. Nothing is necessary in the just man's behavior other than what God has revealed to be necessary; nor is there any way to answer the question as to what the just man should do other than by what is revealed.

And as al-Ghazali asks, again rhetorically, "If He did not announce it how would it be known that there is to be Reward?"[59]

Of course, on Ash'arite premises, it would not and could not be known if He did not announce it. Unlike the Mu'tazilites, al-Ghazali cannot answer that reward could be inferred from the nature of a God whose essence includes the attribute of justice, some sense of which He has imbued in man. And contrary to Mu'tazilite teaching, revelation does not simply *reveal* what is good and evil; it *constitutes* what is good and evil. Therefore, it is the sole source for information on what is to be rewarded.

Why has God decided on punishment for certain acts and reward for others? Because God can issue rules without reason, there can be no answer to this question. But what might the content of this justice be? If one behaves according to this understanding of justice, are there consequences for one's behavior on which one can rely? Since things are *haram* only as a matter of Allah's convention, may Allah arbitrarily decide to reward those who commit such acts, and punish those whose acts are *halal*? This would seem to go directly against the Qur'an in verse 24 of Surah 3: "So how will it be when We assemble them for a Day about which there is no doubt? And each soul will be compensated [in full for] what it earned, and they will not be wronged."

But the Qur'an also states, "He forgiveth whom He pleaseth, and punisheth whom He pleaseth" (2:284). And "He forgives whom He wills, and He punishes whom He wills. And to Allah belongs the dominion of the heavens and the earth and whatever is between them, and to Him is the [final] destination" (5:18). And "He punishes whom He wills and forgives whom He wills, and Allah is over all things competent" (5:40).

Al-Ghazali explains: "Allah's justice is not to be compared with the justice of man. A man may be supposed to act unjustly by invading the position of another, but no injustice can be conceived on the part of Allah. It is in his power to pour down torrents upon mankind and if he were to do it, his justice would not be arraigned. There is nothing He can be tied to, to perform, nor can any injustice be supposed of him, nor can He be under obligation to any person whatever."[60]

No injustice can be conceived on the part of Allah because, according to al-Ghazali, justice means performing an obligation—something that would cause serious harm if not performed. God has no obligations, and cannot be harmed. Good and bad, justice and injustice, pertain to whether something achieves or frustrates a purpose. Since God has no purpose, these terms are superfluous to Him. He can do anything, and there could not possibly be any blame. As the Qur'an states, "He cannot be questioned concerning what He does" (21:23).

In *The Middle Path in Theology*, al-Ghazali states: "We assert that it is admissible for God the Exalted not to impose obligations on His servants, as well as to impose on them unachievable obligations, to cause pain to His servants without compensation and without [preceding] offence [by them]; that it is not necessary for Him to heed what is most advantageous for them, or to reward obedience or punish disobedience."[61] This, of course, is the antithesis of the Mu'tazilite position that God *must* reward good and punish evil, and that He will not impose on man obligations that are beyond his capacity to perform.

Al-Ghazali puts these words into the mouth of God: "These to bliss, and I care not; and these to the Fire, and I care not."[62] As disturbing as this expression of divine indifference may seem, it is clearly based on a supporting Hadith: "Abu Darda' reported that the Holy Prophet said: Allah created Adam when He created him. Then He stroke his right shoulder and took out a white race as if they were seeds, and He stroke his left shoulder and took out a black race as if they were charcoals. Then He said to those who were on his right shoulder: Towards paradise and I don't care. He said to those who were on his left shoulder: Towards Hell and I don't care."[63]

A popular story of a most likely fictional incident, related by the nineteenth-century historian Sir William Muir, illustrates the same point:

When the Caliph Omar journeyed to Jerusalem to receive its surrender, he delivered an address, in the course of which he used this quotation from the Corân: "Whomsoever the Lord desireth to guide, he shall be guided aright; and whomsoever the Lord shall mislead, thou shalt not find for him a patron, nor any guide." "God forbid!" cried a Christian priest from the crowd, interrupting the caliph, and shaking his raiment in token of indignant dissent; "the Lord doth not mislead any one, but desireth rather the right direction of all." Omar inquired what that Christian "enemy of the Lord" was saying. He saith, replied the people, that "God misleadeth no one." Omar resumed his discourse, and a second time the priest interrupted him at the obnoxious words. Omar was angry, and said: "By the Lord! if he repeat this again, I will surely behead him upon the spot." So the Christian held his peace, and Omar proceeded: "Whom the Lord guideth, him none can mislead; and whom the Lord misleadeth, for him there is no guide."[64]

Of course, the words of the priest in this dialogue could have come just as well from a Mu'tazilite.

This view of Allah's arbitrariness has been consistently maintained by Ash'arite and allied schools. In the *Kitab al-Fisal* (*Detailed Critical Examination*), Ibn Hazm (994–1064) asserted, "He judges as He pleases and whatever He judges is just."[65] Ibn Hazm makes clear that "whatever" can mean anything: "If God the Exalted had informed us that He would punish us for the acts of others . . . or for our own obedience, all that would have been right and just, and we should have been obliged to accept it."[66] Ash'arite theologian Al Fakhr al-Razi (1149–1209) declared: "It is possible according to our religion that God may send blasphemers to paradise and the righteous and worshipers to (eternal) fire, because ownership belongs to Him and no one can stop Him."[67] This is, of course, the exact opposite of Abd al-Jabbar's teaching on "the promise and the threat," as it is of multiple verses in the Qur'an which speak of Allah's justice as reliable.

To outsiders, the capricious dimension of this form of Islam was clear as long ago as the Middle Ages. The great Jewish philosopher Maimonides (1135–1204) spoke of his experiences in Egypt to illustrate the way some Muslims think. Every morning the caliph rides through Cairo and every morning he takes the same route, said Maimonides, but tomorrow he could take a different route. Why? Because he is the caliph and he can do as he wills. Every morning the sun rises in the East and sets in the West. It has happened for years; it happened today. But tomorrow it might rise in the South and set in the North. That depends on the will of Allah and there is no saying that it will not. (In fact, some Islamic apocalyptical literature predicts the sun will rise in the West.) Maimonides concluded that "the thing which exists with certain constant and permanent forms, dimensions, and properties [in nature] only follows the direction of habit.... On this foundation their whole fabric is constructed."[68]

Maimonides was not the only one to have noticed that this is a problem. In *Lectures on the History of Philosophy*, Hegel observed that, in this version of Islam, "the activity of God is represented as perfectly devoid of reason."[69] Hegel said, "All we can discern here is the complete dissolution of all interdependence, of everything that pertains to rationality.... [God's activity] is wholly abstract, and that is why the differentiating that has been posited by means of it is wholly contingent. ... The Arabs developed sciences and philosophy in this way, where all is caprice."[70]

In *The Decline of the West*, Oswald Spengler wrote that "Islam is precisely the *impossibility of an I as a free power vis-à-vis the divine*.... In the entire cosmic cave there is only one cause which is the immediate ground of all visible effects: the deity, which itself has no longer any reasons for its acts."[71]

This aspect of Allah was also remarked upon by the Islamist radical Sayyid Qutb in *The Shadow of the Qur'an*: "Every time the Qur'an states a definite promise or constant law, it follows it with a statement implying that the Divine will is free of all limitations and restrictions, even those based on a promise from Allah or a law of His. For His will is absolute beyond any promise of law."[72]

The Loss of Free Will

Just as Ash'arite metaphysics makes any notion of God's justice incomprehensible—as justice is defined as *whatever God does*—it also has a devastating impact on the notion of human freedom. While for the Mu'tazilites, man's freedom is a matter of God's justice, for the Ash'arites, man's freedom is an offense to God's omnipotence. To them, God would not be omnipotent if another being were even potent. Power is indivisible. If man is the cause of his own actions, then how could God be omnipotent? The First Cause must be the only cause. What, then, are the implications for man if he is constituted by space-time atoms that are instantaneously coming into and going out of existence directly by God's command? Do humans retain any capacity to act on their own? In his book, *Al-Ibanah 'an Usul al-Diyanah* (*The Clear Statement on the Fundamental Elements of the Faith*), al-Ash'ari describes God's arbitrary power as overwhelming human initiative:

> We believe that Allah has created everything, by simply bidding it: Be, as He says [in Qur'an 16:42]: "Verily, when we will a thing, our only utterance is: Be and it is"; and that there is nothing good or evil on earth, except what Allah has preordained. We hold that everything is through Allah's will and that no one can do a thing before he actually does it, or do it without Allah's assistance, or escape Allah's knowledge. We hold that there is no Creator but Allah, and that

the deeds of the creature are created and preordained by Allah, as He said [in Qur'an 37:94]: "He has created you and what you make." ... We hold that Allah helps the faithful to obey Him, favors them, is gracious to them, reforms and guides them; whereas He has led the unfaithful astray, did not guide or favor them with signs, as the impious heretics claim. However, were He to favor and reform them, they would have been righteous, and had He guided them they would have been rightly guided.... But it was His will that they should be ungodly [singular: *kafir*], as He foresaw. Accordingly He abandoned them and sealed their hearts. We believe that good and evil are the outcome of Allah's decree and preordination [*qada' wa qadar*]: good or evil, sweet or bitter, and we know that what has missed us could not have hit us, or what has hit us could not have missed us, and that creatures are unable to profit or injure themselves, without Allah.[73]

Man, therefore, can neither originate nor complete an action. According to al-Ash'ari, he can only intend, and it is the intention by which he is judged. Duncan Macdonald sums up al-Ash'ari's view: "No other being than Allah possesses any act at all—*any act at all*. From Allah and of Allah are all acts. In no sense can it be said when, for example, I lift this book, that that act belongs to me.... So the movement of my hand to take hold of this book, its movement up with the book, the movement of the book itself upwards, all involve a series—rapid of course—invisible—of miraculous creations directly by Allah."[74] For al-Ash'ari, according to Macdonald: "Man cannot create a thing; God is the only creator; nor does man's power produce any effect on his actions at all. God creates in His creature power (*qudrah*) and choice (*ikhtiyar*). Then He creates in him his actions corresponding to the power and choice thus created."[75] To give al-Ash'ari's own example, a man picks up a pen and writes. It is, however, God who creates in him the will to write, the power to write, and then the motion of the hand to the paper with the pen. Allah then also causes the figures to appear on the paper as the pen touches it.

In what way, then, can these be man's acts? Al-Ash'ari answers with the curious idea that man "acquires" them from God, who is their real cause. The theory of acquisition is somewhat similar to that of the Jabrite Jahm bin Safwan (d. 745), who said that man's actions can be imputed to him only in the way as one imputes "bearing fruit to the tree." Ash'arite Al Shahrastani (d. 1153) attempted to explain that "God creates, in man, the power, ability, choice, and will to perform an act, and man, endowed with this derived power, chooses freely one of the alternatives and intends or wills to do the action and, corresponding to this intention, God creates and completes the action."[76] Also, Allah creates in the mind of the man acting his acceptance of his action, which means that even his acquisition of his act is directly created by Allah. If a man feels he is acting freely, it is only because Allah has placed that feeling in him.

Al-Ash'ari does not flinch from the unreality of man's acts—in the sense of their not being acts truly produced by man's free will and action—implied in this theory, as he explains that God can create the act and the will to act, as well. "If it is permissible that God create prayer in another person in order that the other person becomes a praying one, why should it not be permissible for Him to create a will in another? [In so doing] that person becomes an intending one. Or [why not create] speech, whereby that person becomes a speaker?" He then states the Mu'tazilite objection that such speech is not speech in reality because of its involuntary character, like someone talking in their sleep. Al-Ash'ari responds: "Nor is the speech of an epileptic or a sleeping person speech in reality; *nor is the speech of a waking person speech in reality.*"[77] Al-Ash'ari equates conscious, rational speech with unconscious, irrational murmurings. The waking person is as little the cause of his speech as the sleeping person is of his, because the only *real* cause and actor is God.

Al-Ash'ari makes this clear in a dialogue format:

> *Question*: Why is it that the occurrence of the act which is an acquisition does not prove that it has no agent save God, just as it proves that it has no creator save God?
>
> *Answer*: That is exactly what we say.
>
> *Question*: Then why does it not prove that there is no one with power over it save God?
>
> *Answer*: It has no agent who makes it as it really is save God, and no one with power over it so that it will be as it really is, in the sense that he creates it, save God.[78]

If man is without the capacity to cause his own acts, free will, of course, makes no sense, nor does the idea of "acquisition." In Averroes's critique of the Ash'arite position, he said that they hold that "although man has the power to 'earn,' what he earns thereby and the act of earning are both created by God." "But this," said Averroes, "is meaningless, because if God Almighty creates both the power to earn and what man earns, then the servant must necessarily be determined to earn it."[79]

In place of free will, the Ash'arites reinforced the traditionalist predilection for predestination. Al-Ghazali said, "Behind this sea [of comprehending God's justice] is the mystery of predestination where the many wander in perplexity and which those who have been illuminated are forbidden to divulge. The gist is that good and evil are foreordained. What is foreordained comes necessarily to be after a prior act of divine volition. No one can rebel against God's judgement. No one can appeal His decree and command."[80] It is interesting to note that al-Ghazali, who rebelled at the idea of deterministic causality in the natural world as a necessary relation between cause and effect, was, nonetheless, a thorough predestinarian who insisted that everything happens necessarily. It appears that causality, as such, did not seem to be the problem, but rather *who* was doing the causing.

How does God's direct action on human behavior work metaphysically? Islam scholar Len Goodman observed: "The Ash'arites conceded that we act by capacities. . . . But capacities, on the Ash'arite account, are created by God at the very moment of the action. They have no prior existence (as mere dispositions or unactualized potentialities), and they are not polyvalent [capable of more than one thing]. If the capacity for an action predated the act, Ash'ari argued, then the act would already have taken place."[81] In other words, everything is instantaneous or, as Goodman suggests, "only the actual is real." Also, potency exists only for a particular act and is not a preexisting power to act in general. As al-Ash'ari said, "No one can do a thing before he does it."[82] Fazlur Rahman illustrates what this means: "Before I raise my arm, I have no power to raise my arm; God creates this power in me at the time I actually raise my arm."[83] The action that takes place is the only action that could have taken place. Al-Ash'ari explained, "It is a condition of created power that its existence includes the existence of the object of the power."[84] The action *had* to happen. In other words, this is the reverse of Fazlur Rahman's formulation of the Jabrite objection that freedom for man is bondage for God. For the Ash'arites, freedom for God means bondage for man.

This Ash'arite position accounts for the preference in many Muslim thinkers to use the terms "substance and accidents" in describing reality and their concomitant aversion to the Aristotelian terms "potency and act" or "matter and form." Potency and act inhere in things having a nature that endures. The nature of a thing defines in potency what it has the capacity to become—in fact, what it ought to become—in actuality, but not yet has. Therefore, an acorn is an oak tree in potency. No matter where the acorn is in its trajectory on its way to becoming an oak, its nature prevents it from becoming a man, or something other than an oak.

This is precisely what the Ash'arites disputed with their insistence on the simultaneity of potency and act. A thing is what is only for the moment in which it is, after which it might become something else, or rather, more accurately, be replaced by something else. The oak tree may *seem* to be the same thing over time but only because the series of moments in which it exists form familiar sequences. For reasons man cannot fathom, God's direct will usually keeps these sequences in a familiar order, but they have no order of, or within, themselves. Even al-Ghazali wondered at the consistency with which God keeps in sequence fire and the burning of cotton, but he shut the door to any inquiry that could produce knowledge concerning it: "The predisposition for receiving forms varies through causes hidden from us, and it is not within the power of flesh to know them."[85] Thus, there is no entelechy, no such thing as "having one's end within," as Aristotle put it. Just as God does not act teleologically, His creatures have no *telos*.

The extraordinary claim of the simultaneity of potency and act comes perilously close to denying the principle of contradiction—that a thing cannot be, and not be, in the same way, at the same time, in the same place—without which everything lapses into incoherence. It is a powerful demonstration of the lengths to which the Ash'arites felt it necessary to go to protect their notion of the radical sovereignty and omnipotence of Allah, for the sake of which they placed all else in metaphysical jeopardy. It also empties the term *potency* of any real meaning, since an atom cannot exist with the potential to be anything other than what it is in its infinitesimal instance of existence. There really is no such thing as potency, only pure, instantaneous act, with Allah as the only actor.

Much is lost with the denial of the existence of potency. Aristotle's notion of potency and act was a solution to the perplexing metaphysical problem of how things could change and still somehow remain the same. Pre-Socratics had proposed either that all was change and nothing remained the same (Heraclitus) or that everything stayed the same and change was an illusion (Parmenides). Both notions ran counter to the daily experience of mankind of things changing but somehow keeping their identity. Something persists through the change. The position of the Ash'arites seems to be a reversion to the pre-Socratic position of Heraclitus. It also shares in the huge epistemological problem that Socrates pointed out to a disciple of Heraclitus, Cratylus: If change is all, how can man know? Socrates asked: "Can we truly say that there is knowledge, Cratylus, if all things are continually changing and nothing remains? For knowledge cannot continue unless it remains and keeps its identity. But if knowledge changes its very essence, it will lose at once its identity and there will be no knowledge."[86]

By subverting the foundation of knowledge in this manner, the Ash'arite position also raises problems with itself: If it were true, how could one know it to be true? How could one notice that everything is changing unless something in the observer of the change remained the same? In other words, how could memory, the basis of identity and civilization, exist?

Since such a view of things could hardly have been arrived at empirically, what might have been the motivation in adopting it—particularly when it seems at such odds with the ordinary experience of reality? Why, one wonders, did the Ash'arites feel it necessary to embrace Greek skepticism to this extent?

Fazlur Rahman suggested, "The Mutakallims rejected the Aristotelian doctrine of matter and form as a prerequisite for rejecting natural causation and restated the early Ash'arite atomism with fresh arguments until affirmation of atomism and denial of natural causation came to be looked upon as almost a cardinal religious dogma regarded as a necessary step to prove the temporal creation of the world and the Islamic eschatology."[87] They began with a conclusion received from revelation, and then deduced what they thought was necessary to support it in metaphysical terms. This drove them to abandon causality in the natural world. In short, the Ash'arites were compelled by their theology to deny reality.

Concerning al-Baqilani and the Ash'arite school in general, Macdonald offered a related hypothesis: "In truth, their philosophy is in its essence a skepticism which destroys the possibility of a philosophy in order to drive men back to God and His revelations and compel them to see in Him the one grand fact of the universe."[88] In other words, Ash'arism's scorched-earth policy toward reason attempted to leave man with no alternative to itself. It is either their God or nothing.

Chapter 4

THE TRIUMPH OF ASH'ARISM

Despite its radicalism, Ash'arism swept through practically the entire Sunni world. Indeed, the *ulema* (Islamic legal scholars) of every school but the literalist Hanbali came to accept Ash'arism. Set against the heretical rationalist Mu'tazilites and the traditionalist Hanbalites, the Ash'arite school became known—rather remarkably—as the "middle way."* This perception developed because the Hanbalites were actually more extreme in their rejection of reason. They disputed even al-Ash'ari's limited use of it in defending or explaining religious dogmas.

When the Hanbalites had the upper hand in Baghdad under vizier al-Kundri, Friday prayers included curses against the Ash'arites. Around 1063, however, Nizam al-Mulk, the powerful vizier to Seljuk sultan Alp-Arslan, had the curses stopped. According to British Islam scholar W. Montgomery Watt, al-Mulk also "began to implement a policy of supporting and strengthening the Ash'arites against the other theological and legal schools."[1] In 1067, al-Mulk opened a college in Baghdad, the Nizamiyya, to propagate Ash'arite teachings,

---

* Scholars such as George Makdisi have disputed this, claiming that the traditionalists actually maintained more influence than the Ash'arites.

and founded at least eight more in places ranging from Mosul
to Herat. "Thus," concludes Watt, "Ash'arite theology became
the form of Islamic doctrine supported by the government."[2] In
1077, al-Ghazali began his studies at the Nizamiyya college in
Nishapur, where he remained until 1085. Later, from 1091 to
1095, al-Ghazali served as the head of the Nizamiyya college
in Baghdad.

With state aid, the influence of the Ash'arite school spread
to become the most influential in the Sunni Arab world. With
its success came the broadly accepted understanding that the
Mu'tazilite school was heretical. In his *El Khutat El Maqrizia*
(*The Maqrizian Plans*), the famous Muslim historian al-Maqrizi
(d. 1442) gives an account of how Ash'arism triumphed, which is
made all the more interesting because of the prominent role of
the famous Saladin, who recaptured Jerusalem from the Cru-
saders:

> The madhdhab [school] of Abu'l-Hasan al-'Ash'ari
> spread in Iraq from around 380 AH* and from there
> spread to Sham [the Levant]. When the victorious
> king Salahuddeen Ysuf bin Ayyub took control over
> Egypt, his main judge Sadruddeen 'Abdul Mallik bin
> 'Isa bin Darbas al-Marani and himself were adher-
> ents to this school of thought. The madhdhab was
> also spread by the just ruler Nuruddeen Mahmood
> bin Zinki in Damascus. Salahuddeen memorised a
> text authored by Qutbuddeen Abu'l-Ma'ali Mas'ood
> bin Muhammad bin Mas'ood an'Naysaburi and this
> (Ash'ari) text was then studied and memorised by
> Salahuddeen's offspring. This gave prominence and
> status to the madhdhab [attributed] to al-'Ash'ari and
> was taken on board by the people during their rule.

* AH stands for *anno Hegiare*. The Muslim calendar starts from the Hijra,
Muhammad's emigration from Mecca to Medina. This occurred in A.D.
622 (common time).

This was continued by all of the successive rulers from Bani Ayyub (the Ayyubid) and then during the rule of the Turkish kings (Mamluks). Abu 'Abdullah Muhammad bin Tumart, one of the rulers of the al-Maghrib (Morocco), agreed with this (Ash'ari) trend when he travelled to al'-Iraq. He took the 'Ash'ari madhdhab on board via Abu Hamid al-Ghazali and when Ibn Tumart returned to al-Maghrib he caused a clash and began to teach the people of the land the 'Ash'ari madhdhab and instituted it for the people.[3]

Al-Ghazali and the Attack on Philosophy

While Ash'arite influence effectively suppressed Mu'tazilite teachings in the Sunni world, it was al-Ghazali who extended the Ash'arite critique to philosophy itself. Al-Ghazali is a titanic figure, considered by many Muslims to be the second most important person in Islam, next only to Muhammad. He has been called the "Proof of Islam" and was considered a *Mujaddid* (reviver or reformer), who Muhammad promised would arrive every century to revitalize Islam. Al-Ghazali is widely revered to this day. In large part, it is because of his influence that Ash'arism became Sunni orthodoxy and that philosophy suffered its coup de grâce. It was also al-Ghazali who integrated Sufism, the mystical side of Islam, into the orthodox Sunni world, where it had been held highly suspect for its neglect of Islamic duties and it propensity to pantheism.

The assault on philosophy, led by al-Ghazali, naturally grew out of the objections Ash'arites raised against a rational theology and a rational ethics. Such objections applied equally to philosophy, because they are objections to the role of reason itself. But beyond these general issues, al-Ghazali spelled out a number of objections specific to philosophy that ensured it would not gain wide adherence in the Muslim world.

Al-Ghazali's intention was to demonstrate that, on a philosophical basis, the major positions of the philosophers (and particularly those of Avicenna [981–1037], the foremost philosopher and physician of his time) could not be proved by reason. Even further, he wished to show that philosophy and reason were incapable of providing intellectual certitude. In fact, he asserted, philosophy has no truths of its own to offer.[4] In *The Incoherence of the Philosophers*, he said, "What . . . we assert is that the philosophers are unable to know these things by rational demonstration. If these things were true, the prophets would know them through inspiration or revelation; but rational arguments cannot prove them." Therefore, he announced, "I have been led to reject philosophic systems."[5] After undermining the path of reason, al-Ghazali turned toward Sufism, where, he claimed, he found the certitude he sought in mystical experiences.

In his autobiography, *Deliverance from Error*, al-Ghazali first takes to task the Materialists, who deny a Creator, and then Naturalists, who, while admitting a Creator, deny the immortality of the soul. Both these schools were refuted by the Theists, among whom al-Ghazali counts Socrates and Plato. Aristotle improved upon Socrates and Plato, "but he could not eliminate from his doctrine the stains of infidelity and heresy which disfigure the teaching of his predecessors. We should therefore consider them all as unbelievers, as well as the so-called Muslim philosophers, such as Ibn Sina [Avicenna] and Al Farabi, who have adopted their systems." Aristotle's philosophy, al-Ghazali says, can be divided into three portions: "the first contains matter justly chargeable with impiety, the second is tainted with heresy, and the third we are obliged to reject absolutely."[6]

While admitting the validity of mathematics, logic, and physics as inoffensive to faith, al-Ghazali charges that metaphysics is the most offensive because it is "the fruitful breeding-ground of errors of the philosophers." These errors he reduces to "twenty propositions: three of them are irreligious, and the other seventeen heretical." The three most egregious propositions are: (1) "Bodies do not rise again; spirits alone will be rewarded or punished; future punishments will be therefore spiritual and not physical"; (2) "'God takes cognizance of universals, not of specifics.' This is manifestly irreligious"; and (3) "They maintain that the universe exists from all eternity and will never end."[7] These three propositions, he maintains, are in direct contradiction to the Islamic teachings of bodily resurrection; physical suffering in hell and pleasure in paradise; God's omniscience; and creation ex nihilo. In taking on each argument, al-Ghazali demonstrates the uncertainty of *any* position on these matters reached by reason.

While the philosophers claimed that only the soul is immortal, al-Ghazali asserts that God can recreate the body at the resurrection, just as He had created the body in the first place—either exactly as it was, or analogously. God could easily recreate what He had made nonexistent. The mistaken objection to this possibility comes from those who do no accept God as the immediate and direct cause of everything. Within Ash'arite atomistic metaphysics, bodily resurrection is not a problem.

The philosophers held that God could know only universals and not particulars, because knowledge of particulars implies some change in God, which is impossible. He does not know particulars, which are the conditions of time and place, because these are objects of sense experience of which God, as spirit, cannot partake. Al-Ghazali's rebuttal is that God is omniscient, so He must know particulars, as well. Al-Ghazali defends the Qur'anic doctrine that "the smallest particle in heaven or on earth" does not escape God's knowledge. Change in the object of knowledge, he claims, does not imply change in the Knower, who has known all things simultaneously in eternity.

For orthodox Islam, the major stumbling block in Aristotle is the eternity of matter, which was accepted by almost all the Muslim philosophers, with exception of al-Kindi. Al Farabi and Avicenna embraced the view that the heavens were eternally and necessarily produced by God. Not only does a necessary, eternal world compromise creation ex nihilo, but it unavoidably leads to pantheism.

Al-Ghazali spends almost a quarter of his famous book *The Incoherence of the Philosophers* on this issue. He finds particularly objectionable the idea that the world exists necessarily, as an emanation from God, like the rays from the sun. The philosopher's position was driven by the consideration that God's creation of the world at a particular moment in time would imply a change in God, which is impossible. A perfect being cannot change. Therefore, the world must have always existed, eternally emanating from God.

To al-Ghazali, the philosophers' claim contradicts God's freedom to create or not to create; in other words, an eternal world is a denial of God's free will. Al-Ghazali responds to the philosophers' position by saying that it is inconsistent, that they could not disprove the possibility of creation ex nihilo. Aristotle argued for the existence of God as the First Cause because an infinite regress of uncaused causes is impossible. This argument falls apart, says al-Ghazali, if the world is eternal, because, if bodies are eternal, they require no cause. An infinite series would not be impossible; in fact, the eternity of the world would require that an infinite series of causes and effects, fathers and sons, had already come and gone.

Where within this infinite series could one insert a First Cause? asks al-Ghazali. It would clearly be impossible. Therefore, the philosophers who hold this position cannot demonstrate the existence of God as the First Cause. Also, one cannot properly speak of a Creator of a universe that is eternally emanating from the Creator. How could there be a causal relationship between two eternally existing things?

With this syllogism, al-Ghazali neatly dispatches the case for the eternity of the world: "An actual infinite cannot be completed by successive addition. The temporal series of past events has been completed by successive addition. The temporal series of past events cannot be an actual infinite."[8]

While this brief summary is inadequate to the merits of the arguments, it is meant to demonstrate the general point of al-Ghazali's emphasis on the inadequacy of reason to arrive at certainty. He wished to show that what the philosophers held was not the result of reason, but was really a different form of faith, antithetical to one based upon Islamic revelation, because the philosophers "oppose the principles of religion." Unlike Islam, their faith was groundless.

Sample chapter headings in *The Incoherence* illustrate his purpose in debunking the ability of philosophers to prove anything:

> IV. To show their inability to prove the existence of the creator of the world;

> V. Of their inability to prove by rational arguments that God is one, and that it is not possible to suppose two necessary being each of which is uncaused;
>
> . . .

> IX. Of their inability to prove by rational arguments that there is a cause or creator of the world;
>
> . . .

> XII. To show their inability to prove that God knows Himself either;
>
> . . .

> XIV. To show their inability to prove that the heaven is living, and obeys God through its rotatory motion;
>
> . . .

> XVIII. Of their inability to give a rational demonstration of their theory that the human soul is a spiritual substance which exists in itself.[9]

It is quite beside the point as to whether al-Ghazali actually defeated the philosophers on these issues. In *The Incoher-*

ence of the Incoherence, a spirited rebuttal of al-Ghazali, Averroes certainly disputed that he had. The point remains, however, that al-Ghazali was generally seen as having done so rather thoroughly.

The Triumph of Skepticism: The Uncertainty of Knowledge

After the thorough drubbing of the philosophers, the question remained: Of what, then, can man be sure and how is he to know? This is the intriguing question that al-Ghazali puts to himself in his autobiographical account in *Deliverance from Error.* He audaciously announces to the reader that he will relate "my experiences while disentangling truth lost in the medley of sects and divergencies of thought, and how I have dared to climb from the low levels of traditional belief to the topmost summits of assurance."[10] Al-Ghazali immodestly claims that, to prepare for the enterprise, he mastered the sum total of relevant knowledge: "There is no philosopher whose system I have not fathomed, nor theologian the intricacies of whose doctrine I have not followed out. Sufism has no secrets into which I have not penetrated."[11] He is the master of all.

Al-Ghazali relates that he left behind "the fetters of tradition and freed myself from hereditary beliefs" at a young age. He then sets out "in the first place to ascertain what are the bases of certitude." He defines certitude in an extraordinary way: "certitude is the clear and complete knowledge of things, such knowledge as leaves no room for doubt nor possibility of error and conjecture, so that there remains no room in the mind for error to find an entrance."[12] This certitude must be so solid that even a miracle could not shake it. "All forms of knowledge which do not unite these conditions [imperviousness to doubt, etc.] do not deserve any confidence, because they are not beyond the reach of doubt, and what is not impregnable to doubt can not constitute certitude."[13] This standard would seem to carry within itself a recipe for disaster; by definition, human beings would find it impossible to attain such certain knowledge.

From where, one wonders, might al-Ghazali have gotten his criteria for certitude? How could anything be *that* certain? Then an echo sounds from a similar assertion of certitude. It comes from the real source from which he was working and to which he returned in triumph. The answer is at the beginning of the second Surah of the Qur'an, which states: "This is the Book about which there is no doubt, a guidance for those conscious of Allah" (Qur'an 2:2). It seems, then, that the thing about which there is no doubt is the Qur'an. But how is one to arrive at this realization? What are the means for achieving this certitude? It would seem that one must be "conscious of Allah." We will shortly see how al-Ghazali pursued this state of consciousness and reached the kind of certitude he needed to fulfill the wish expressed in Surah 102: "If you only knew with the knowledge of certainty . . ."

Al-Ghazali's stated demands for certitude are so strict that there is little suspense in his explorations of the various fields of knowledge to see whether they will produce results that meet his requirements. Of course they will not; it is more or less a forgone conclusion. Al-Ghazali's dogmatic skepticism is too corrosive to allow anything to withstand its dissolvent powers. But dogmatic skepticism is simply that—another kind of dogma, not any more convincing than any other dogma. In fact, it is less convincing, because its premises cannot withstand being applied to itself. One can easily object that al-Ghazali should have been more skeptical of his skepticism. However, he is radically skeptical to a purpose; his skepticism has to be understood in terms of the desired destination to which it took him.

Al-Ghazali begins to take stock of the things he thinks he knows. "I then examined what knowledge I possessed, and discovered that in none of it, with the exception of sense-perceptions and necessary principles, did I enjoy that degree of certitude which I have just described. I then sadly reflected as follows: 'We can not hope to find truth except in matters which carry their evidence in themselves—that is to say, in sense-perceptions and necessary principles.'"[14] He discovers, however, that his confidence in sense perceptions is misplaced. For example, "the eye sees a star and believes it as large as a piece of gold, but mathematical calculations prove, on the contrary, that it is larger than the earth. These notions, and all others which the senses declare true, are subsequently contradicted and convicted of falsity in an irrefragable manner by the verdict of reason." Therefore, "my confidence in them was shaken."[15]

He goes on: "Then I reflected in myself: 'Since I cannot trust to the evidence of my senses, I must rely only on intellectual notions based on fundamental principles, such as the following axioms: Ten is more than three. Affirmation and negation can not coexist together. A thing can not both be created and also existent from eternity, living and annihilated simultaneously, at once necessary and impossible.'"[16]

Next to go was his confidence in these necessary principles, including the indispensable one of the principle of contradiction. His systemic doubt made the following objections: "Who can guarantee you that you can trust to the evidence of reason more than to that of the senses? You believed in our testimony till it was contradicted by the verdict of reason, otherwise you would have continued to believe it to this day. Well, perhaps, there is above reason another judge who, if he appeared, would convict reason of falsehood, just as reason has confuted us. And if such a third arbiter is not yet apparent, it does not follow that he does not exist."[17]

Al-Ghazali wonders if this is not like when "asleep you assume your dreams to be indisputably real? Once awake, you recognize them for what they are—baseless chimeras. Who can assure you, then, of the reliability of notions which, when awake, you derive from the senses and from reason? In relation to your present state they may be real; but it is possible also that you may enter upon another state of being which will bear the same relation to your present state as this does to your condition when asleep. In that new sphere you will recognize that the conclusions of reason are only chimeras."[18]

Of course, speculations such as these reduce everything to gibberish and make it impossible to think. Once you negate the reliability of the senses and jettison the principle of contradiction, all meaningful discourse comes to a halt. Not surprisingly, the effect on al-Ghazali was an acute mental, if not psychological, crisis: "This unhappy state lasted about two months, during which I was not, it is true, explicitly or by profession, but morally and essentially, a thorough-going skeptic." Then "God at last deigned to heal me of this mental malady; my mind recovered sanity and equilibrium, the primary assumptions of reason recovered with me all their stringency and force. I owed my deliverance, not to a concatenation of proofs and arguments, but to the light which God caused to penetrate into my heart—the light which illuminates the threshold of all knowledge."[19] Al-Ghazali was, he claims, healed not by reason but by grace.

Sane again, he embarks upon an examination of the respective claims of the different seekers after truth. The first are the orthodox theologians. They have merit as apologists who "preserve the purity of orthodox beliefs from all heretical innovation," but have their limitations. "Their principal effort was to expose the self-contradictions of their opponents and to confute them by means of the premises which they had professed to accept. Now a method of argumentation like this has little value for one who only admits self-evident truths. Scholastic theology could not consequently satisfy me nor heal the malady from which I suffered."[20]

Next come the philosophers. We have already seen al-Ghazali's objections to them in *The Incoherence*. "All, in spite of their diversity, are marked with the stamp of infidelity and irreligion." He concludes that, for the general run of mankind, "the reading of philosophic writings so full of vain and delusive utopias should be forbidden, just as the slippery banks of a river are forbidden to one who knows not how to swim."[21] Al-Ghazali did, however, incorporate Aristotelian syllogistic logic into his theology, which had a lasting effect on *kalam*.[22]

The Solution of Sufi Mysticism

Lastly, al-Ghazali takes up the Sufis and describes their aim: "To free the soul from the tyrannical yoke of the passions, to deliver it from its wrong inclinations and evil instincts, in order that in the purified heart there should only remain room for God and for the invocation of his holy name." This, then, was not so much an intellectual as a spiritual exercise. "It became clear to me that the last stage could not be reached by mere instruction, but only by transport, ecstasy, and the transformation of the moral being." Therefore, says al-Ghazali, "I saw that Sufism consists in experiences rather than in definitions, and that what I was lacking belonged to the domain, not of instruction, but of ecstasy and initiation."[23]

Knowing this path and following it proved to be two different things, and the disparity between them provoked the next spiritual crisis in al-Ghazali's life. Though he "saw that the only condition of success was to sacrifice honors and riches and to sever the ties and attachments of worldly life," he could not quite bring himself to do it. He kept resolving to give up his prestigious teaching position in Baghdad, and then failing to keep his resolution. At last, "God caused an impediment to chain my tongue and prevented me from lecturing. Vainly I desired, in the interest of my pupils, to go on with my teaching, but my mouth became dumb. The silence to which I was condemned cast me into a violent despair; my stomach became weak; I lost all appetite; I could neither swallow a morsel of bread nor drink a drop of water."[24]

He recovered from this dire state, for which the physicians had no cure, only upon taking "refuge in God as a man at the end of himself and without resources." He then resigned from the Baghdad Nizamiyya college in 1095, left provisions for his family, gave away everything else, and wandered off to live as an ascetic in Syria, Palestine, and, finally, Mecca. He reports: "Ten years passed in this manner. During my successive periods of meditation there were revealed to me things impossible to recount. All that I shall say for the edification of the reader is this: I learned from a sure source that the Sufis are the true pioneers on the path of God; that there is nothing more beautiful than their life, nor more praiseworthy than their rule of conduct, nor purer than their morality."[25] In 1105, al-Ghazali was back in his native city of Tus (eastern Iran), where he established a Sufi hostel. In 1106, he resumed teaching, this time at the Nizamiyya college in Nishapur, at the request of the vizier of the Seljuk prince of Khurasan. In 1109, he retired and returned to Tus, where he died in 1111.

What can seem hubristic in al-Ghazali's work, such as his extravagant claims in *Deliverance*, was actually part of a strategy to vindicate Sunni orthodoxy and revelation. By demonstrating that none of the rational arguments on vitally important issues is conclusive, al-Ghazali impelled recourse to revelation as the only authority left, and then substantiated it through mysticism. His Sufi quest showed that it is through the supra-rational that the certainty of the Book is confirmed.

He ended *Deliverance*, as he ended his life, with a beautiful spiritual prayer that helps explain the deep reverence in which al-Ghazali is held in the Islamic world to this day. It reads: "I pray God the Omnipotent to place us in the ranks of his chosen, among the number of those whom He directs in the path of safety, in whom He inspires fervor lest they forget him; whom He cleanses from all defilement, that nothing may remain in them except Himself; yea, of those whom He indwells completely, that they may adore none beside Him."[26] Even those within Islam who criticized al-Ghazali, such as Ibn Taymiyya, did not doubt his sincerity.

Al-Ghazali's excursion into Sufism (from *suf*, the rough wool from which Sufi clothes were made) was not without its dangers. The orthodox Sunni *ulema* looked upon Sufism with suspicion because it had developed beyond pious exercises in spiritual purgation into some extravagant and highly heterodox claims. It had also become very popular. The rigid legalism of Sunni Islam and its emphasis on mandatory ritual observances make the appeal of Sufism easy to understand. Just as the denial of cause and effect by Ash'arite theologians could not prevent the average Muslim from sensibly starting a fire to cook a meal, the depersonalized Ash'arite deity—placed beyond morality, inscrutable and unapproachable—did not keep Muslims from envisaging something more. In reaction to this spiritually sterile depiction of God, Sufism arose. It offered a more personal, loving encounter with God. In Sufism, Muslims sought and claimed to find the merciful, compassionate Allah, who knew them and with whom they could have a personal experience— even, if one dare say it, a union.

Al-Ghazali addressed both the subject of love and the sterility of the Sunni *ulema*:

> Love for God is the furthest reach of all stations, the sum of the highest degrees, and there is no station after that of love, except its fruit and its consequences . . . nor is there any station before love which is not a prelude to it, such as penitence, longsuffering, and asceticism. . . . Yet some of the "*ulam*" deny the possibility of love for God, and say that it means nothing more than persevering in obedience to God, be He exalted, while true love of God is impossible except metaphorically or in very unusual circumstances. And, since they deny the possibility of loving God, they also deny any intimacy with Him, or passionate longing for Him, or the delight of confiding in Him, and the other consequences of love. Thus we must of

necessity deal with this matter here, and mention in this book the proofs of the Law on love, and propound its reality and its occasioning features.[27]

One may note that al-Ghazali speaks only of man's love for God, not of God's love for man. Loving is a particularly problematic attribute for Allah to possess because it places Him in relation to a contingent being. How can a totally transcendent Being love a creature infinitely below Him? How can God desire? A Sufi tradition, well outside of what is allowable in Sunni orthodoxy, exquisitely expresses God's yearning for man: "I was a hidden treasure, being unknown. Then I desired to be known. So I created creatures and made myself known to them; and by Me they knew Me." This side of Sufism, al-Ghazali could not allow.

"When there is love," said al-Ghazali, "there must be in the lover a sense of incompleteness; a recognition that the beloved is needed for complete realization of the self." For God this is impossible, as He is complete in Himself. "The love of God means that he removes the veil from the heart of man; that God wills and has willed, from all eternity, that man should know Him, and that God causes man to know Him. There is no reaching out on the part of God. He only affects man so that man turns and goes out to Him; there can be no change in God; no development in Him; no supplying of a lack in Himself. He only affects man so that man comes to God."[28]

Despite the many citations in the Qur'an about God's love for his obedient servants, this must be understood as God's predilection, an expression of His will. He may *favor* man when he obeys Him, but He does not love him. The Christian idea of *agape*, an overflowing, unconditional divine love for man, is completely foreign to al-Ghazali's version of Islam—but not to Sufism.

Two other problems seemed to place Sufi mysticism outside the pale of Sunni orthodoxy. One was the monism into which the Sufi adept (meaning practitioner) merged and became one with God. This notion was blasphemous. Man was not divine and could not become divine by uniting with God. The other was the authoritative knowledge such Sufis claimed from their unique experiences that placed them above or beyond the *shari'a*. These claims reached their extreme in figures like Abu Yazid al-Bistami (d. 875), who first personified these dangers with his declaration: "Then He changed me out of my identity into His selfhood. . . . Then I command with Him with the tongue of His Grace, saying 'how fare it with me with Thee?' He said: 'I am thine through Thee; there is no God but Thee.'"[29] While al-Bistami claimed self-extinction in the ecstatic encounter with God, he also implied a self-identification with the divine in his exclamation: "Glory be to me, how great is my worth"[30] and "Within this robe is naught but Allah."[31] Mansur al-Hallaj (c. 858–922) took this to the point of saying: "I am the truth,"[32] a shocking claim when one realizes that "truth" is one of God's ninety-nine names. Unlike other Sufis who feigned madness to escape Sunni censure, al-Hallaj insisted he was completely sane. He also spoke openly to the crowds: esotericism for the masses. An extraordinary tribunal in Baghdad took his declaration as a literal claim to be God, and he was eventually subjected to a most gruesome execution for blasphemy.

The problem of special or esoteric Sufi knowledge was manifested in a statement attributed to al-Tustari (d. 896), who said, "Lordship has a secret which, if manifested, would destroy Prophethood; and Prophethood has a secret, which if divulged, would nullify knowledge; and the gnostics have a secret which, if manifested by God, would set the law at naught."[33] Setting the law at naught was exactly what the *ulema* feared—an abrogation of the divine law upon which the Muslim community was founded by something claiming to be superior to it. What could be more dangerous? The *ulema* observed certain Sufis exempting themselves from the ritual observances of Islam with the excuse that they had transcended such rituals. Indeed, some even claimed that the truth (*al haqq*) they had reached transcended confessional differences: "I am neither Christian, nor

Jew, nor Muslim."[34] Or even worse, "Until belief and unbelief are quite alike, no man will be a true Muslim."[35]

Also, the Sufi emphasis on a personal quest for God through contemplation was not congruent with the idea of the *umma* (community of believers) as a political/religious/social order for the salvation of the community. Personal salvation should not trump the communal undertaking to realize the project of a universal Islam.

Intuition Replaces Reason

Nonetheless, al-Ghazali took the risky plunge into Sufi mysticism because there did not appear to be any terms of rational discourse left for him to pursue. It may be no wonder that he turned inward and became a mystic. One could say that he not so much escaped into mysticism as boxed himself into it. Since reason was not a reliable path to reality or to God, how was one to know the truth of revelation? What did al-Ghazali have left after devastating the philosophers and blocking the road of reason to reality? Although his skepticism is sometimes seen as a presage of David Hume's, al-Ghazali's moral agnosticism did not extend to God and revelation. For al-Ghazali, according to Fazlur Rahman, "only that knowledge directly conducive to the success in the hereafter deserves the name in the true sense of the word. This knowledge is totally esoteric and explores the depths of the Sufi encounter with God."[36] The conclusion of the partial verse from Surah 102 that states "If you only knew with knowledge of certainty ..." is estimated to be "... you would not have been distracted from preparing for the Hereafter." Having attained that certainty of knowledge, al-Ghazali's attention was now fixed.[*]

It is hardly strange that someone who thought God's creation was unmediated by secondary causes—that each moment

---

[*] By the Saheeh International-Riyadh translation of the Qur'an—since the actual text ends as indicated, the translator speculates, rather authoritatively, on the ending.

was alive with a direct act of God's will—would finally conclude that the only *sure* knowledge comes from experience, without the intermediary of the intellect. God creates without mediation, so any experience of Him must be direct. Intuition replaces reason. All reason can do is bring you to this realization. All reason can know is its own limits. "One knows necessarily that he has reached a point beyond the intellect," al-Ghazali writes, "and there opens for him the eye from which the unseen is disclosed and which only the few perceive."[37]

And what is disclosed?

They come to see in the waking state angels and souls of prophets; they hear their voices and wise counsels. By means of this contemplation of heavenly forms and images they rise by degrees to heights which human language can not reach, which one can not even indicate without falling into great and inevitable errors. The degree of proximity to Deity which they attain is regarded by some as intermixture of being (*haloul*), by others as identification (*ittihad*), by others as intimate union (*wasl*). But all these expressions are wrong, as we have explained in our work entitled, "The Chief Aim." Those who have reached that stage should confine themselves to repeating the verse—*What I experience I shall not try to say; Call me happy, but ask me no more.* In short, he who does not arrive at the intuition of these truths by means of ecstasy knows only the name of inspiration. . . .

This possible condition is, perhaps, that which the Sufis call "ecstasy" (*hal*), that is to say, according to them, a state in which, absorbed in themselves and in the suspension of sense-perceptions, they have visions beyond the reach of intellect.[38]

"Beyond the reach of the intellect" in terms "which human language cannot reach" is the key point. Certain knowledge is supra-rational. In *Deliverance from Error*, al-Ghazali explains that this inspiration or revelation "belongs to a category of branches of knowledge which cannot be attained by reason," and that "the perception of things which are beyond the attainment of reason is only one of the features peculiar to inspiration."[39] Man must reach a higher plane of reality "by which he perceives invisible things, the secrets of the future and other concepts as inaccessible to reason as the concepts of reason are inaccessible to mere discrimination and what is perceived by discrimination of the senses."[40]

What, then, is the point of correspondence "beyond the intellect" between man and God? As we have seen, al-Ghazali repeatedly emphasizes that it is not reason. There is no *Logos* here, or there. If it is not man's reason that is the receptacle for the message of God, what is? How is it that man can know God, who is incomparably above him, at all? If man can know God, there must be something in him corresponding to the divine. Within Judaism and Christianity, this is not a problem, because in Genesis it states that man was "created in God's image," and the Book of Wisdom declares that "God formed man to be imperishable; the image of his own nature He made him" (Wisdom 1:13–15) But this is blasphemy in orthodox Sunni Islam. The doctrine of *tanzih* means precisely that there is no correspondence. There is one Hadith that seems to give an opening by echoing Genesis: "God created man in his image." But as Father Samir Khalil Samir points out, "In reality, the meaning of the adjective 'his' in Islam is 'in the image of man.'"[41] Thus, the explicated passage reads, "God created man in man's image." How can man relate to God if there is no similarity between them?

The Triumph of the Will

Obviously, the source of the relationship cannot be reason, since reason does not abide in God and is an inferior faculty in man. It will be no surprise that the Ash'arites, having reduced God to pure will, find the will as the only point of correspondence between God and man. For al-Ghazali, according to Arab scholar De Lacy O'Leary, "The essential element of this [man's] soul is not the intelligence which is concerned with the bodily frame, but the will: just as God is primarily known not as thought or intelligence, but as the volition which is the cause of creation."[42]

Duncan Macdonald gives essentially the same analysis: Al-Ghazali's "primary conception is, *volo ergo sum* [I will; therefore I am]. It is not thought which impresses him, but volition. From thought he can develop nothing; from will can come the whole round universe. But if God, the Creator, is a Willer, so, too, is the soul of man. They are kin, and, therefore, man can know and recognize God."[43]

And this relationship is what one discovers in the higher state of consciousness that Sufi experience alone produces. In *Gem of the Qur'an*, al-Ghazali reports that the higher state reveals that "indeed, there is nothing in existence except God and His acts, for whatever is there besides Him in His act."[44] Pure will produces pure act. In *The Niche for Lights*, al-Ghazali writes that mystics "are able to see visually that there is no being in the world other than God and that the face of everything is perishable, save His face (Qur'an 28, 88), not in the sense that it perishes at some time or other, but rather in the sense that it is perishing eternally and everlastingly and cannot be conceived to be otherwise. Indeed, everything other than He, considered in itself, is pure nonbeing. . . . Therefore, nothing is except God Almighty and His face."[45] Of this sort of assertion, Paul Valéry (1871–1945) quipped, "God made everything out of nothing, but the nothingness shows through."[46] In respect to itself, nothing really exists. This is the result not simply of the creation ex nihilo doctrine of Islam but also of the monism of its theology.

Al-Ghazali may have barely skirted the pantheism into which other Sufis had fallen and would continue to fall, but one can wonder how fine a line it is between saying that nothing exists except God and saying that all that exists is God. G. B. MacDonald observed that "it is part of the irony of the history of Muslim theology that the very emphasis on the transcendental unity should lead thus to pantheism."[47] W. H. T. Gairdner called Islam "a pantheism of pure force."[48] An overemphasis on God as One can easily morph into God as the only One, which then ineluctably incorporates everything into the only One, with nothing outside of it. We are left with either monism or pantheism.

The Loss of Reality

Gairdner explained the logic behind this intractable dilemma: "And in fact we often see, in the history of Islamic thought, men who have in their very insistence on absolute *tanzih* [pure transcendence] positively asserted this very thing, namely, that only Allah exists, and that all other existence is illusory, a semblance. This is the thought that underlies their name for God—Al Haqq [the only Reality]. They mean that no other being has reality or existence. These men, whether they know it or not, are pure pantheists, their belief resembling the Indian philosophic pantheism, whereby all that we see is Maya [illusion]. Thus easily does pure *tanzih* fall to its extreme opposite. In the language of these men, *tawhid* did not merely mean calling God the One, but calling Him the Only—that is, denying reality or even existence to all phenomena whatsoever."[49] The metaphysical proposition operating here seems to be that unless something is the cause of its own existence, there can be no reality in it. Since only God is the cause of His own existence, only God exists; what He has created then must be an illusion.

If God is the only Reality, then accepting the reality of the world becomes a form of polytheism—placing the real in competition with the only Real. However, denying the reality of the world for this reason boomerangs back into pantheism by then making the world part of the only Reality. The almost inescapable pull of pantheism from Islam's doctrine of *tanzih*, despite the clear Qur'anic injunctions against it, makes particularly ironic al-Ghazali's expulsion of philosophy from Sunni Islam on the grounds that it embraced pantheism through Aristotle's emanationism.

The significance of al-Ghazali's embrace of Sufism for our general topic is that the insubstantiality of reality in Sufism makes reason all the less important, just as it elevates that which is beyond reason—*Al Haqq*. Also, that which is beyond reason is not communicable. It cannot be taught. It is beyond language. Al-Ghazali's spiritual experience is inherently ineffable and therefore private.

Hans Jonas, the German expert on Gnosticism, diagnosed the type of knowledge to which al-Ghazali alluded as Gnostic in nature: "It is closely bound up with revelatory experience, so that *reception* of truth either through sacred or secret lore or through inner illumination replaces rational arguments and theory."[50] Although al-Ghazali railed against Gnosticism, it is far from clear that he did not engage in it himself. In *The Niche for Lights*, he speaks of the mystic "state" of al-Hallaj, and other "inebriates," and the expressions they emit in their mystic intoxication—"behind which truths," al-Ghazali says, "also lie secrets which it is not lawful to enter upon."[51] Had he trespassed upon this forbidden territory?

In *The Niche for Lights*, al-Ghazali claims that the end of the quest for truth is "an Existent who transcends ALL that is comprehensible by human Insight . . . transcendent of and separate from every characterization that in the foregoing we have made."[52] In a footnote to this statement, the translator and commentator, W. H. T. Gairdner, offers an extremely penetrating insight into al-Ghazali: "In Ghazzâlî [*sic*] the most extreme Agnosticism and the most extreme Gnosticism meet, and meet at this point; for, as he says, 'things that go beyond one extreme pass over to the extreme opposite.' For him 'Creed because Incredible' becomes 'Gnosis because Agnoston.' What saved the

Universe for him from his nihilistic theologizing was his ontology. What saved *God* for him from his obliterating agnosticism was the experience of the mystic leap, his own personal *mi'râj*. This may have been non-rational, but it was to him experience. Even those who regard the sensational experience of Sûfism as having been pure self-hypnotism cannot condemn them and the sense of reality they brought, in relation to the man who had thought his way out of both atheism and pantheism, and yet would have been left at the end of the quest, by his thinking alone, with an Unknown and Unknowable Absolute."[53]

Al-Ghazali made it safe to be a Sufi by assimilating Sufism into Sunni orthodoxy. For this synthesis, he is credited with revitalizing Islam. Although al-Ghazali certainly seems to have flirted with Gnosticism, he resolved the difficulty of including Sufism within Sunni Islam by saying that, according to Fazlur Rahman, "Sufism has no *cognitive content or object but the verities of the Faith*. He, therefore, disallowed the pretension of the theosophic mysticism and castigated the men of ecstatic delirium [emphasis in original]."[54] Despite this achievement, the *ulema* remained suspicious of Sufism and found ample cause to be so with one of the most famous Sufis, Ibn al-Arabi (d. 1240), whose teachings were thoroughly monistic and pantheistic.

Beyond Reason

The main point here is that the incorporation of Sufism hardly enhanced the status of reason within Sunni Islam, as its principal access to the divine is through means "beyond reason" that simply affirmed through mystical experiences the truths of the faith. "Notice in your heart the Prophet's knowledge, without book, without teacher, without instructor," said Jalal al-Din Rumi, the great thirteenth-century Persian Sufi poet.[55] As Fazlur Rahman wrote, "Sufism proclaimed that only God exists. Both Ash'arism and Sufism taught passivity vis-à-vis God, since both subscribed to the inanity of natural and human voluntary causations."[56] In this way, certain tendencies within Sunni Islam were reinforced. The Ash'arite absolute dependency upon the will of God was now joined with the Sufi tendency to discount this world. The unreality of this world transmitted an indifference to it. The resulting passivity easily translated into quietism.

We end up with a double disparagement of reason—first by Ash'arism and then by Sufism. One may object to the conclusion that Sufi mysticism denigrated reason. Something "beyond reason" is not necessarily unreasonable, and this is certainly true.* Sound reason admits its own limits. God is infinite and the human mind finite. Some form of mysticism exists in all religions. But al-Ghazali's mysticism has to be seen within the context of his having first undermined the authority of reason to know reality at all. Reason is not left as a safeguard against potential delusions in mysticism; only the dogma of revelation is. One is then left with no means to address the more basic inquiry that the Mu'tazilites tried to undertake: Is the revelation itself reasonable? Al-Ghazali destroyed the standard by which to judge an answer to this vital question, or even to ask it in the first place.

In *Deliverance from Error,* al-Ghazali states: "The only beneficial function of intellect is to teach us that fact [that prophets are the doctors of heart ailments], bearing witness to the veracity of prophecy and its own incompetence to grasp what can be grasped by the eye of prophecy; it takes us by the hand and delivers us to prophecy as the blind are delivered to guides and confused patients to compassionate doctors. Thus far is the progress and advance of intellect; beyond that it is dismissed."[57] Obviously, al-Ghazali rejected the Mu'tazilite position that there is no faith without reason, or that faith requires rational assent, since for him reason is "blind."

Thus, al-Ghazali praised the *Hajj*—the obligatory pil-

---

* Beyond reason does not necessarily mean against reason unless it insists on the acceptance of something directly contrary to it—such as that the world does not really exist, as is the contention of some Sufis.

grimage to Mecca—precisely because it is beyond reason. He highlighted its irrationality in order to emphasize the self-sufficiency of revelation as its justification. In *The Revival of the Religious Sciences*, he wrote, "The pilgrimage is the most irrational thing in Islam. There we perform gestures and rites that are absolutely irrational. For this reason, the pilgrimage is the place where we can, better than in any other place, demonstrate our faith because reason does not understand anything at all of it and only faith makes us do those actions. Blind obedience to God is the best evidence of our Islam."[58]

On similar grounds al-Ghazali objected to the claims of Muslim ethical philosopher Ibn Miskawayh (940–1030) concerning the significance of communal prayer and other rituals. As summarized in *A History of Islamic Philosophy*, "Al-Ghazali was infuriated by Ibn Miskawayh's suggestion that the point of communal prayer is to base religion upon the natural gregariousness of human beings in society. This seemed to al-Ghazali to disparage the religious enterprise, since he argued that the significance of religious rituals is that they are specified by the religion, and there can be no other reason. Their rationale is that they are unreasonable. God indicates the huge gap that exists between him and us by setting us unpleasant and difficult tasks. For Ibn Miskawayh, the reason for the ritual is that it has a part to play in helping us adapt to religious life, using the dispositions that are natural to us, so that the rules and customs of religion are essentially reasonable."[59] This notion, of course, was inimical to al-Ghazali's conception of religion as inaccessible to the intellect. Irrational rules are more efficacious in bringing man into submission to God.

Judah ha-Levi, a Jewish follower of al-Ghazali, wrote an attack on philosophy, entitled *Kuzari*, in which he concluded that man ought to approach revelation from God precisely by dismissing the intellect: "I consider him to have attained the highest degree of perfection who is convinced of religious truths without having scrutinized them and reasoned over them."[60] For al-Ghazali, the notion of God as pure will ineluctably leads to the elevation of incomprehensibility as a virtue. As Rémi Brague explains in his recent book *The Law of God*, "Some [Islamic] authors even specify that 'enslavement' (to God) formally excludes the search for the reasons behind the commandments (*ta'lil*)."[61] Reason is irrelevant to the required subjection and, in fact, an obstacle to it.

A contemporary version of this view of reason's irrelevance to faith is related by Dr. Tawfik Hamid in his account of terrorist recruitment, *The Development of a Jihadist's Mind*. To appreciate the story, one must know that the donkey is considered a symbol of inferiority in Arab culture (which is why Christians were ordered to ride donkeys, and not horses, under early Muslim rule). When Hamid was a medical student in Cairo, he was approached by Muchtar Muchtar from the foremost terrorist group in Egypt, Jemaah Islamiyah. Hamid recounts: "On the way (to the mosque) Muchtar emphasized the central importance in Islam of the concept of *al-fikr kufr*, the idea that the very act of thinking (*fikr*) makes one become an infidel (*kufr*). He told me, 'Your brain is just like a donkey that can get you only to the palace door of the king (Allah). To enter the palace once you have reached the door, you should leave the donkey (your inferior mind) outside.' By this parable, Muchtar meant that a truly dedicated Muslim no longer thinks but automatically obeys the teachings of Islam."[62]

Muchtar's tale is ultimately rooted in al-Ghazali's dismissal of the intellect in *Munqidh*. The Muchtar episode is the *reductio ad absurdum* of the idea of God as pure will, unbound by reason. In Muchtar's parable, reason—the donkey—has no relationship to God, the king, the all-powerful pure will.* The irrelevance of reason easily turns into antipathy toward it, as

---

* By this comparison, I do not mean to suggest the al-Ghazali would be in sympathy with terrorism, any more than I would say that Nietzsche was a Nazi. Nonetheless, both had their teachings vulgarized to a level where their emphasis on the primacy of the will had unfortunate results.

seen in placards posted in Afghanistan by the Taliban religious police: "Throw reason to the dogs—it stinks of corruption."[63] In Islam, dogs are considered unclean animals and, therefore, the proper recipients of corrupt reason.

Chapter 5
THE UNFORTUNATE VICTORY OF
AL-GHAZALI AND THE
DEHELLENIZATION OF ISLAM

Al-Ghazali's influence in the Arab and Muslim world was overwhelming. The overall impact of his thought has been much remarked upon due to its enormous consequences. His ultimate significance may be that, in the words of Pakistani philosophy professor M. Abdul Hye, he "made the Ash'arite theology so popular that it became practically the theology of the Muslim community in general and has continued to remain so up to the present time."[1] Assured by al-Ghazali, the ascendancy of the Ash'arite school spelled the effective end of the attempted assimilation of Greek thought into Sunni Islam. *The Incoherence of the Philosophers*, according to contemporary thinker Seyyed Hossein Nasr, "broke the back of rationalistic philosophy and in fact brought the career of philosophy ... to an end in the Arabic part of the Islamic world."[2] As Fazlur Rahman said, "Having failed to satisfy orthodox requirements, [philosophy] was denied the passport to survival."[3]

Through the teaching that nothing certain can be known by reason, al-Ghazali inflicted incalculable harm on Sunni Islamic posterity. Caliph al-Ma'mun's dream of Aristotle ("the good is what is rationally good") turned into a nightmare. Man could not know what is good and must subject his life and mind to blind obedience. While al-Ghazali certainly incorporated some philosophical tools into theology, he used those tools to undermine philosophy as an independent study. In *The Encyclopaedia of Islam*, G. B. MacDonald says: "Al-Ghazali taught that intellect should only be used to destroy trust in itself."[4] Duncan Macdonald concluded, "When he has finished there is no intellectual basis left for life; he stands beside the Greek skeptics and beside Hume. We are thrown back on revelation, that given immediately by God to the individual soul or that given through prophets."[5] What use, then, did they find for reason? Macdonald answered: "Its use, they found, was to demonstrate that it was not of any use. . . . They cut away the possibility of dealing with religion by means of reason. . . . They used reason to cut away the possibility of philosophizing about the world and about life, and, then, having driven philosophy off the field and any possibilities on that side, they fell back upon what their fathers had told them and upon what came to them in their own religious experience."[6] The attempted hellenization of Islam provoked its opposite.

Almost one hundred years after al-Ghazali's *The Incoherence of the Philosophers*, Averroes (1126–1198) tried to launch a counterattack against al-Ghazali's disparagement of philosophy with *The Incoherence of the Incoherence* (1180), which is an almost line-by-line refutation of al-Ghazali's book. After all the damage that had been done by the Ash'arites and al-Ghazali, Averroes attempted to restore parity between reason and revelation of the kind that had been espoused by al-Kindi. He also insisted, somewhat like the Mu'tazilites, that the study of philosophy is commanded as an obligation in divine law. In *The Book of the Decisive Treatise*, Averroes stated that since "their [the ancients'] aim and intention in their books is the very intention to which the Law urges us . . . whoever forbids reflection upon them by anyone suited to reflection upon them . . . surely bars people from the door through which the Law calls them to cognizance of God."[7] Averroes also correctly diagnosed the ethical subjectivism inherent in Ash'arism as similar to that of the Greek sophists (the difference being a divine ruler arbitrarily setting the rules in Ash'arism, and a human ruler in sophism). "All these are views like those of Protagoras!" he exclaimed.[8]

But it was too late. It is Averroes's books that ended up being burned, not al-Ghazali's. In 1195, in the town square of Cordoba, 108 of Averroes's books were incinerated and the teaching of philosophy was banned. As one of the greatest interpreters of Aristotle, Averroes had a far greater impact upon medieval Europe than upon his own world. In fact, most of his works survived because they were preserved in Europe. As Father Joseph Kenny notes, "Most of his important commentaries on Aristotle, except that on the *Metaphysics*, are lost in Arabic, having been burned by his enemies, but they are preserved in Latin or Hebrew translations, thanks to Jewish and European fascination with his thought at the beginning of the 13th century."[9]

Dehellenization of Islam

The "intruding sciences" would intrude in Islam no more. They were expelled. As a result, notes Professor Joel Kraemer of the University of Chicago, "the assimilation of the Greek heritage in the Orient may be termed a 'tragic sterility.'"[10] Professor of Arabic and Near Eastern studies G. E. von Grunebaum stated, "The far-reaching importance of the Greek contribution to Islamic cultures should not lead one to suppose that it effected a fundamental change in its vitality or its concept of man. There are few traces of the Greek spirit in the human ideal within even those sects which, like the [Shiite] Isma'iliyya, were most open to the influence of the Greek element in the interest of its own theologico-philosophic system." Thus, he concluded, "The fundamental structure of Islamic thinking has been left untouched by Hellenistic influence."[11]

Here are two more critical assessments of the results of al-Ghazali's success from twentieth-century Muslims. "While the fierce debates between those believing in free will (the Qadarites) and the predestinarians (the Jabrias) were generally resolved in favor of the former," Pervez Hoodbhoy avers, "the gradual hegemony of fatalistic Ash'arite doctrines mortally weakened . . . Islamic society and led to a withering away of its scientific spirit. Ash'arite dogma insisted on the denial of any connection between cause and effect—and therefore repudiated rational thought."[12]

Fazlur Rahman concurs that the earlier disputes concerning predestination were not fatally injurious, "but with Ash'arism a totally new era of belief dawned upon Muslims. From then on, they could not act in reality; human action, indeed, became a mere metaphor devoid of any real meaning. Al-Ashari explicitly stated that even a waking person cannot speak in reality. . . . The truth is that Ash'arism held its sway right up until the twentieth century and holds sway even now in the citadels of Islamic conservatism."[13] The deadening effects, says Rahman, included the loss of human initiative, activity, and imagination—a devastating tally, as we shall see when we examine the state of the Arab world today.

The damage was evident in immediate aftermath of al-Ghazali's triumph. In *Testament*, Al Fakhr al-Razi, a critic of Avicenna and twelfth-century follower of al-Ghazali, stated reason's obituary in the following terms: "I have explored the ways of *kalam* and the methods of philosophy, and I did not see in them a benefit that compares with the benefit I found in the Qur'an. For the latter hurries us to acknowledge that greatness and majesty belong only to Allah, precluding us from involvement into the explication of objections and contentions. This is for no other reason than because human minds find themselves deadened in those deep, vexing exercises and obscure way [of *kalam* and philosophy]."[14]

Further calcification was evident in the early thirteenth century. Ibn-as-Salah (d. 1251), the head of the Dar al-Hadith al-Ashrafiya in Damascus, one of the most prestigious institutions for the study of Hadith in the Islamic world, was asked if it was permissible to study or teach philosophy and logic, the latter of which al-Ghazali had at least allowed. He responded with a *fatwa* in which he described philosophy as "the foundation of folly, the cause of all confusion, all errors and all heresy. The person who occupies himself with it becomes colourblind to the beauties of religious law, supported by brilliant proofs. . . . As far as logic is concerned, it is a means of access to philosophy. Now the means of access to something bad is also bad. . . . All those who give evidence of pursuing the teachings of philosophy must be confronted with the following alternatives: either execution by the sword, or conversion to Islam, so that the land may be protected and the traces of those people and their sciences may be eradicated."[15]

The degeneration continued with Ibn Taymiyya (1263–1328), who profoundly influenced Ibn Abd al-Wahhab, the founder of Wahhabism, the strict Hanbalite form of Islam practiced in Saudi Arabia and whose thought has been resuscitated by the Islamists today. Ibn Taymiyya said that man's job is simply to obey. Submit. Reason plays no role. According to Lebanese scholar Majid Fakhry, he "insured the victory of Neo-Hanbalism over scholastic theology and philosophy."[16] Al-Ghazali's more finely tempered view becomes lost, and now even theology becomes a path to perdition. Ibn Taymiyya did to theology what al-Ghazali did to philosophy; he exiled it. He cited predecessors who had devoted their lives to these sciences, but who later recanted, such as Al-Shahrastani, who "confessed that it was folly to discuss theology." He relished Abu Yusuf, "who said that he who would seek knowledge by the help of scholastic theology (*kalam*) would turn into an atheist," and Imam Shafi'i, who held that "theologians should be beaten with shoes and palm-branches, and paraded through the city so that people may know the consequence of the study of theology."[17]

The narrowing of knowledge is evident in the jurist Abu Ishaq al-Shatibi's (d. 1388) pronouncement that "investigation into any question which is not a basis for an action is not recommended by any proof from the *Shari'a*. By act I mean both mental and physical acts." Al-Shatibi added: "And so is the case with every branch of learning that claims a relationship with the *Shari'a* but does not (directly) benefit action, nor was it known to the Arabs."[18] In other words, the only thing worth knowing is whether a specific action is, according to the *Shari'a*: obligatory, recommended, permitted, discouraged, or forbidden. The rest is irrelevant.

In the seventeenth century, Turkish author Katib Chelebi (d. 1657) complained of further decay: "But many unintelligent people . . . remained as inert as rocks, frozen in blind imitation of the ancients. Without deliberation, they rejected and repudiated the new sciences. They passed for learned men, while all the time they were ignoramuses, fond of disparaging what they called 'the philosophical science,' and knowing nothing of earth or sky. The admonition 'Have they not contemplated the kingdom of Heaven and Earth?' (Qur'an, VII, 184) made no impression on them; they thought 'contemplating the world and the firmament' meant staring at them like a cow."[19]

More recently, Georges Tarabishi, a prominent liberal Syrian intellectual living in France, spoke directly to Fazlur Rahman's accusation of intellectual suicide, with which this book began. In a January 2008 interview with the London Arabic daily *Al-Sharq Al-Awsat*, he said: "Philosophy is a product of the mind. [But] what prevails today in Arab culture is the [Arab] mentality [instead of the critical mind]. Thus, I could almost say that it is impossible today for Arab philosophy to exist. Perhaps there is some degree of generalization in this sentence—but nonetheless, give me one single example of an Arab philosopher worthy of the name. And I do not exempt myself from this judgment. This is saddening, since we know that what created Western modernity was first and foremost philosophy. Should we not attribute the failure of Arab modernism, at least in part, to the absence of Arab philosophers?"[20]

What, then, of the achievements of Muslim philosophy in Ibn Rushd (Averroes), Ibn al-Haytham, Ibn Sina (Avicenna), al-Razi, al-Kindi, al-Khawarizmi, and al-Farabi? Reformist thinker Ibrahim Al-Buleihi, a current member of the Saudi Shura Council, responds, "These [achievements] are not of our own making, and those exceptional individuals were not the product of Arab culture, but rather Greek culture. They are outside our cultural mainstream and we treated them as though they were foreign elements. Therefore we don't deserve to take pride in them since we rejected them and fought their ideas. Conversely, when Europe learned from them it benefited from a body of knowledge which was originally its own because they were an extension of Greek culture, which is the source of the whole of Western civilization."[21]

In fact, the rejection continues to this day. Muslim scholar Bassam Tibi states that "because rational disciplines had not been institutionalized in classical Islam, the adoption of the Greek legacy had no lasting effect on Islamic civilization."[22] Indeed, "contemporary Islamic fundamentalists denounce not only cultural modernity, but even the Islamic rationalism of Averroes and Avicenna, scholars who had defined the heights of Islamic civilization."[23]

The contemporary Egyptian reformist thinker Tarek Heggy neatly summarizes the conflict and its outcome: "The world of Islam was the scene of a battle of ideas between Abu Hamid Al-Ghazzali (Algazel) [sic], a strict traditionalist who did not believe the human mind capable of grasping the Truth as ordained by God, and Ibn Rushd (Averroes), who championed the primacy of reason. The exponents of these two schools waged a bitter battle. . . . But despite his [Averroes's] spirited defense [of rationality], the outcome of the battle was clearly in Al-Ghazzali's favour, and the great majority of Islamic jurists adopted his ideas, interpreting the precepts of Islamic law by appeal to the authority of tradition and spurning deductive reasoning altogether. Islamic jurisprudence was dominated by the Mutakallimun, or dialectical theologians, who asserted the primacy of tradition (*naql*), as advocated by Al-Ghazzali, over that of reason (*'aql*), as advocated by Ibn Rushd."[24]

Al-Ghazali's influence was, and is, so important that a modern thinker of Fazlur Rahman's stature could say that "without his work . . . philosophic rationalism might well have made a clean sweep of the Islamic ethos."[25] One can only imagine how different the world would have been had that happened.

Chapter 6
DECLINE AND CONSEQUENCES

Were it not for al-Ghazali, Averroes and rationalism might have won the battle for the Muslim mind. But it did not happen, and, as a result, the Sunni Muslim mind suffered the consequences. It closed.

Reformist thinker Tarek Heggy states: "Exalting a man who did not believe the human mind capable of grasping the Truth as ordained by God set into motion a process that continues to this day with devastating effects on the Arab mindset, which has become insular, regressive and unreceptive to new ideas."[1] With the supremacy of *fiqh* (jurisprudence) assured, this mindset turned in upon itself and spun out ever more refined interpretations of the *shari'a* until every application to every situation had been ruled upon and enumerated, and then even that stopped. The gates to *ijtihad* (independent reasoning) shut. *Taqlid* (imitation) reigned. Philosophy was dead (removed from the syllabus at al-Azhar until attempts to revive it in the late nineteenth century).[2]

Like Fazlur Rahman, the Egyptian cultural historian Ahmad Amin (1886–1954) speculated that: "If the Mu'tazili tradition had continued until the present time the position of the Muslim community in history would have been far different from what it is. Fatalism weakened the Islamic community and drained its energy while *tawakkul* [trust only in God] led to a static condition."[3]

How different is "far different," one wonders. We shall examine the possible answers to this question in terms of aborted political development, dysfunctional behavior and thinking, descent into fantasy and conspiracy theories, and ruined development in almost every sphere of life, as recounted by Arabs themselves.

The Logic of Despotism

The triumphant moral agnosticism of the Ash'arite form of Islam has had and still has enormous consequences for political development, and is responsible for its retardation. Hassan Hanafi, professor of philosophy at the University of Cairo, suggested that the effect of "al-Ghazali's critique of rational sciences [was] giving the Ruler an ideology of power."[4] Speaking of how overwhelmingly the balance of forces was weighted in favor of determinism in the Middle Ages, Fazlur Rahman said that "increasing despotism both sustained and was sustained by this theoretical attitude."[5] A backhanded tribute to the power of al-Ghazali's influence is the fact that Kemal Ataturk, in his attempt to modernize and democratize Turkey, forbade the translation of al-Ghazali's works into Turkish.

Many wonder why democracy did not develop indigenously in the Muslim world and ask whether it can still develop today. The answer is that, so long as the Ash'arite (or Hanbalite) worldview is regnant, democratic development cannot succeed for the simple reason that this view posits the primacy of power over the primacy of reason. Those who might contend that Ash'arism is already irrelevant in the Middle East then need to provide some other explanation for its dysfunctional character. I do not assert that Ash'arism is a living force in the sense that people consciously seek solutions to the problems of Islam in the modern world through it, although "it is still taught at the Azhar in Cairo and other colleges of Islamic theology."[6] Rather, it functions as an embedded dead weight that inhibits the reasonable search for such solutions. Even worse, it is Hanbalism, which al-Ash'ari originally rose to defend, that is gaining traction today in the form of Wahhabism, which is even more inimical to the primacy of reason than Ash'arism. As for the growing Islamist movement, Wilfred Cantwell Smith's words apply: "The new Islamic upsurge is a force not to solve problems but to intoxicate those who cannot longer abide the failure to solve them."[7]

The primacy of reason, theologically and philosophically understood, is the prerequisite for democracy. Otherwise, what could serve as its legitimating source? Along with it must come metaphysical support for natural law, which provides the foundations not only for modern science but also for the development of constitutional government. Therein lies the source for "the laws of Nature and of Nature's God," on which constitutional edifices are built. The primacy of power in Sunni Islamic thought undermines a similar prospect. If one does not allow for the existence of secondary causes, one cannot develop natural law. If one cannot develop natural law, one cannot conceive of a constitutional political order in which man, through his reason, creates laws to govern himself and behave freely.

If man lives in a world of which he can make no sense, an irrational world without causality, he can choose only to surrender to fate or to despair. Reason and freedom become irrelevant. If man is not a political creature endowed with reason in a world accessible to his mind, why attempt to order political life based upon deliberation and representation? In such circumstances, man will not go about writing constitutions, for constitutions by their very nature imply a belief in a stable external order, in man's reasonability, and in his ability to formulate and establish a rational mode of government, grounded in a rational creation. Law is reason, as John Courtney Murray said, which is why we discuss reasons for laws. Ultimately, law is reason because God is *Logos*.

However, if man cannot apprehend right and wrong through his reason, the moral foundation for man-made law is fatally subverted. On what would such laws then be based? If "reason is not a Legislator," why have legislation? Man's laws can only be, and be seen as, arbitrary expressions or impositions of human will, which is to say no foundation at all, especially when stacked up against divine will. If the capacity to know the good does not exist, there is no justification for democracy. Democracy cannot develop within this epistemology. If God is not *Logos*, then man's law is unreasonable. The only form of democracy we are legitimately left with is: one God, one vote. And, as an Algerian fundamentalist said, "one does not vote for God. One obeys Him."[8] Since in Ash'arite (and Hanbalite) Islam God is *not Logos*, it is no surprise to see a lack of democracy at the political level. This is reflected in the *2010 Freedom House Survey* of the Middle East and North Africa, in which no Arab country is listed as "free." Only Morocco, Lebanon, and Kuwait are labeled as "partly free"; the rest of the Arab countries, which include 88 percent of the region's people, are designated as "not free."[9] As in past years, Israel continues to be the only country in the region listed as "free."

The problem is that democracy is the answer to a question that the Arab Islamic world has not asked. As Middle East analyst Elie Kedourie remarked, "There is nothing in the political traditions of the Arab world which might make familiar, indeed intelligible, the organizing ideas of constitutional and representative government."[10] This is why, until recent neologisms, there were no words in Arabic for "citizen," "democracy," "conscience," or "secular." It is also why, as Bassim Tibi explains, "in the ideology of Islamic fundamentalism—or for that matter, in the minds of Islamic peoples—democracy is not an important issue."[11] How could it be otherwise? This led to the frustration of various reformers such as Muhammad 'Abduh, who said, "The Orient needs a despot who would force those who criticize each other to recognize their mutual worth,"[12] and Kemal Ataturk, who famously declared, concerning his efforts to impose democracy in Turkey, "For the people, despite the people."[13]

Further, there is no subsidiarity in voluntarism. There is no room for it. There is no hierarchy of responsibilities and actions corresponding to it—i.e., leaving each action delegated to the smallest unit of society capable of undertaking it, beginning with the individual. God does it all—directly. Allah is in charge of everything. Therefore, the inclination is to submit and do one's duty as one is told to do it. Power equals authority, human or divine. Therefore, the one in power, ipso facto, has authority (so long as he is not an outright apostate).* This is what I take Hassan Hanafi to have meant by "an ideology of power." Since reason has no standing on its own, it simply becomes the servant to power, which in turn serves the ruler's will. If God is force, then force becomes one's God. Within this view, power becomes self-legitimating.

To think that the only obstacles to democracy in such cultures are the autocracies that rule them is delusional. If God is pure will, how ought his vice regents on earth behave and rule? It is no accident that the embraced view of a tyrannical god produces tyrannical political orders. Syrian poet Ali Ahmad Sa'id, known as Adonis, sarcastically characterized this connection as follows: "If we are slaves, we can be content and not have to deal with anything. Just as Allah solves all our problems, the dictator will solve all our problems."[14] The rule of power is the natural, logical outcome of a voluntaristic theology that invests God's shadow on earth—the caliph or ruler—with an analogous force based on God's will. Within the voluntaristic outlook, man's only responsibility is to obey. Tunisian poet Basit

---

* This is not the case in mainstream Shi'ism, which has not granted de jure legitimacy to any ruler after the occultation of the twelfth imam.

bin Hasan describes the resulting mindset: "They [see themselves as] a people that can only live . . . in a state of submission to a redeemer [i.e., a leader whom they believe will lead them to redemption]."[15] In the face of this, can Arab Muslims create a political culture that is capable of embracing human rights, freedom of conscience, rule of law, etc.? It would seem not without first addressing the problem of the cult on which Arab culture is based.

Without a different theology, can one have democracy? Iranian philosopher Dr. Abdulkarim Soroush explicitly answered this question: "You need some philosophical underpinning, even theological underpinning in order to have a real democratic system. Your God cannot be a despotic God anymore. A despotic God would not be compatible with a democratic rule, with the idea of rights. So you even have to change your idea of God."[16] Elsewhere, Dr. Soroush wrote, "some of the understandings that exist in our society today of the Imams or of the *Mahdaviyat* (Shi'a belief in the twelfth Imam's return) or even of the concept of God are not particularly compatible with an accountable state and do not allow society to grow and develop in the modern-day sense."[17]

There is another way to state the problem. Within the Islamic understanding of revelation, is one authorized at any point to state the fundamental principle of democracy: that all people are created equal? Although there are a few intimations in the Qur'an that man is somehow made in God's image or has something of God's spirit in him—and therefore that each person is individually inviolable—this is quickly set aside by Muslim theologians as trespassing on the unbridgeable gulf of *tanzih*. Surah 15:28–29 quotes Allah speaking to the angels: "I will create a human being out of clay from an altered black mud. And when I have proportioned him and breathed into him my [created] soul, then fall down to him in prostration." The footnote to "soul" in the Saheeh International translation of the Qur'an from Riyadh, Saudi Arabia, typically explains, "The element of life and soul which Allah created for that body, not His own spirit or part of Himself (as some mistakenly believe)."[18] Further inquiries into this matter are rebuked with the Qur'an's admonition, "The spirit is the affair of thy Lord; not of thee."

Certainly, all Muslims are created equal, as was evident from the beginnings of Islam, when any slave who converted was immediately manumitted. The deep sense of Muslim equality is on display each year during the *Hajj* when the Ka'ba is circumambulated by pilgrims, all dressed in a white cloth (*ihram*) that resembles the Islamic funeral shroud. The rich, the poor, the young, the old, and people of many races are indistinguishable in the surging, circling masses. In fact, even corpses are brought along on litters, erasing the distinction between the living and the dead.[19] Why have Muslims been largely unable to expand upon this profound experience of Muslim equality to embrace all of humanity?

The answer is that there is neither a basis in revelation on which to do so nor an acceptance of "the laws of Nature and of Nature's God," which would require it. The equality of Muslims is not "self-evident," but only the product of faith. In short, there is no ontological foundation for equal human rights in Islam, which formally divides men and women, believer and unbeliever, and freeman and slave. This is fatal for democratic development and, concomitantly, equality before the law. Since, in Islam, man is not made in the image of God, he cannot be sovereign. Unless man is made in God's image, the sovereignty of God and the sovereignty of the people are mutually exclusive. To suggest that sovereignty resides in man is *shirk*, a blasphemous affront. Within this theology, sovereignty of the people, residing in the inviolable dignity of the individual, is inconceivable. As stated in 1997 by Professor Saeed, when head of the Jamaat Dawa-wal-Ishad in Pakistan: "the notion of sovereignty of the people is un-Islamic—only Allah is sovereign."[20]

Where, then, does this leave non-Muslims? These are the *dhimmi*; they are ruled in a different way according to the

Shar'ia. And what of the Muslim who chooses to change his religion? He is declared an apostate and forfeits his Muslim wife (who must divorce him), if not also his life. Even the injunction from the Hadith to love one's neighbor in Islam traditionally means to love one's fellow Muslim, not someone of another religion. Indeed, one is enjoined by the Qur'an not to make friends with them (17:87). Also, the Muslim obligation for charitable giving, *zakat*, is only for other Muslims, and must not be used for non-Muslims.

In light of this, it is not surprising that the 2003 United Nations Arab Human Development Report finds that "the majority of the Arab states have signed the international human rights conventions—all of them refer to respect for fundamental freedoms—yet those conventions have neither entered the legal culture nor have they been incorporated into the substantive legislation of those states. The conventions have remained nominal, as is apparent from the fact that they are rarely raised before the judiciary for implementation."[21]

Six years later, the 2009 UN Arab Human Development Report confirms that "state constitutions do not adhere in several key respects to the international norms implicit in the charters to which Arab countries have acceded. This gravely compromises levels of human security in the countries concerned. Many Arab countries' constitutions adopt ideological or doctrinal formulas that empty stipulations of general rights and freedoms of any content and which allow individual rights to be violated in the name of the official ideology or faith."[22]

Nothing makes clearer how un-Islamic the notion of equality is than "The Cairo Declaration on Human Rights in Islam," signed by forty-five foreign ministers of the Organization of the Islamic Conference on August 5, 1990. The Cairo Declaration was issued as an appendix to the UN Universal Declaration of Human Rights to make explicit Muslim differences with the UN declaration, which espouses universal, equal rights. The last two articles in the Cairo Declaration state that "all rights and freedoms stipulated in this Declaration are subject to the Islamic *Shari'a*" (Article 24) and that "the Islamic *Shari'a* is the only source of reference for the explanation or clarification [of] any of the articles of this Declaration" (Article 25). Elsewhere it declares that "no one in principle has the right to suspend . . . or violate or ignore its [Islam's] commandments, in as much as they are binding divine commandments, which are contained in the Revealed Books of God and were sent through the last of His Prophets. . . . Every person is individually responsible—and the Ummah collectively responsible—for their safeguard."[23]

The source of human dignity, according to the Cairo Declaration, is God's bestowal of a vice regency upon man (Qur'an 2:30). However, this is a delegated authority, not one inherent in man's nature, and it is not clear that it obtains to anyone other than the vice regent (caliph). This understanding comports with the only other use of the word in the Qur'an, when God says, "O David, We have made thee a vice regent in the earth" (Qur'an 38:26). The vast distance between this Muslim vice regency and the Judeo-Christian notion of man "created in the image and likeness of God" explains the gulf between the UN's and the Cairo Declaration's understanding of human rights.*

Under the dispensation of the *Shari'a*, what does respect for human rights look like? In June 2000, the grand sheikh of al-Azhar, the highest jurisprudential authority of the Sunni world, Muhammad Sayed Tantawi, offered Saudi Arabia as the model. He said: "Saudi Arabia leads the world in the protection of human rights because it protects them according to the *shari'a* of God. . . . Everyone knows that Saudi Arabia is the leading country for the application of human rights in Islam in a just and objective fashion, with no aggression and no prejudice."[24]

This is a stunning statement, because as Dr. Muhammad

---

* It is symptomatic of the difference in the two views of man that, in Genesis, it is Adam who names the animals, while in the Qur'an it is God who does so. Naming was a sign of power over the thing or person named. Muslim man did not have this power; only Allah did.

al-Houni, a Libyan intellectual living in Italy, says, "Islamic law was not familiar with equality or civil rights, because it was a product of its times."[25] How then is *Shari'a* their protector? *Shari'a* does not contain the concept of citizenship, for which there was no word in Arabic. In its terms, the inequality between believers and unbelievers appears to be unbridgeable. This is evident from the rigid discrimination against non-Muslims in Saudi Arabia, a *Shari'a* state, and in the vulgarly expressed opinions of Islamists like Abu Hamza, who wishes to impose *Shari'a* in Great Britain. He declared, "Only the most ignorant and animal minded individuals would insist that prophet killers (Jews) and Jesus worshipers (Christians) deserve the same rights as us."[26] As mentioned before, Islam is considered the *din al-fitra*, the religion that is "natural" to man. It was Adam's religion and would be everyone's religion were they not converted as children to apostasy in their upbringing by Christians, Jews, Hindus, or others. Therefore, restoring everyone to Islam is the only path to true "equality."

An article by Dr. Ahmad Al-Baghdadi, titled "Defending the Religion through Ignorance," gives a practical example of the consequences of the *Shari'a* understanding of human rights. The author noted the intention of "the Kuwaiti Ministry of Education to omit Article 18 of the International Declaration of Human Rights from the human rights curriculum for high school students, since it stipulates that every individual has freedom of thought, which includes the freedom to change one's religion and beliefs. The head of the technical council for the curriculum and professor of law, Rashid al-'Anzi, said that the reason why Article 18 of the [Declaration of] Human Rights will no longer be taught is that it is contrary to the Islamic *shari'a*, saying that we [in Kuwait] are a conservative Islamic society, in which we must instill religious, Islamic beliefs in accordance with the Islamic *shari'a*, and thus this article is not in keeping with how we want the students to be."[27]

The general difficulty in dealing with the subject of

human rights was addressed by Tunisian intellectual Basit bin Hasan: "Whenever the Arab discourse comes close to accepting new concepts [of human rights] heralding freedom and equality, it immediately runs into [a barrier of] suspicion and doubt regarding the practical benefit of these concepts and the extent of their rootedness in our 'cultural identity.' It was only for brief moments in [Arab] history that the discourse on liberation was inspired by human rights concepts. [This discourse appeared briefly] as part of the discussions during the [Arab] revival, among the anti-colonial national liberation movements, and during the period in which [the Arab] human rights organizations formed and developed. [However, in all other periods,] the issue of human rights came under severe attack by many political currents and in different writings—not only conservative ones but 'progressive' ones as well. This created much confusion regarding the concept, and made it even harder to grasp for the Arabs."[28]

The reason for this resistance goes to the heart of Islam. In *The Crisis of Islamic Civilization*, Ali Allawi, a distinguished former minister of both finance and defense in the new Iraq, gives an explanation that is worth quoting at length because, without ever mentioning Ash'arism, it nevertheless reveals how completely saturated Islamic thinking is by this school, to include the Ash'arite idea of man's acquisition of his actions. In fact, without an understanding of Ash'arite theology, one would be unable to explicate this statement accurately or to grasp fully its significance.

> In classic Islamic doctrine, the problem of the nature of the individual as an autonomous entity endowed with free will simply does not arise outside of the context of the individual's ultimate dependence on God. The Arabic word for "individual"—*al-fard*—does not have the commonly understood implication of a purposeful being, imbued with the power of rational

choice. Rather, the term carries the connotation of singularity, aloofness or solitariness. The power of choice and will granted to the individual is more to do with the fact of acquiring these from God, at the point of a specific action or decision—the so-called *iktisab*—rather than the powers themselves which are not innate to natural freedoms or rights. *Al-fard* is usually applied as one of the attributes of supreme being, in the sense of an inimitable uniqueness. It is usually grouped with others of God's attributes (such as in the formula *al-Wahid, al-Ahad, al-Fard, al-Samad*: The One in essence, state and being, and the everlasting), to establish the absolute transcendence of the divine essence. Man is simply unable to acquire any of these essential attributes. Therefore, to claim the right and the possibility of autonomous action without reference to the source of these in God is an affront. . . . The entire edifice of individual rights derived from the natural state of the individual or through a secular ethical or political theory is alien to the structure of Islamic reasoning.[29]

Note carefully that "the power of choice" is "not innate" to man—meaning that it is not part of his nature. He acquires it at the point of his action—which makes nonsense of any idea of freedom of choice. Allawi's last sentence is a tribute to the thoroughness of al-Ghazali's destruction of moral philosophy, here referred to as "secular ethical theory." This, as we have seen in earlier chapters, is, indeed, "alien to the structure of Islamic reasoning," as it was shaped by the Ash'arites and al-Ghazali. The end result, as Allawi says, is that the question of human rights does not even arise within the Muslim mind. How could it? How could man have a "right" to anything he does not possess by nature? Unless rights are "innate," democracy cannot form the moral basis of government. Advocates of democracy promotion in Muslim countries need to read Allawi's statement to appreciate fully what they are up against.

If within the Muslim world there is no principle of equality that embraces all human beings, there is no philosophical foundation for democracy. According to Raphael Patai, a revealing proverb from the Levant states: "Nothing humiliates a man like being subject to somebody else's authority."[31] This is so when there is no rational basis upon which to give one's assent to the authority of another because that authority itself is not based upon reason, but only power.

How, then, can one acknowledge that all people are created equal if this is not expressed in one's revelation? An avenue is open to this realization through philosophy and the recognition that *every* person's soul is ordered to the *same* transcendent good or end—which is what we mean by human nature in the first place. For this to happen, however, the culture in which it takes place must be open to reason or, more exactly, to reason's authority in its ability to apprehend reality. As we have seen, the effort to open Arab culture to reason had only a temporary success, while the expulsion of philosophy from it seems to have formed, or deformed, it in a permanent way.

Those wishing to influence the Islamic world through public diplomacy and the media should take heed of Lawrence Freedman's admonition: "Opinions are shaped not so much by the information received but the constructs through which that information is interpreted and understood."[30] Unless and until the Sunni world reembraces philosophy, it is difficult to imagine through what "constructs" it could receive the promotion of equal human rights in a favorable way.

Unfortunately, there is no room in this kind of Islam (Ash'arite or Hanbalite) for the individual to assert a version of the good based upon the authority of reason—to which standard he could then call others. This lack undermines the prospect for civil society and for peaceful change. The only way left to dispute the ruling order is to claim a more authentic understanding of Islamic scripture than the one on which the ruling order is based. Religious revolutionaries, who have nothing but their religion through which to assert their claims, usually settle their contests through sectarian violence. What other recourse is there? Only reason is nonsectarian. Once, however, the primacy of power is asserted—which is what primacy of the will means—violence is the only path left open. (As we will see later, this disposition was reinforced in the worst way by the adoption of Western totalitarian ideologies in the twentieth century by Arab secular states.)

Moroccan intellectual Fatima Mernissi explains how this syndrome functions: "As intellectual opposition was repressed and silenced, only political rebellion and terrorism had any success, as we see so well today. Only the violence of the subversive could interact with the violence of the caliph. This pattern, which is found throughout Muslim history, explains the modern reality, in which only religious challenge preaching violence as its political language is capable of playing a credible role. . . . From then [the suppression of the Mu'tazilites] on, fanatical revolt was the only form of challenge which survived within a truncated Islam."[32] Mernissi gets close to the source of this syndrome of violence with her mention of the suppression of the Mu'tazilites, but she fails to make explicit that the rationalization for this violence in a "truncated Islam" comes from a "truncated" theology. We will see the force of Mernissi's point, however, when we examine the ideology of today's Islamists.

George Hourani gives a similar, but even richer, perspective on the dynamics of violence in the Islamic world, which is worth quoting at length. He explains: "Ethical voluntarism put the determination of ethical questions firmly in the hands of experts in the interpretation of the *shari'a*, which was supposed to give guidance in every sphere of practical life. These experts were the *'ulama*,' the professional Islamic scholars who included the staffs of the *madrasas*, mosque preachers, qadis [judges for administering Islamic law], muftis [Muslim scholars who interpret the *Shari'a*] and theoretical jurists. Private lay people were discouraged by these tendencies as well as by autocratic sultans from proposing reforms in a state or organizing secular groups such as our labour unions, charitable organizations and especially political parties. Thus all *peaceful* change in society had to be initiated from the top by the heads of state who most times were satisfied with the way things were. The only other path to change was through revolutionary movements. But the only forces strong enough to gather supporters were religious leaders, claiming to be *mahdis* ringing in a golden age."[33]

As formidable, or even overwhelming, as these obstacles to democratic development appear, they are not insuperable, as has been shown in other parts of the Muslim world, such as Turkey and Indonesia. There are also reformers like the Libyan scholar Muhammad Abdelmottaleb al-Houn, who has the courage to say, "If we must choose between human rights and *shari'a*, then we must prefer human rights."[34] However, one must at least have as a starting point the admission contained in the statement by Columbia University scholar Richard Bulliet that "finding ways of wedding [Islam's traditional] protective role with modern democratic and economic institutions is a challenge that has not yet been met."[35]

Unreality in the Loss of Causality

In attacking the Mu'tazilites, the Ash'arites, in the words of Muhammad Khair, wished "to free God's saving power from the shackles of causality."[36] The price for this liberation was the loss of rationality, which, in turn, promotes irrational behavior. In short, as mentioned before, Ash'arite theology compelled its followers to deny reality. Saudi writer and reformist Turki Al-Hamad describes the symptoms thusly: "Unfortunately, we are regressing in a superstitious and unreasonable manner. . . . Today's world is ruled by logic. It operates according to a certain logic, which views the future according to certain criteria and considerations. We, on the other hand, have forsaken this future for the sake of myth. We live in the world of the supernatural, not in the real world, which we have completely neglected."[37] Modern manifestations of the resulting confusion are many. As Albert H. Hourani observed, Arabs "tend to see acts in themselves, as fitting an occasion rather than as links in a chain of cause and consequence."[38] It is not difficult to see from where this disposition developed. Even if only anecdotally, the following examples will give some flavor as to how the effects of the loss of causality play themselves out even in daily life.

Less than a decade ago, an imam in Pakistan instructed physicists there that they could not consider the principle of cause and effect in their work. Dr. Pervez Hoodbhoy, a Pakistani physicist and professor at Quaid-e-Azam University in Islamabad, said that "it was not Islamic to say that combining hydrogen and oxygen makes water. 'You were supposed to say that when you bring hydrogen and oxygen together then by the will of Allah water was created.'"[39]

There are people in Saudi Arabia today who still do not believe man has been on the moon. This is not because they are ignorant; it is because accepting the fact that man was on the moon would mean also accepting the chain of causal relationships that put him there, which is simply theologically unacceptable to them.

The denial of reality, however, can become explicit. Syrian philosopher Sadik Jalal al-'Azm recounts that "in Ibn Baz's [grand mufti of Saudi Arabia from 1993 until his death in 1999] book, published in 1985, he . . . completely rejected the idea that the earth orbits the sun. I own the book and you can verify what I am saying. And so, the earth does not orbit the sun, rather it is the sun that goes around the earth. He brought [us] back to ancient astronomy, to the pre-Copernican period. Of course, in this book Ibn Baz declares that all those who say that the earth is round and orbits the sun are apostates. At any rate, he is free to think what he wants. But the great disaster is that not one of the religious scholars or institutions in the Muslim world, from the East to the West, from Al-Azhar to Al-Zaytouna, from Al-Qaradhawi to Al-Turabi and [Sheikh Ahmad] Kaftaro, and the departments for *shari'a* study—no one dared to tell Ibn Baz what nonsense he clings to in the name of the Islamic religion. The fact that you tell me that this is a sensitive matter—this means that I cannot reply to the words of Ibn Baz when he says that the Earth is flat and does not go around the sun, but rises and sets, in the ancient manner. This is a disaster. The greatest disaster is that we cannot even answer them."[40]

The effects of the denial of secondary causality permeate even the most practical aspects of daily life. For instance, former British Islamist Ed Husain relates, "Hizb ut-Tahrir believed that all natural events were acts of God (though in some actions man could exercise free will), hence insurance polices were *haram*. . . . Hizb members could not insure their cars."[41] Likewise, the use of seatbelts is considered presumptuous. If one's allotted time has arrived, the seatbelt is superfluous. If it has not, it is unnecessary. One must realize that the phrase "insha' Allah [God willing]" is not simply a polite social convention, but a theological doctrine.

Those involved in training Middle Eastern military forces have encountered a lackadaisical attitude to weapon maintenance and sharp-shooting. If God wants the bullet to hit the target, it will, and if He does not, it will not. It has little to do with human agency or skills obtained by discipline and practice. Likewise, the conduct and outcome of the 2006 conflict between Israel and Hezbollah in Lebanon was characterized as a "divine victory" by Hezbollah because of what its leader, Hasan Nasrallah, called "divinely guided missiles." Though Hezbollah is a Shi'ite group, it shares the same point of view of God (or His direct agents) as the sole cause. "We believe that God's angels and the Mahdi were there, protecting our boys," said the brother of one fallen Hezbollah fighter, Mahmoud Chalhoub. "Even the Israelis talk about a man all in white [the Mahdi], riding a white horse, who cut off the hand of one of

their soldiers as he was about to launch a missile. The Israelis pretend that Hezbollah possesses satellites and this is how
its fighters were able to aim at military targets. We don't have
satellites, we have missiles guided by God."[42] Again, what may
seem to Westerners as crude war propaganda is grounded in
a deeply theological perspective. It is the twenty-first century
equivalent of the Qur'anic verse: "When you shot, it was not
you who shot but God" (8:17).

The enormous influence of Saudi Arabia today in the Muslim world is often thought by Westerners to be almost completely due to its oil wealth—petro-Islam. However, this dis-
counts the fact that many Muslims, including in countries like
Egypt, which are traditionally opposed to Saudi Arabia, see
this wealth as a direct gift from Allah. Can it be only an accident that these treasures are under the sands of this particular
country? No, they must be there as a reward to the Saudis for
following the true path. Why else would the oil be there?—a
question that has to be answered not by geologists, but within
the understanding that God has directly placed the oil there as
He directly does all things. The presence of petroleum gives
credence to the Saudi claim that its Wahhabi form of Islam is
the legitimate one. It is because of the oil that other Muslims
are willing to give this claim consideration. This is why Wahhabism has spread so significantly, even in parts of the world like
Indonesia that would seem, from their cultural backgrounds, to
have little sympathy with its radical literalism. Therefore, it is
not only *through* Saudi oil largess but also *because* of where the oil
is that Wahhabism enjoys such prominence.

A Kurdish acquaintance told me that he went on the *Hajj*
with a devout friend who was very much taken by the Ash'arite
teaching of God as the only cause. At the Ka'ba under the hot
Saudi sun, his friend touched the black stone, which was cool.
See, he said, this is God's direct miraculous action; how else
could this stone be so cool in this heat? My Kurdish acquaintance looked around until he found stairs descending to a

refrigeration unit. He then took his friend down to see it, and explained to him, "This is why the stone is cool." His friend's reaction to this lesson was outrage. Rational knowledge was a threat to his religious certainty. The refrigeration unit, a product of rational knowledge, was an assault on his theology.

In Taliban-controlled portions of Pakistan, "Polio vaccinations have been declared *haram* by the *ulema*, and the government campaign has subsequently stalled."[43] Like car insurance, vaccinations are a form of presumption. Only with the expulsion of the Taliban from the Swat Valley in the late summer of 2009 was the Pakistani government able to resume vaccinations.*

The Logic of Unreality: A Discourse of Conspiracies

Freed from cause and effect, the Islamic world reverts to a pre-philosophical, magical realm where things happen unaccountably due to mysterious, supernatural forces. In the place of reasonable explanations—or of explanations subject to reason—conspiracy theories reign, along with superstition. The daily Islamic press is rife with them. Conspiracy theories are the intellectual currency of an irrational world. Muslims are transformed from actors into victims—usually of some Jewish or Western conspiracy. Otherwise, events are assigned directly to God as their sole cause, again removing them from the realm in which man's actions can have any effect. As Tunisian poet Basit bin Hasan, describes it: "The prevailing discourse among us is accustomed to blaming the hegemonic and tyrannical 'other' for our misfortunes, for the hideousness that surrounds us, for our cultural emptiness, and for our problems. It acquits [us of responsibility for] our tragedies through the dualism of the evil 'other' and 'us,' the innocent victims."[44]

Natural disasters are, of course, explicable only in terms of God's direct action. On television, Sheikh Salih Fawzan al-

---

* Curiously, the Afghan Taliban encourage vaccinations.

Fawzan, a high functionary of the Saudi regime, opined that the 2004 tsunami "happened at Christmas, when fornicators and corrupt people from all over the world come to commit fornication and sexual perversion. That's when this tragedy took place, striking them all and destroyed everything."[45] On a Muslim website, the Arabic script spelling "Allah" was super-imposed on the satellite photo of the tsunami wave in such a way that it matched it, graphically suggesting the message of direct divine intervention. The wave itself spelled "Allah."

When Hurricane Katrina hit the southern United States, a typical article in the Arab press announced that "Katrina is a wind of torment and evil from Allah sent to this American empire" and that "the terrorist Katrina is one of the soldiers of Allah."[46] Further, "the only reason for this disaster is that Allah is angry at them."[47] Most Americans see this as simple propaganda without realizing it stems from a theological perspective that requires an understanding of the event as the direct result of the First Cause. It is the necessary view of people who must interpret it in this way because their theology does not allow for the existence of secondary causes.

Pervez Hoodbhoy reports, "When the 2005 earthquake struck Pakistan, killing more than 90,000 people, no major scientist in the country publicly challenged the belief, freely propagated through the mass media, that the quake was God's punishment for sinful behavior.* Mullahs ridiculed the notion

---

* In stark contrast, the New Testament makes clear that disasters and physical afflictions are not God's direct punishment for sin, significantly leaving open the possibility of other explanations, such as natural causes. In John 9:2, for example, the apostles ask Christ, "Rabbi, who hath sinned, this man or his parents, that he should be born blind?" Christ answers, "Neither this man nor his parents sinned." Likewise, in the death of eighteen people from the collapse of the tower of Siloam, Christ refuted the explanation that they died as punishment for their sins (Luke:4–5). This difference in understanding between Christian and Muslim revelation was extremely important for the development of Western civilization, as it was for the lack of development in Islamic civilization.

that science could provide an explanation; they incited their followers into smashing television sets, which had provoked Allah's anger and hence the earthquake. As several class discussions showed, an overwhelming majority of my university's science students accepted various divine-wrath explanations."[48]

Unreality in Perception and Press

The loss of rationality and the divorce from reality are also amply reflected in the press, which is rife with conspiracy theories and fantastical accounts of natural events. The 2003 UN Arab Human Development Report's take on Arab media stated: "News reports themselves tend to be narrative and descriptive, rather than investigative or analytic, with a concentration on immediate and partial events and facts. This is generally true of newspapers, radio bulletins and televised news. The news is often presented as a succession of isolated events, without in-depth explanatory coverage or any effort to place events in the general, social, economic and cultural context."[49] If your metaphysics is atomistic, most likely your reportage will also be of "a succession of isolated events," without the continuity that causal relationships would give it. This fits exactly George Hourani's observation, quoted earlier, that Arabs fail to see acts "in a chain of cause and consequence."

There almost seems nothing too ridiculous to appear in the Arab and Muslim press or to be published in the Arab world, including calculations for the speed of light according to a Qur'anic formula and accounts of Columbus encountering Arabic-speaking natives. In Saudi Arabia, a book published by the state press, *Brotokolat Ayat Qumm Hawla al-Haramayn al-muqaddasayn* (*The Protocols of the Ayat of Qumm Concerning the Two Holy Cities* [Mecca and Medina]), by Dr. 'Abd Allah al-Jafar, contended that the Shi'ites were a result of a plot by the Jews to subvert Islam. The Shi'ites were instrumental in all the invasions of the Islamic world and they also created the Freemasons, which will be news to many Europeans. The title is a takeoff from *The Pro-*

tocols of the Elders of Zion, a long-discredited nineteenth-century Czarist secret police forgery that still circulates in the Islamic world as a genuine document of Jewish perfidy. A more recent example of this perspective, this time from the Shi'ite angle, was offered by Mahmoud Musleh, a prominent Hamas member of the Palestinian legislature, who said of the massive demonstrations in Iran protesting Mahmoud Ahmadinejad's supposed reelection in June 2009, "Israel is standing behind what's going on in Iran."[50] An example from further afield comes from Indonesia, where two books by Herry Nuri, published in 2007, were titled *Signs of Freemasons and Zionists in Indonesia* and *Resurgence of Freemasons and Zionists in Indonesia.*[51]

There also does not seem to be anything too absurd to believe. The explanations for 9/11 are a prime example. Around the time of the eighth anniversary of those attacks, Mshari Al-Zaydi offered a satirical revue of some of the popular conspiracy theories in *Al-Sharq Al-Awsat* (September 9, 2009):

> Those who carried out the 11 September 2001 attacks—were they extremist Serbian nationalists? No it was the Israeli Mossad—no, pardon me, it was a U.S. group of Seventh Day Adventists! Not at all, the one who carried out the terrible attacks was the U.S. Central Intelligence Agency [CIA]! The suggestions and imaginary illusions continue to pour in the direction of evading the real consequences of the reality—which is that those who carried out the September 11 attacks were Muslim youths who believed in a hard-line interpretation of Islam, who are led by Osama bin Laden, and who are encouraged, and were then encouraged, by millions of Muslims. The idea that the Serbs were the ones who carried out the September 11 attacks in revenge for U.S. interference in the Serbs' war against Bosnia and the Croats was pronounced by Hasanayn Haykal, the symbol of Arab

political journalists who follow the pan-Arab direction. He said this days after the explosions took place (in the Lebanese *Al-Safir* newspaper, October 1, 2001). The idea that the attacks were carried out by the Israeli Mossad (the source of all evils and of mysterious events that some do not have the stamina to investigate and scrutinize) was suggested by Islamist writer Fahmi Huwaydi, who believed that Al-Qaeda could not carry out such an operation, but that the Mossad could (Kuwaiti *Al-Watan* newspaper, September 25, 2001). As for the idea that the explosions were carried out by a U.S. group called the Seventh Day Adventists, this was pronounced by Mustafa Mahmud, host of the "Science and Belief" program (*Al-Ahram*, Egypt, September 22, 2001).[52]

As late as 2006, despite repeated claims of credit by al-Qaeda, a *growing* number of Muslims believed that Arabs did not carry out the September 11, 2001, attacks on the United States. According to the *Washington Post*, "A report last year by the Pew Global Attitudes Project, however, found that the number of Muslims worldwide who do not believe that Arabs carried out the Sept. 11 attacks is soaring—to 59 percent of Turks and Egyptians, 65 percent of Indonesians, 53 percent of Jordanians, 41 percent of Pakistanis and even 56 percent of British Muslims."[53] A January 2006 study by *L'Economiste* revealed that 44 percent of Moroccans aged sixteen to twenty-nine believe that al-Qaeda is not a terrorist organization, 38 percent "don't know," and only 18 percent say it is a terrorist group.[54] In other words, there is no correlation between the evidence available and the opinions held.

For those unacquainted with the level of unreality in the daily Muslim press, here are samples taken from the media monitoring work of the Middle East Media Research Institute (MEMRI). What is notable is not so much the outlandishness of the accusations or stories as the lack of any concern over evidence as to whether they are true or false, or of any procedure to reach such a conclusion, which a fundamental regard for reality would seem to require. Despite the impression they create, the citations below are not from the equivalent of American tabloids at grocery store checkouts. Numerous citations are given not in order to create the impression that this is the whole of the Muslim press, but to show that it is a significant part of it. (This is not to say that there are not superb Arab and Muslim journalists.) The full texts and video excerpts can be obtained at the MEMRI website: www.memri.org. All titles come from MEMRI:

- *"Egyptian Cleric Ahmad Abd Al-Salam: Jews 'Infect Food with Cancer and Ship it to Muslim Countries,'"* February 24, 2009[55]

  Although a seemingly outlandish claim, this headline is not simply a form of sensationalist journalism designed to draw in readers. The quote is from a video address given by al-Salam: "The Jews conspire day and night to destroy the Muslims' worldly and religious affairs. The Jews conspire to destroy the economy of the Muslims. The Jews conspire to infect the food of the Muslims with cancer. It is the Jews who infect food with cancer and ship it to Muslim countries." Al-Salam further accuses the Jews of sexually abusing Muslim women and conspiring to bring about the downfall of Islam.

- *"Iranian Filmmaker Nader Talebzadeh Denies the Holocaust and States: Al-Qaeda and the Mossad Carried Out 9/11 Together,"* April 3, 2008[56]

  September 11 conspiracy theories are rampant in the Muslim world. There is even one theory that says George W. Bush himself executed and masterminded the attacks of September 11.

- *"Iranian TV: Swine Flu—A Zionist/American Conspiracy,"* May 12, 2009[57]

  Here are excerpts from another Iranian TV report on swine flu, which aired on IRINN, the Iranian news channel, on May 6, 2009: "In his speech, Barak [*sic*] Obama mentioned a medicine called Tamiflu—but what exactly is Tamiflu? Who are the compassionate manufacturers of this medicine? This great pharmacist is none other than Rumsfeld, the former American secretary of defense. He is one of the shareholders, and an active and influential member on the board of directors of Gilead Science, which is the main provider of medicine for this disease. . . . It should be noted that the Gilead Sciences is a Jewish company. Its name, in Hebrew, means 'holy place,' and all its shareholders are Zionists."

- *"Egyptian Cleric Safwat Higazi Calls to Shut Down Starbucks in the Arab and Islamic World: Jewish Queen Esther Serves as Their Logo,"* January 25, 2009[58]

  Higazi, in an address that aired on Egyptian television, stated frankly: "The girl in the Starbucks logo is Queen Esther. Do you know who Queen Esther was and what the crown on her head means? This is the crown of the Persian kingdom. This queen is the queen of the Jews. She is mentioned in the Torah, in the Book of Esther. The girl you see is Esther, the queen of the Jews in Persia." Despite the fact that Higazi mistakes the identity of the "Starbucks girl"—she is actually a siren from medieval French mythology—he calls for the eradication of all Starbucks in the Muslim world, because "it is inconceivable that in Mecca and Al-Madina, there will be a picture of Queen Esther, the queen of the Jews."

- *"Hamas TV Scientist Dr. Ahmad Al-Muzain: Bayer Derived Its Treatment for AIDS From Prophet Muhammad's Hadith About the Wings of Flies,"* November 13, 2008[59]

- *"Arab Columnists: The Economic Crisis—A Conspiracy by U.S. Government, American Jews,"* October 22, 2008[60]

Dr. Mustafa al-Fiqqi of Egypt writes: "The Bush administration was trained and impelled, by the American conservative right and by Jewish circles, to carry out this mission [in two stages]—at the beginning of [Bush's] first term in office, and at the end of his second term in office. The aim is to achieve two major goals—a global political [goal] in 2001, and a global economic [goal] in 2008." The first prong of the mission was, of course, the attacks of September 11. According to al-Fiqqi, and many others, the 9/11 attacks and the global economic crisis are premeditated missions by powerful Americans and Westerners in an effort to attain global dominance.

- *"Iranian TV Documentary Series Traces Zionist Themes in Western Movies:* Saving Private Ryan,*"* June 30, 2008[61]

Among the claims made by Iranian film critic Dr. Majid Shah-Hosseini that American movies (*Saving Private Ryan* in particular) undeservedly and perhaps heavy-handedly exalt the Jewish-American soldier is this claim: "Moreover, names may be selected for their rhyming value. 'Zion' sometimes becomes 'Ryan,' as in *Saving Private Ryan.* They exploit even the similarity of names."

- *"New Conspiracy Theory in Egypt: It Wasn't Saddam But His Double Who Was Executed,"* January 30, 2007[62]

- *"In TV Interview, Pakistani Security Expert Accuses Western Zionists, Hindu Zionists of Planning 11/26 Mumbai Terror Attacks,"* December 4, 2008[63]

- *"Cultural Advisor to Iranian Education Ministry and Member of Interfaith Organization Lectures on Iranian TV:* Tom and Jerry—*A Jewish Conspiracy to Improve the Image of Mice, Because Jews Were Termed 'Dirty Mice' in Europe,"* February 24, 2006[64]

This quote from a lecture Dr. Hasan Bolkhari, a member of the Film Council of Islamic Republic of Iran Broadcasting and an advisor to the Iranian Education Ministry, is worth citing extensively to demonstrate the vast depth and breadth of unreality so prevalent in Muslim world:

> There is a cartoon that children like. They like it very much, and so do adults—*Tom and Jerry.*
>
> […]
>
> Some say that this creation by Walt Disney [*sic: Tom and Jerry* is a Hanna Barbera production] will be remembered forever. The Jewish Walt Disney Company gained international fame with this cartoon. It is still shown throughout the world. This cartoon maintains its status because of the cute antics of the cat and mouse—especially the mouse.
>
> Some say that the main reason for making this very appealing cartoon was to erase a certain derogatory term that was prevalent in Europe.
>
> […]
>
> If you study European history, you will see who was the main power in hoarding money and wealth, in the 19th century. In most cases, it is the Jews. Perhaps that was one of the reasons which caused Hitler to begin the antisemitic trend, and then the extensive propaganda about the crematoria began.... Some of this is true. We do not deny all of it.

Watch *Schindler's List.* Every Jew was forced to wear yellow star on his clothing. The Jews were degraded and termed "dirty mice." *Tom and Jerry* was made in order to change the Europeans' perception of mice. One of terms used was "dirty mice."

I'd like to tell you that.... It should be noted that mice are very cunning ... and dirty.

[...]

No ethnic group or people operates in such a clandestine manner as the Jews.

[...]

Read the history of the Jews in Europe. This ultimately led to Hitler's hatred and resentment. As it turns out, Hitler had behind-the-scenes connections with the *Protocols [of the Elders of Zion].*

Tom and Jerry was made in order to display the exact opposite image. If you happen to watch this cartoon tomorrow, bear in mind the points I have just raised, and watch it from this perspective. The mouse is very clever and smart. Everything he does is so cute. He kicks the poor cat's ass. Yet this cruelty does not make you despise the mouse. He looks so nice, and he is so clever. . . . This is exactly why some say it was meant to erase this image of mice from the minds of European children, and to show that the mouse is not dirty and has these traits. Unfortunately, we have many such cases in Hollywood shows.

- *"Saudi Cleric Muhammad Al-Munajid: Mickey Mouse Must Die!"* August 27, 2008[65]

In the latest of his controversial statements and fatwas, well-known Saudi Islamist lecturer and author Sheikh

Muhammad Al-Munajid stated, on Al-Majd TV on August 27, 2008, that mice were Satan's soldiers and that "according to Islamic law, Mickey Mouse should be killed in all cases."

- *"Egyptian Cleric and Former Islamic Lecturer in the U.S. Hazem Sallah Abu Isma'il on Al-Risala TV: Lectures on the Jews' Conflicts with Islam's Prophet Muhammad, Stating U.N. Documents Assert '82% of All Attempts to Corrupt Humanity Originate from the Jews,'"* May 10, 2006[66]

Isma'il is an Egyptian cleric. He has a weekly television show called *The Raids* in which he discusses Muhammad's battles. In one segment, he spoke of how, according to a UN report, Jews were responsible for 82 percent of the world's video clips, which led him to conclude: "Eighty-two percent of all attempts to corrupt humanity originate from the Jews. You must know this so that we can know what should be done."

- *"Saudi Author Dr. Muhammad Al-'Arifi on Show Produced by Saudi Ministry of Religious Endowments: Women in the West Marry Dogs and Donkeys; 54% of Danish Women Do Not Know Who Fathered Their Babies,"* April 6, 2006[67]

- *"Saudi Urologist Offers Lizard Kidneys (Dried and Ground) to Treat Impotence and Concludes: Birth Control Increase STDs,"* May 23, 2005[68]

In addition to these, there are many other videos and articles that make similar claims and subscribe to similar conspiracy theories. The Middle East Media Research Institute (from which the above stories and videos are taken) offers a wealth of information on both their video page and their Special Dispatch section.[69]

While the amount of this kind of delusional material is nearly overwhelming, there are TV stations such as Al Arabiya, headed by Adbul Rahman al-Rashed, one of the finest journalists in the Arab world, and newspapers such as *Asharq Al-Awsat*, published out of London, that serve as models for what Arab journalism could become.

Chapter 7

THE WRECKAGE:
MUSLIM TESTIMONIALS

Today, according to Arabs themselves, the condition of the Arab Muslim world is dysfunctional. This is hardly news. In the late nineteenth century, Sayyid Jamal al-Din al-Afghani (1839–1897) stated: "It is permissible . . . to ask oneself why Arab civilization, after having thrown such a live light on the world, suddenly became extinguished; why this torch has not been relit since; and why the Arab world still remains buried in profound darkness."[1] The question was repeated by Shakib Arslan in the title to his 1960s book *Why Are Muslims Backward While Others Have Advanced?* Contemporary Arab thinkers continue to speak of the darkness which al-Afghani described.

Syrian poet Ali Ahmad Sa'id (b. 1930), known by his pseudonym "Adonis," a 2005 candidate for the Nobel Prize for Literature, said: "If I look at the Arabs, with all their resources and great capacities, and I compare what they have achieved over the past century with what others have achieved in that period, I would have to say that we Arabs are in a phase of extinction, in the sense that we have no creative presence in the world." Sa'id proffered that a people becomes extinct when it loses its creative capacity to change its world. He pointed to the Sumerians, the ancient Greeks, and the Pharaohs—all extinct. The clearest sign of an Arab extinction, he said, is that "we are facing a new world with ideas that no longer exist, and in a context that is obsolete."[2]

In his book *Contre-Prêches* (*Counter-Preaching*), Tunisian thinker Abdelwahab Meddeb invites his audience to imagine a meeting of representatives of the various civilizations, European, American, Japanese, Chinese, Indian, African, Arab, and Muslim: "Each [representative] would be asked what his civilization could contribute to the humanity's present and future. What could the Arab Muslim offer? Nothing, except for Sufism, perhaps.... Unless they take a new direction, one can reasonably assume that the Arab [civilization], constrained by the framework of Islamic faith, will join the great dead civilizations."[3]

In a January 2008 interview with the Qatari *Al-Raya* daily, eminent Syrian philosopher Sadik Jalal al-'Azm said that Islamic thinkers no longer even attempt to "deal with the problems and questions of modern science." Having abandoned rational judgment for a kind of moral infantilization, Islamic religious thought is in "an even deeper state of impoverishment" than before. "Today," he said, "we have arrived at issues like the *fatwa* of breast-feeding adults." This is a reference to the infamous May 2007 *fatwa* saying that the only way an unmarried man and a woman could work alone in the same room together would be if they established a familial relationship. This they could do if the woman breastfed the man. As al-'Azm pointed out, this *fatwa* "was not issued by any ordinary sheikh, but by the head of the Hadith Department at Al-Azhar University," the most prestigious Muslim institution in the Arab world. (After a public outcry, the *fatwa* was withdrawn.)

Another example comes from the book *Religion and Life—Modern Everyday Fatwas,* by the mufti of Egypt, Dr. Ali Gum'a, who wrote that the companions of Muhammad would bless themselves by drinking his urine, saliva, or sweat. (A public uproar caused Gum'a to withdraw the book.) Ali Gum'a has also offered *fatwas* against sculpture and ones forbidding women to wear pants and soccer players to show their legs. Al-'Azm also points out that the Arab world is now rife with reiterations of "the Hadith of the fly." (The Prophet said, "If a house fly falls in the drink of anyone of you, he should dip it [in the drink], for one of its wings has a disease and the other has the cure for the disease" [*Sahih Al-Bukhari*: Volume 4, Book 54, Number 537].) This was thought to have some application to a cure for AIDS. According to al-'Azm, "the spread of this superstitious manner of thinking . . . represents an additional deterioration over and above the impoverishment" that he had written about in the late 1960s.[4]

A contemporary cry of desperation comes from Indian Muslim thinker Rashid Shaz: "We Muslims live with a paradox. If we are really the last chosen nation entrusted to lead the world till end time, why it is so that we are unable to arrest our own decline? Despite the fact that the Muslim nation today constitute [*sic*] almost two billion strong population and they are strategically located in energy-rich lands on which depends the future of the world, they are reduced to mere consumers. The new technology has revolutionised the way we live and it is still forcing us to live differently, but we as a nation have almost no share in this process and hence have completely lost control of the happenings around us."[5]

These voices sound so forlorn because things have been getting worse, not better, over the past fifty years. The trajectory is away from reform, not toward it. One barometer is the work of Khalid Muhammad Khalid, an Egyptian thinker, who wrote a seminal work, *Here We Start*, in 1950. The book, which was reprinted ten times in less than fifteen years, spelled out the relationship between religion and politics that is necessary for effective reform: "We should keep in mind that the religion ought to be as God wanted it to be: prophecy, not kingdom; guidance, not government; and preaching, not political rule. The best we can do to keep religion clear and pure is to separate it from politics and to place it above [politics]. The separation between religion and the state contributes to keeping religion [free of] the shortcomings of the state and its arbitrariness."[6] In 1989, however, Khalid renounced all of this, collapsed the very distinction he had insisted upon, and called for *din wa dawla*, the unity of religion and state, and for Islamic world government, which is precisely the goal of the Islamists.[7]

The Wreckage in Human Development: Muslim Testimonies

The Arab world's underdevelopment has been bluntly reported in a series of invaluable United Nations reports that began in 2002. It should be noted that only Arab scholars write the UN's Arab Human Development Reports—a wise choice by the UN that makes it difficult to dismiss the conclusions as biased or as the product of Western intellectuals infamously known as "Orientalists."

The second report, from 2003, states, "In being connected with and at the same time contradictory to knowledge, Arab intellectual heritage nowadays raises basic knowledge problems."[8] The report is bold enough to refer to a lack of scientific perspective and "sometimes a disregard of reality" in the Arab heritage. It gets close to suggesting that the origin of the "knowledge problems" is fundamentally theological in nature by saying, "Finally, it [Arab consciousness] has been cloaked in the supernatural, which in reality signified an absence of consciousness and an abandonment of the scientific and intellectual basis that underpinned the Arab classical cultural experience."[9]

The UN report is right to identify "basic knowledge problems" in the Arab intellectual heritage, which grew straight out of the developments chronicled in this book. But the UN paper does not get the reason for them exactly correct. The difficulty does not really consist in being "cloaked in the supernatural"; rather, it is the *kind* of supernatural in which consciousness is "cloaked" that is decisive for science and everything else. As we have seen, the denial of natural law, occasioned by a certain conception of God, removed the very objective of science from the Muslim mind. Since the effort of science is to discover nature's laws, the teaching that these laws do not, in fact, exist (for theological reasons) obviously discourages the scientific enterprise. The Ash'arite school, by diminishing the worth of the world as having no status in and of itself, marginalized the attempts to come to know it.

The extent of the discouragement and the paucity of scientific research this has produced is, if predictable, still astonishing. While the UN reports testify to this, Pakistani physicist Pervez Hoodbhoy is particularly trenchant on the subject. In the August 2007 issue of *Physics Today*, he notes that after the major scientific contributions of Islam's Golden Age in the ninth to thirteenth centuries, "science in the Islamic world essentially collapsed. No major invention or discovery has emerged from the Muslim world for well over seven centuries now. That arrested scientific development is one important element—although by no means the only one—that contributes to the present marginalization of Muslims and a growing sense of injustice and victimhood."[10]

Hoodbhoy cites an array of statistics that lay bare the lack of scientific inquiry in the Muslim world. According to a study conducted by the International Islamic University Malaysia, Islamic countries have only 8.5 scientists, engineers, and technicians per 1,000 population, barely 20 percent of the world average (40.7 per 1,000), and just 6 percent of the average for countries in the Organisation for Economic Cooperation and Development (139.3). Meanwhile, India and Spain *each* produce a larger percentage of the world's science literature than forty-six Muslim countries *combined*. Hoodbhoy also cites official statistics showing that "Pakistan has produced only eight patents in the past 43 years."

The 2003 UN Human Development Report expands on these distressing figures. Scientific papers, measured by papers per million inhabitants, are "roughly 20 percent of that of an industrial country. South Korea produces 144 per million; Arab countries 26 per million." In comparing the number of patents registered in the twenty-year period from 1980 to 2000, the report shows Korea with 16,328, and nine countries in the Middle East, including Egypt, Syria, and Jordan, with 370, with even many of these patents registered by foreigners.[11]

This dire situation was made even worse by Muslim countries attempting to reinvigorate science by making it "Islamic." "In the 1980s," Hoodbhoy writes, "an imagined 'Islamic science' was posed as an alternative to 'Western science.' The notion was widely propagated and received support from governments in Pakistan, Saudi Arabia, Egypt, and elsewhere." Supporters of this "new science," says Hoodbhoy, announced that "revelation rather than reason would be the ultimate guide to valid knowledge."

The results of "Islamic science" were predictable. As Hoodbhoy recounts, so-called scientists took verses from the Qur'an and tried to utilize them as "literal statements of scientific fact." So, for example, "Some scholars calculated the temperature of Hell, others the chemical composition of heavenly djinnis. None produced a new machine or instrument, conducted an experiment, or even formulated a single testable hypothesis."[12]

To say that there is an *Islamic* (or a Christian or Hindu) science is, of course, to deny that there is such a thing as science, as what stands scientifically must be the same everywhere for everyone. Is hydrogen *Islamic*? Is there an *Islamic* lightbulb? The claim for a specifically Islamic science comes from a point of view grounded in al-Ghazali's statement that "the science that the Qur'an brings is all science."[13] Applied literally, this teaching means practically *no* science for Sunni Muslims.

More UN Reports on Arab Underdevelopment

The devastation extends far beyond science. Were it not for sub-Saharan Africa, the Arab world would find itself at the bottom of the scale in almost every category of human development—health, education, per-capita GDP, and productivity.

Again, the UN Arab Human Development Reports relate the grim results. For instance, the 2002 report notes that "GDP in all Arab countries combined stood at $531.2 billion in 1999—less than that of a single European country, Spain ($595.5 billion)."[14] If oil exports are stripped out, the Middle East exports less than Finland. The report also states that the Arab world, for all its oil riches, has experienced "a situation of quasi-stagnation" since 1975, with real per-capita income growing by only about 0.5 percent annually when the global average increase was more than 1.3 percent a year. As the UN reported, "only sub-Saharan Africa did worse than the Arab countries." During the same time period, purchasing power parity declined considerably in the Arab world, from 21.3 percent to just 13.9 percent. Unemployment, too, remained stubbornly high across the Arab world, hovering at about 15 percent—"among the highest rates in the developing world," according to the UN.[15] This is hardly surprising given the paucity of investment in research and development, which does not exceed 0.5 percent of gross national product, well below the world average.[16] For instance, it is even lower than in Cuba at 2.35 percent in 1995.[17]

Further, "Despite the popular perception that Arab countries are rich, the volume of economic product in the region is rather small. Overall GDP at the end of the 20th century (US $604 billion) was little more than that of a single European country such as Spain (US $559 billion) and much less than that of another European country, Italy (US $1,074 billion) (UNDP 2002)."[24]

According to the Arab Human Development Report, productivity in the Arab world is woefully low. Including the Arab world's oil production, the productivity level in the richest Muslim countries is just over half of that of Argentina or South Korea. Further, in the Arab countries that produce little oil, the productivity level is less than one-tenth that of Argentina or South Korea.[25]

In 2005, the U.S. treasury undersecretary for international affairs, John B. Taylor, citing the work of Professor Guido Tabellini, noted that "productivity actually fell in the Middle East in the last 20 years, by 0.7 percent per year. In contrast, this is a period when productivity was increasing in the United States, Europe and East Asia.... Regional unemployment levels are 15 percent and reach 30 percent among younger workers."[18]

Out of a combined population of around 300 million, some 65 million Arabs are illiterate, two-thirds of them women. According to the 2009 Arab Knowledge Report, this figure has improved slightly since 2002 but it is still above 60 million.[19]

In terms of what it enumerates as the "freedom deficit," the report states that "out of seven world regions, Arab countries had the lowest freedom score in the late 1990s figures."[20] Little has changed since then.

According to the UN, the production of scholarly and literary books is severely lacking in the Muslim world. Muslims publish just over 1 percent of the world's books despite constituting 5 percent of the world's population. Further, their share of literary or artistic books stands at just *under* 1 percent. Even more telling is that of books published in the Arab market, 17 percent are religious in nature. That's 12 percent more than the average in other parts of the globe.[21] "Turning to UNESCO statistics on the volume of world publications shows that, in 1991, Arab countries produced 6,500 books compared to 102,000 books in North America, and 42,000 in Latin America and the Caribbean."[22]

Finally, the number of books translated in the Arabic world is five times less than of those translated in Greece. In fact, in the past one thousand years, since the reign of al-Ma'mun, the Arab community has translated only 10,000 books, or roughly the number that Spain translates in one year.[23]

A sad epitaph to this grim litany of failure comes from Syrian philosopher Sadik Jalal al-'Azm:

When we simply look at the Arab world, we see that it consumes everything but that it produces nothing apart from raw materials. What can we expect from the Arabs? Look at the Arab world from one end to the other; there is no true added value to anything. There is a structure that seems not to encourage production and to not be for it. What do we produce? What do we export? [This is true] whether you are talking about material, economic, scientific, or intellectual production, or any other kind. Look at oil production, for example. What is the Arabs' relation to the oil industry? They own the oil, but they have nothing to do with its extraction, refinement, marketing, or transport. Look at the huge installations for prospecting oil, extracting it, and refining it. Look at the Arab satellite, what in it is Arab? I doubt the ability of the Arabs to produce a telephone without importing the parts and the technologies it requires, and perhaps even the technicians.[26]

In terms of education, things do not look much better. In a *Wall Street Journal* article, Sheikh Muhammad bin Rashid al Maktoum, prime minister of the United Arab Emirates and ruler of Dubai, notes that more than half of the Arab population of 300 million is under the age of twenty-five. He then asks rhetorically, "And how much do we spend on education? The per capita expenditure of our region's 22 nations [members of the Arab League] has shrunk in the last 15 years to 10% from 20% of what the world's 30 wealthiest countries spend."[27]

Making Sense of the Wreckage: The Seeds of Islamism

It is a long way from the resplendent Baghdad court of Caliph al-Ma'mun to conditions in the Arab world today. Ali Allawi laments, "The creative output of the twenty or thirty million Muslims of the Abbasid era dwarfs the output of the nearly one-and-a-half billion Muslims of the modern era."[28] Poignantly, the 2003 UN report uses a quote from the first Arab philosopher, al-Kindi, a thinker sponsored by al-Ma'mun, to encourage acceptance of the truth, no matter from where it might come, a subtle suggestion that the Arab world needs to catch up with its past. To repeat al-Afghani's question: "It is permissible, however, to ask oneself why Arab civilization, after having thrown such a live light on the world, suddenly became extinguished; why this torch has not been relit since; and why the Arab world still remains buried in profound darkness." (It was not as "sudden" as al-Afghani suggested.)

The question must be addressed within the context of a very long period of decline. As is usual in the decline of empires, Islam's loss of intellectual vitality preceded its loss of political vitality. Islam as a global civilization with the Arabs at its center gradually collapsed in on itself (with the help of the Mongols, who destroyed Baghdad in 1258). There is no reason here to recite the history of decline. It was not uninterrupted, as is known from the great achievements of the Ottomans, who succeeded the Arabs in the Middle East. However, eventually the decline became so pronounced that it raised disturbing questions. This happened principally because of the incursions of advanced Western powers into the sacrosanct lands of Islam.

As Ibn Khaldun wrote in *The Muqaddimah* (*Introduction to History*), Muslims "are under obligation to gain power over other nations."[29] Had not Allah promised, "Our soldiers will be those who overcome" (Qur'an 37:173)? And did not the astonishing success of Islam in its first centuries confirm the prophecy for its believers? Failure is particularly galling when there is a theological imperative to succeed. Loss of power is egregious because Islam is driven by a theology of empire. "But when you don't have an empire you have something that has gone seriously wrong."[30]

Things began to go seriously wrong in 1798, when Napoleon defeated the Egyptian armies at the Battle of the Pyramids (or even before, when the Ottoman Empire was forced to sign the Treaty of Küçük Kaynarca in 1774 with Russia). As Abd al-Rahman al-Jabarti observed at the time, the proper order of things as divinely ordained had been overturned. The Muslim world began to experience enormous theological, philosophical, and political confusion. How could this defeat possibly have happened in the house of Islam?

Things got much worse after World War I, with the collapse of the caliphate in 1924, the secularization of Turkey, and the almost complete colonization of the Levant and the Maghreb. There was the old enemy, the West, ruling over Muslims. In strict Islamic teaching, a non-Muslim is not allowed to rule an Islamic country. It is a scandal for an infidel to rule over a believer.[31] Suddenly, a huge part of the Islamic world was being ruled by the West. How could this be understood within the tenets of the faith and what was to be done about it?

There were two distinct answers from Muslims. One was that Islamic thinking had calcified, and this was the cause of its decline. Thus, it needed to modernize and to learn from the West. To allow for this, Islam could be reinterpreted to show that its fundamental teachings and principles were, in fact, not simply compatible with modern science and other achievements, but already underlay those achievements. Islam had led the way in the Middle Ages, only to be stifled by its own clerical establishment. Meanwhile the West had built upon Islam's own achievements to surpass it. Now Islam had to reclaim its legacy from the West and develop it further. This response was given well before the end of the caliphate under the experience of Western imperial domination of Muslim lands in Egypt and India.

Jamal al-Din al-Afghani, a pan-Islamist, insisted that there was no conflict between faith and reason in Islam, and sought Islam's modernization in order to strengthen it against the West. The West's superiority was seen principally in its vastly greater scientific knowledge and in the power that issued from it. He was scathing in his address to the *ulema* of India: "They do not ask: Who are we and what is right and proper for us? They never ask the causes of electricity, the steamboat, and railroads. . . . Our ulema at this time are like a very narrow walk on top of which is a very small flame that neither lights its surroundings nor gives light to others."[32] In an exchange with French writer Ernest Renan, al-Afghani wrote, "A true believer must, in fact, turn from the path of studies that have for their object scientific truth. . . . Yoked, like an ox to the plow, to the dogma whose slave he is, he must walk eternally in the furrow that has been traced for him in advance by the interpreters of the law. Convinced, besides, that his religion contains in itself all morality and all sciences, he attaches himself resolutely to it and makes no effort to go beyond. . . . Whereupon he despises science." "In truth," said al-Afghani, "the Muslim religion has tried to stifle science and stop its progress."[33] As a result, he said, referring to Western colonization of Islamic lands, "ignorance had no alternative to prostrating itself humbly before science and acknowledging its submission."[34]

In turn, al-Afghani taught the Egyptian Muhammad 'Abduh (1849–1905) in the rationalism of early Islamic thought, including Avicenna. Although 'Abduh had received a traditional education, including four years at al-Azhar, he rebelled at the rote learning and the lack of philosophy and theology in the al-Azhar curriculum. A conservative al-Azhar professor, Sheikh 'Ulaysh, confronted him, asking "if he had given up Ash'arite teaching to follow the Mu'tazilite." 'Abduh responded: "If I give up blind acceptance (*taqlid*) of Ash'arite doctrine, why should I take up blind acceptance of the Mu'tazilite?"[35] This was a clever answer, as "blind acceptance" is exactly what the Mu'tazilites taught against, and it would have been dangerous for 'Abduh to admit openly to Mu'tazilite sympathies. As it was, 'Abduh was sent into exile for his attempts at reform. While in Beirut, he wrote *Risalat al-tawhid* (*Treatise on [Divine] Unity*). In the first edition of the book, 'Abduh went so far as to embrace the Mu'tazilite position that the Qur'an was created—*Khalq al-Qur'an*—and not coeternal with God. However, because of the controversy this caused, he removed it in subsequent editions.[36]

Returning from Beirut, 'Abduh still found formidable obstacles to reform at al-Azhar in teaching even Ibn Khaldun's undisputed classic of Arabic thought from the fourteenth century. "After my return from exile, I tried to convince Sheikh Muhammad al-Anbabi, then Sheikh al-Azhar, to accept certain proposals, but he refused. Once I said to him, 'Would you agree, O Sheikh, to order that the *Muqaddimah* (*Introduction*) of Ibn Khaldun be taught at al-Azhar?' And I described to him whatever I could of the benefits of this work. He replied, 'It would be against the tradition of teaching at al-Azhar.'"[37]

In addition to its embrace of a created Qur'an, *Risalat* contains other passages that are very redolent of Mu'tazilite teaching and sound as if they could have been written by Abd al-Jabbar: "[How] then can reason be denied its right, being, as it is, the scrutineer of evidences (*adilla*) so as to reach the truth within them and know that it is Divinely given? . . . Yet this obligation (of recognizing revelation) does not involve reason in accepting rational impossibilities such as two incompatibles or opposites together at the same time and point. . . . But if there appears something which appears contradictory reason must believe that the apparent is not the intended sense. It is then free to seek the true sense by reference to the rest of the prophet's message in whom the ambiguity occurred."[38] Revelation was given "to help fallible reason by defining some of the good and bad acts on the basis of the utility principle."[39]

'Abduh said he wished "to liberate thought from the shackles of *taqlid* [imitation or emulation] . . . to return, in the acquisition of religious knowledge, to its first sources, and to weigh them in the scales of human reason, which God has created in order to prevent excess or adulteration in religion . . . and to prove that, seen in this light, religion must be accounted a friend to science, pushing man to investigate the secrets of existence."[40]

'Abduh rose to become the mufti of Egypt—the highest authority on Islamic jurisprudence. As entranced as he was by both Leo Tolstoy and Herbert Spencer, whom he went to London to meet, 'Abduh was not willing to go as far as the Mu'tazilites in "subjecting God's power to the principle of justice."[41] As we have seen earlier, his position was that "reason quite lacks the competence to penetrate to the essence of things. For the attempt to discern the nature of things, which necessarily belongs with their essential complexity, would have to lead to the pure essence and to this, necessarily, there is no rational access."

It is interesting to note the reason why 'Abduh did not approve of the Tanzimat reforms in the Ottoman Empire that granted equality before the law to Muslims and non-Muslims alike. He did not oppose the substance of these reforms but objected that they had been "instituted not by and through religion, as they should have been, but in defiance of it. . . . All changes so attempted must fail in Islam because they have in them the inevitable vice of illegality."[42] Even for 'Abduh, then, "reason is not a legislator," and Islam remains the sole source of legitimacy.

In India, Sayyid Ahmad Khan (1817–1898) went further than 'Abduh in insisting on the primacy of reason and the createdness of the Qur'an. "If people do not shun blind adherence, if they do not seek that light which can be found in the Qur'an and the indisputable Hadith, and do not adjust religion and the sciences of today, Islam will become extinct in India."[43] Founded by Khan, Aligarh University, modeled on Cambridge, became a major center for intellectual renewal. "Of the different religious books which exist today and are used for teaching, which of them discusses Western philosophy or modern scientific matters using principles of religion? From where should I seek confirmation or rejection of the motions of the Earth, or about its nearness to the sun? Thus it is a thousand times better not to read these books than to read them. Yes, if the Mussulman be a true warrior and thinks his religion right, then let him come fearlessly to the battleground and do unto Western knowledge and modern research what his forefathers did to Greek philosophy. Then only shall the religious books be of any real use. Mere parroting will not do."[44] He insisted that "today we are as before in need of a modern theology (*'ilm al-kalam*) by which we should either refute the doctrines of the modern world or undermine their foundation, or show that they are in conformity with the articles of Islamic faith."[45]

Ahmad Khan rejected *Shari'a* and said that the Qur'an should be reinterpreted to conform to known facts of physical reality. He not only echoed the Mu'tazilites but also embraced the Islamic philosophers, including their Aristotelian description of God as the "First Cause."[46] His disciple, Sayyid Ameer Ali (1849–1924), blamed al-Ashari, Ibn Hanbal, al-Ghazali, and Ibn Taymiyya for the collapse of Islamic science and culture. Ahmad Khan's message was deeply resented by the *ulema* and he was vilified among the orthodox, who boycotted Aligarh University, but who were eventually able to foist upon it their own religious instruction. As for Khan, "The *mutawalli* (keeper) of the Holy Kabba declared him to be an enemy of Islam and *wajib-i-qatl* (deserver of death)."[47] Even al-Afghani considered Khan a heretic.[48]

The efforts of al-Afghani, Muhammad 'Abduh, Ahmad Khan, and others like them were ultimately unsuccessful in terms of reorienting Islamic culture so it could successfully absorb modern science and rationality, and still retain its religious orthodoxy. The reason for this may be that, as intimated by 'Abduh's objection to the Tanzimat reforms, they were not seen as emanating from Islam and therefore suffered from the "inevitable vice of illegality." One must remember that, by the late nineteenth and early twentieth centuries, Ash'arism had had a thousand years to seep into every nook and cranny of

Arab culture. Its influence could hardly be abrogated in the space of a mere fifty years, or more.

Perhaps the most important reason for failure, according to Bassam Tibi, is that "Islamic modernism never went beyond dogma and remained basically scripturalist, acting exclusively within dogmatic confines. Because it did not engage in a reason-based response to the question Arslan asked ('Why are Muslims backward?'), no cultural innovation was accomplished."[49] David Pryce-Jones explains that "Afghani built into the definition of progress a contradictory regression to the Islamic past."[50] Ironically, these reformers laid the foundations for the Salafist movement. If one traces the genealogy of the ideology of today's Islamists back to al-Afghani, one can see the force of this insight in their insistent calls to return to the ways of the Companions of the Prophet.* (The lineage goes from al-Afghani to Muhammad 'Abduh to Rashid Rida to Hassan al-Banna to Sayyid Qutb to Osama bin Laden and Ayman al-Zawahiri.) The problem with a return to the past is that the past is impervious to change. In these terms, reform in the late nineteenth and early twentieth centuries was unfortunately stillborn. In 2008, Saudi author and reformist Turki al-Hamad gave this epitaph for reform: "From the early 20th century to this day, we constantly hear people say: We should adopt the good things [from the West] and ignore the bad. You cannot do such a thing. When you consider the products of modern civilization—the car, the computer, and so on—these are all products of a certain philosophy, a certain way of thinking. If you adopt the product, but ignore the producer—you have a problem. You cannot do such a thing. [For us,] the product is new, but the thought is not. We move forward with our eyes looking backward."

---

* The force of regression is somewhat endemic to Islam based upon the Qur'an's description of Medina in the early seventh century: "You are the best community produced [as an example] for mankind" (3:110). If this is so, emulating Medina, even fourteen hundred years later, ineluctably becomes the goal of reform.

Chapter 8
THE SOURCES OF ISLAMISM

The other answer to al-Afghani's question about the decline of Islamic civilization had nothing to do with the loss of science or the need to catch up with the West. It understood the crisis as a rebuke from Allah because Muslims had not followed His way. Just as success is a validation of faith, failure is a personal rebuke. Did not Allah promise, "You shall be uppermost if you are believers" (3:139)? The corollary to this must be that, if you are not uppermost, you must not be believers. Within this theological viewpoint, defeat by a superior power must be interpreted as a judgment from Allah that Muslims have deviated from His path. This is the perspective that was seized upon by the Islamists.

A narrative of grievance and potential recovery exists throughout the Muslim world, but particularly among the Islamists, who are still in a state of shock over the abolition of the caliphate by Kemal Ataturk in 1924. With the collapse of the Ottoman Empire at the end of World War I, the caliphate was but a shell of itself. Nevertheless, its abandonment left some Muslims completely adrift. It was as if the Vatican had abjured its authority to represent the church. How could the end of the caliphate be explained? Its abolition called into existence the first Islamist organizations such as the Muslim Brotherhood, the *al-Ikhwan al-Muslimun*, dedicated to its restoration. While most Muslims may not share in the Islamist mythology regarding the caliphate, which did not exist continuously from the time of Muhammad, they nonetheless do require an explanation for the decline of their civilization.

A somewhat similar situation existed in Germany after World War I, which Adolf Hitler was able to exploit with the Nazi Party. In fact, there are striking parallels to this sense of grievance that can be found in *Mein Kampf.* The comparison is not adventitious. There were associations between the Nazis and the early Islamists going back to the 1930s, when Hassan al-Banna, the founder of the *Ikhwan*, modeled the Muslim Brotherhood on the Brownshirts. The German sense of grievance came from defeat in World War I and the metaphysical shock of the collapse of the Second Reich. This loss was inconceivable to them. The world had somehow been turned upside down. To comprehend the loss, Hitler and his companions explained it in terms of first the internal enemy and then the external enemy. Germany was stabbed in the back. Where was the rot in German society from which this betrayal came? The racist Nazi answer was the Jew. Germany must expunge the Jew and purify itself for the battle against the external enemy in order to bring about the millenarian vision of the Third Reich and the supremacy of the Aryan race.

Similarly, Islamists try to focus the widely shared sense of grievance and humiliation in the Muslim world on the loss of the caliphate because they wish to restore it. Their explanation for the decline of their civilization is, as indicated above, a loss of faith. The solution to this problem is obviously not imitating the West, but restoring Muslim faith to a pristine condition, as defined by them. They, too, began looking for the internal enemy and then the external enemy. Osama bin Laden's deputy, Ayman al-Zawahiri, gives typical expression to this formulation in describing "the apostate domestic enemy and the

Jewish-crusader external enemy."[1] It is here, at the heart of the effort to restore past glory, that the questions asked in the introduction reappear.

Are the Islamists of today something new or a resurgence of something from the past? How much of this is Islam and how much is Islamism?* Is Islamism a deformation of Islam? If so, in what way and from where has it come? And why is Islam susceptible to this kind of deformation?

Quite some time ago, an answer to the first question was proffered by the famous British author Hilaire Belloc. In *The Great Heresies*, published in 1938, he predicted the resurgence of Islam in the following way: "Since religion is at the root of all political movements and changes and since we have here a very great religion physically paralysed but morally intensely alive, we are in the presence of an unstable equilibrium which cannot remain permanently unstable."[2] A few pages later Belloc wrote: "That [Islamic] culture happens to have fallen back in material applications; there is no reason whatever why it should not learn its new lesson and become our equal in all those temporal things which now *alone* gives us our superiority over it— whereas in *Faith* we have fallen inferior to it."[3]

Belloc saw the coming resurgence of Islam within the context of Islamic history from the seventh to the seventeenth centuries, at the end of which the Turks were stopped for the second and final time outside the gates of Vienna. A revived Islam, he seemed to say, would be more of the same, yet now equipped with modern technology. It would be an even more lethal foe against a West weakened by its loss of faith.

As prescient as Belloc may seem, can one adequately understand what is happening today in the terms he suggested?

---

* *Islamism* is used here as a form of shorthand for Muslim totalitarian ideology. It is in some ways an unsatisfactory term, as there are self-proclaimed Islamists who would not subscribe to this meaning of the term. However, it is useful to designate the transmogrification of Islam into an ideology.

The centuries-long expansion of Islam came from the center of an extraordinary dynamic that thrust out to the boundaries of its potential, but then slowly subsided into quiescence. As already stated, the Islamic world was jolted out of its several centuries of torpor only by intrusions from the West. By the early nineteenth century, the West had demonstrated such a decisive superiority over Islamic culture that Islam's defensive attempts to recover from its influences have been indelibly marked by the very things against which Muslims were reacting. To resist the West, they became, in a way, Western. As Raphael Patai pointed out in *The Arab Mind*, the very standards by which Muslims measure their own progress are Western. This is amply evident in the UN Arab Human Development Reports, written by Arabs themselves. In a final irony, the most rabid ideological reactions against this state of affairs in the Muslim world are also infused with Western ideology. Islamists practice a perverse kind of homeopathy which uses the very disease from which they are suffering to combat it, but with dosages that are lethal. Belloc did not foresee this.

Islamist authors cannot be accurately understood in the terms of Islam simply, but only within the perspective of the twentieth-century Western ideologies that they have assimilated, most especially those based on Nietzsche and Marx. (We shall shortly see how thorough the assimilation was.) The seminal thinkers in Islamism, like Sayyid Qutb in Egypt, were very well versed in Western philosophy and literature. Qutb went to the United States for two years of postgraduate studies (1949–50). He was completely repelled by what he saw as a materialist culture. For example, he thought that the way Americans cared for their lawns was a sign of materialism and that the parish dances he witnessed were examples of sexual degeneracy. His exposure to the West intensified his hatred of it. The solution to what he diagnosed as Western alienation was Islam. Islam could overcome the relativism and the moral degeneracy that he had observed. Islam would save the West as well as the East.

In order to do this, Qutb said that Muslims must emulate the behavior of the Companions of the Prophet to prepare for the struggle ahead. But he used Leninist terms and means, espousing a "vanguard" of the faithful which would lead the restoration of the caliphate. (In fact, Qutb, though he despised Marxism, was the Muslim Brotherhood's liaison to the Communist Party in Egypt and to the Communist International.) Because of his opposition to the Egyptian government, Qutb was hanged by Nasser in 1966. He is said to have gone to the gallows smiling, leaving that iconic image to inspire his followers today.

The highly heterogeneous world of contemporary Islam stretches from the Atlantic to the Pacific, from Morocco to the southern Philippines. There are very few things that one can say about this world that are true in all these places. Of the forty-four predominantly Muslim countries in the world, twenty-four do not use Islamic law as their primary source of laws. While Muslims everywhere observe the five pillars of Islam, they are culturally very different in, say, Indonesia and the Arab world. However, this highly heterogeneous character is in danger of being homogenized. The engine for the homogenization is Qutb's Islamist ideology, which has demonstrated tremendous cross-cultural appeal. Qutb's writings are considered the new writ, along with those of Pakistani writer Maulana Maududi and Hassan al-Banna, the founder of the Muslim Brotherhood. Qutb's teachings are at the foundation of, for instance, the Justice and Prosperity Party (PKS), which is the fastest-growing and only dues-paying party in Indonesia (although it has suffered some recent setbacks), as well as the more explicitly violent Jemaah Islamiyah. The Hizb ut-Tahrir organization, which is banned in most Muslim countries, has had quite an impact in central Asia and western Europe. The foundation of its ideology is also Sayyid Qutb. The people at whom Hizb ut-Tahrir aims are the intelligentsia and the upper middle class across the Islamic world. Hizb ut-Tahrir does not explicitly advocate violence and terrorism, but prepares the intellectual foundations for it by using Qutb's teachings. On the other hand, al-Qaeda, also spawned by Qutb's ideology, explicitly promotes violence in the fifty-some nations in which it has a presence. Qutb's brother, Muhammad, taught Osama bin Laden at Abdul Aziz University in Jeddah, Saudi Arabia. Islamic Jihad in Palestine, another Qutb clone, advocates violence. Iran's Supreme Leader, Ayatollah Ali Khamenei, translated substantial parts of Qutb's works into Farsi, demonstrating the impact of Qutb's thought across the Sunni-Shi'ite divide. In other words, this is not a local phenomenon. The cross-cultural appeal of this ideology reflects a deeper crisis within Islam itself. It is in its most exacerbated form in the Arab world, but it exists everywhere in the Muslim universe or *umma*.

Why is Qutb so popular and influential? There is a two-fold answer. Part of the explanation comes from the abiding sense of Muslim grievance and humiliation to which Qutb's ideology plays. This part stems from Islam itself, which takes as its model for success the Companions of the Prophet, who blazed the way to glory and empire. So, said Qutb, Muslims must remove the accretions of the ages and go back to that original community, model themselves on the Companions and prepare to do what they did—to retake the world, and to reestablish the caliphate. The instrument for doing this, depending on which Islamist you talk to, is a combination of persuasion (*dawa*) and *jihad*, both of which are grounded in traditional Islam, or simply *jihad*.

Qutb blamed the Jews in Istanbul for conspiring in the collapse of the caliphate ("The Jews have always been the prime movers in the war declared on all fronts against the advocates of Islamic revival throughout the world"),[4] and labeled impious Muslims as the internal enemy, who must be vanquished so that the infidel West could be confronted and overcome. This much of the program can be understood from Islam alone, without any contamination by Western ideology.

The rest of the appeal stems from the results of the ancient struggle within Islam over the primacy of power versus the primacy of reason, which has been the subject of this book. As we have seen, the outcome of this contest decisively affected the character of the Islamic world in which Qutb could find such a ready audience for his ideology. The infection of Western millenarian ideological thought from Nietzsche and Marx would not have made Islamism the attraction it is unless Islamism was not also able to claim legitimacy by drawing upon something within the traditions of Islam itself. For this, Islamist thinkers selectively chose one, albeit a primary one, of the many theological and philosophical traditions within Islam's rich history. The nexus between this school of thought and Western totalitarian ideology was the primacy of will.

The Totalitarian Connection

The Ash'arite demotion of reason at the theological level is Islamism's connection with modern secular ideology and its denigration of reason, and the subsequent celebration of the use of force. Modern Western ideology also asserts that the primary constituent of reality is will. This is at the heart of Nietzsche, of course, and his analysis of Socrates and Greek philosophy. Philosophy is simply a rationalization for an assertion of the will, the will to dominate, the will to power. Nietzsche set up a metaphysical project to make everything the object of the will, which would then transform it. The instrument of pure will is force. The political vulgarization of this project was the Nazi Party. (As Hans Friedrich Blunk, president of the Reich's Chamber of Literature, 1933–35, put it: "This government [was] born out of opposition to rationalism.") The same demotion of reason took place in Marxism-Leninism. In *The German Ideology*, Marx said that reason is an excrescence of material forces.[5] It has no legitimacy. One does not argue with man; one does not persuade people. In order to change humanity, one must get hold of all the means of production, alter them, and then change man's thinking through force.

Ineluctably, if will and power are the primary constituents of reality, one will, in a series of deductive steps, conclude to a totalitarian regime. There is no other way out of it. The curious thing is that it does not matter whether one's view of reality as pure will has its origin in a deformed theology or in a totally secular ideology, such as Hegel's or Hobbes's; the political consequences are the same. As Father James Schall has shown, the notion of pure will as the basis of reality results in tyrannical rule. Disordered will, unfettered by right reason, is *the* political problem.

As mentioned earlier, when facing the challenge from the West, many Muslims sought to imitate it. Why, of all things, did they choose as their models the worst of what the West had to offer, fascism and communism? Why, with few exceptions, did they not try to imitate a constitutional democratic order? In *The Middle East*, Bernard Lewis suggests it was because these ideologies were anti-Western and anti-Christian, but also because "the ideologies and social strategies that were being offered corresponded in many ways much more closely to both the realities and the traditions of the region."[6] However, Lewis does not spell out what that correspondence is, beyond saying the West is "individualistic" in orientation and the Middle East "collective." In *The Closed Circle*, David Pryce-Jones gets closer by suggesting that "Nazism and Arab power challenging had in common the belief that life is an unending struggle in which the victor works his will upon the loser by virtue of his victory."[7] The fuller answer is that they were naturally drawn to fascism and communism as more compatible with what they already believed because these models are based upon the primacy of the will and the denigration of reason. A political order that presumes the primacy of reason did not appeal. This natural affinity helps explain the easy passage to Islamism of leftist nationalists and communists like prominent Egyptian writer Dr. Mustafa Mahmud and well-known Islamist Shi'ite writer Samih Atef El-Zein.

Islamism as Ideology

Neither communism nor fascism has worked for the Arabs—because they have not worked for anyone—but the Islamists have ingested their totalitarian programs and mixed them with their Ash'arite interpretation of Islam. That is why one can compare the features of these ideologies and even some of the language they use almost exactly. As Maulana Maududi wrote, "In reality Islam is a revolutionary ideology and programme which seeks to alter the social order of the whole world and rebuild it in conformity with its own tenets and ideals. 'Muslim' is the title of that International Revolutionary Party organized by Islam to carry into effect its revolutionary programme. And 'Jihad' refers to that revolutionary struggle and utmost exertion which the Islamic Party brings into play to achieve this objective."[8] With changing only two words, "Islam" and "Muslim," to either "Nazism" or "communism," and then rereading the sentence above, one will immediately see the nearly complete ideological affinity among them, as no other word changes are necessary to represent the Nazi or communist revolutionary points of view. This can be done with a number of Maududi's statements. For instance, "Islam wishes to destroy all States and Governments anywhere on the face of the earth which are opposed to the ideology and programme of Islam regardless of the country or the Nation which rules it. The purpose of Islam is to set up a State on the basis of its own ideology and programme, regardless of which Nation assumes the role of the standard bearer of Islam or the rule of which nation is undermined in the process of the establishment of an ideological Islamic State."[9] Statements like these are inconceivable without the influence of Western totalitarianism.

This is evident, as well, in Qutb's description of Islam as an "emancipatory movement" and "an active revolutionary creed."[10] Islamism is inevitably on the march, proclaims Sudan's Hasan al-Turabi, because, much as communism used to be, "it's a wave of history." This is familiar rhetoric, but not from Islam.

Islamism definitely has a new element in it. Modern radical Islamism and twentieth-century Western totalitarian movements are not simply akin, moving in parallel to each other. There was a good deal of ideological cross-pollination, and they had real working connections. This is not news in respect to Nazism and Hitler's mufti, Amin al-Husayni, but such relations also existed with the Soviet Union, as outlined in Laurent Murawiec's book *The Mind of Jihad*.[11] In fact, Qutb said all liberation movements were welcome to his revolution: "The Islamic doctrine adopts all struggles of liberation in the world and supports them in every place."[12]

Like twentieth-century Western ideologies, Islamism places the burden of salvation upon politics, a total politics that, only through its control of every aspect of life, can bring about their version of God's kingdom on earth. Islamism is not a religion in the traditional sense. Most religions, in fact all monotheistic ones, put before man a revelation from God that is similar in certain essential respects. The revelation contains a moral code by which man is expected to live if he wishes to achieve eternal life in paradise. Paradise is located in the hereafter—never on this earth. So is the hell to which man will be sent if he is disobedient. The terrestrial and the transcendent are distinct—the city of man and the city of God, as St. Augustine put it. Life here is a test. The ultimate resolution of the problem of justice is not in this vale of tears, but before the throne of God in the next world. Man's ultimate destiny is in the transcendent. This general view is shared by Judaism, Christianity, and Islam, all of which see perfect justice as being established by God's final judgment.

Islamism is an ideology in the classic sense in that it offers, or rather insists upon, an alternative "reality"—one that collapses the separate realms of the divine and the human, and arrogates to itself the means to achieve perfect justice here in this world or, as Qutb said, "to abolish all injustice from the earth."[13] This notion of the inner perfectibility of history—the achievement of perfect justice here—is the very heart of ideology, whether sacred or profane. It places alongside reality its false version and insists that reality conform to its demands. Its adherents live in the magical world of this second reality and obey its laws. They may seem to live and move in the realm of the real world, but they are already transposed into the second, false reality. When they behave according to its laws—such as in slaughtering innocent people without remorse—others are surprised and disturbed because they do not know the contours of this second reality, which has just been so shockingly imposed on them.

Jessica Stern, the author of *Terror in the Name of God*, reflected the puzzlement that initially strikes almost everyone encountering Islamist terrorism until they come to understand its ideology as a pseudoreligion rather than as a political movement. She writes: "I have come to see that apocalyptic violence intended to 'cleanse' the world of 'impurities' can create a transcendent state. All the terrorist groups examined in this book believe—or at least started out believing—that they are creating a more perfect world. From their perspective, they are purifying the world of injustice, cruelty, and all that is antihuman. When I began this project, I could not understand why the killers I met seemed spiritually intoxicated. Now, I think I understand. They seem that way because they are."[14] The joint commissioner of the Mumbai police, Rakesh Maria, said of the captured terrorist Muhammad Ajmal Kasab, the only surviving perpetrator of the 2008 mass murder in Mumbai, India, "He was led to believe that he was doing something holy."[15]

With scathing sarcasm, Abdelwahab Meddeb, the Tunisian reformist, said of Islamist terrorists, "No criminal is more despicable than one who not only fails to feel any guilt after [committing] his crime, but also harbors the illusion that this [crime] will bring him . . . divine reward. This conversion of bad into good not only spares him guilt, but also turns an unhappy person into a happy soul."[16]

Thus, terrorism is not simply terror—some people doing terrible things on the spur of the moment. It is murder advanced to the level of a *moral* principle, which is then institutionalized in an organization—a cell, a party, or a state—as its animating principle. It is the rationalization that allows, as Meddeb said, "the conversion of bad into good," on which the organization is based. In order to act, terrorists must first firmly believe that their violence is moral or "holy," that it will achieve some higher good. Therefore, the very first thing one must understand is the ideology incarnated in the terrorist organization that allows terrorists to do this; it is the source of their moral legitimacy. Without it, they or their organization cannot exist. It is the "ism" in terrorism. In the case of radical Islam*ism*, already mentioned, the trinity of thinkers behind the ideology is Sayyid Qutb, Hassan al-Banna, and Maulana Maududi.

The means for the transformation of reality into the alternative reality is, as in all ideologies, total control based upon absolute power, exercised to annihilate the old order. Qutb said that "only a radical transformation with the complete destruction of old systems could guarantee the flourishing of the ideal society under God's suzerainty."[17] Maududi stated that Islam is a "comprehensive system which envisages to annihilate all tyrannical and evil systems in the world and enforces its own programme of reform which it deems best for the well-being of mankind."[18]

While most ideologies are secular attempts to displace religion as the main obstacle to fulfillment, Islamism is based upon a deformed theology that nonetheless shares in the classical ideological conflation of heaven and earth into one realm. It is exactly in these terms that its chief ideologue, Sayyid Qutb, spoke: "Islam chose to unite earth and heaven in a single system."[19] This means that "the patent purpose of establishing God's law on earth is not merely an action for the sake of the next world. For this world and the next world are but two complementary stages. . . . Harmonizing with the divine law does not mean that man's happiness is postponed to the next life, rather it makes it real and attainable in the first of the two stages."[20] In other words, transcendent ends will be achieved by earthly means, as Qutb said, "to reestablish the Kingdom of God upon earth"[21] or "to create a new world."[22] This is obviously not a political objective but a metaphysical one. Its achievement will bring about a condition, predicted Qutb, which sounds eerily similar to that proclaimed by Marx for his classless society: "Universal adoption of the Divine law would automatically mean man's complete emancipation from all forms of enslavement."[23] To reach this goal, announced Maududi, "Islam wants the whole earth and does not content itself with only a part thereof. It wants and requires the entire inhabited world."[24]

It should be no surprise that, in its political manifestation, Qutb's "single system" duplicates the features of the totalitarian regimes of the twentieth century's secular ideologies and of Socrates' proto-totalitarian city in Plato's *Republic*. In *The Republic*, Socrates showed the limits of the political by transposing the order of the soul into the political order and letting us see, in the form of an imaginary state, what such a transposition would mean. He asked, in effect: If we tried to realize politically a perfect state according to the order of the soul, what would we get? The answer was: the garrison state, the destruction of the family, regimentation, the abolition of the private, eugenics, state education, etc. In other words, the political order cannot satisfy the highest needs of man. Politics cannot meet the goal of the human soul, for it cannot achieve perfect justice; if it is made the vehicle for doing so, it will end in a horrendous tyranny. This is the profound error into which both the Western totalitarians and the Islamists fell.

Therefore, it is only logical that "in such a state," as described by Qutb's ideological soul mate, Maulana Maududi, "no one can regard any field of his affairs as personal and private. Considered from this aspect the Islamic state bears a kind of resemblance to the Fascist and Communist states."[25] It is, he remarked, "the very antithesis of secular Western democracy." In a line worthy of Robespierre, Sayyid Qutb said that a "just dictatorship" would "grant political liberties to the virtuous alone."[26] Hassan al-Banna, whose bedside reading was al-Ghazali, also regarded the Soviet Union under Stalin as a model of a successful one-party system.

So long as some part of the world eludes the control of the Islamist revolutionary, conflict continues—with the *dar al-harb* (the abode of war)—just as perpetual revolution was proclaimed by Marxists until the complete overthrow of the bourgeois order or by the Nazis until the eradication or enslavement of inferior races. Since total control is never achieved, an excuse is always available for why the kingdom has not arrived, just as it was with the ever-receding prospects of a classless society for the Marxists. The excuse for not having achieved the utopia of God's kingdom on earth, or of the Thousand-Year Reich, or of the classless society, is always the same, and roughly analogous: An infidel has escaped our grasp, a Jew has escaped, or a capitalist has eluded us. Thus, paradise is forever postponed, and the war continues as part of a permanent revolution. As Qutb proclaimed, "This struggle is not a temporary phase but a perpetual and permanent war."[27] And Hassan al-Banna said, "What I mean with jihad is the duty that will last until the Day of Resurrection."[28]

The Foundation of Hatred

The fuel for the permanent war is the same for Islamism as it was for Marxism-Leninism and Nazism; it is hatred. Only the object of hatred changes—from race hatred in Nazism and class hatred in communism to hatred of the infidel in radical Islamism, to include any Muslim who does not conform to its version of Islam. "We must hate," Lenin counseled; "hatred is the basis of communism."[29] Bin Laden's parallel doctrine is equally explicit: "As to the relationship between Muslims and infidels, this is summarized by the Most High's Word: 'We [Muslims] renounce you [non-Muslims]. Enmity and hate shall forever reign between us—till you believe in God alone' [Qur'an 60:4]. So there is an enmity, evidenced by fierce hostility from the heart. . . . If the hate at any time extinguishes from the heart, this is great apostasy! . . . Battle, animosity, and hatred—directed from the Muslim to the infidel—is the foundation of our religion."[30]

The most successful megaphone for this message today is the Internet, which radical Islamists use to create what Dr. Jerrold M. Post, a professor of psychiatry, political psychology, and international affairs at George Washington University, calls "a virtual community of hatred."[31]

The Evil of Democracy

As already intimated by Maududi, democracy is antithetical to the Islamist project, as the primacy of reason is antithetical to the primacy of power. The antirational view not only makes democratic, constitutional order superfluous, it also renders it inimical to Islamists as the form of blasphemy they fear the most. Al-Qaeda author Yussuf al-Ayyeri (killed in a gun battle in Riyadh, June 2003) wrote in his last book, *The Future of Iraq and the Arabian Peninsula after the Fall of Baghdad*: "It is not the American war machine that should be of the utmost concern to Muslims. What threatens the future of Islam, in fact its very survival, is American Democracy."[32] Because democracies base their political order on reason and free will, and leave in play questions radical Islamists believe have been definitively settled by revelation, radical Islamists regard democracies as their natural and fatal enemies. Man-made law is a form of *shirk* in that its purported authority impinges upon that of the divine law that has already been prescribed for every situation. It places man's laws on the level of God's. Thus it appears to divinize man and is seen not so much as a form of political order but as a competing, false religion. This is why Sayyid Qutb declared in *Milestones*, "Whoever says that legislation is the right of the people is not a Muslim."[33]

In his book *Democracy: A Religion!*, Abu Muhammad al-Maqdisi, the Palestinian-Jordanian theologian, confirms Qutb's view that "democracy is a religion but it is not Allah's religion." Thus, as a religious obligation, Muslims must "destroy those who follow democracy, and we must take their followers as enemies—hate them and wage a great jihad against them."[34]

The Indonesian Islamist cleric Abu Bakar Bashir, who was released from prison in July 2006 after having been charged with complicity in the Bali terror attacks of 2002, echoes Qutb: "There is no democracy in Islam, so do not try to interpret the Qu'ran and turn Islam into a democracy to suit your needs. God's law comes first. It is not up to the will of the people to decide what is right and how to live. Rather the will of the people have [*sic*] to be bent to suit the will of God. It is not democracy that we want, but Allah-cracy! The principles of Islam cannot be altered and there is no democracy in Islam or nonsense like 'democratic Islam.' . . . Democracy is *shirk* [blasphemy] and *haram* [forbidden]."[35]

Al-Qaeda spokesman Suleiman Abu Gheith said, "America is the head of heresy in our modern world, and it leads an infidel democratic regime that is based upon separation of religion and state and on ruling the people by the people via legislating laws that contradict the way of Allah and permit what Allah has prohibited."[36] For radical Islamists, as we have seen, democracy itself is a blasphemous act of impiety and must be destroyed.

Therefore, as Islamic cleric Sheikh Omar Abdel Rahman (the "blind sheikh") exhorted, "Muslims everywhere [should] dismember [the American] nation, tear them apart, ruin their economy, provoke their corporations, destroy their embassies, attack their interests, sink their ships, . . . shoot down their planes, [and] kill them on land, at sea, and in the air. Kill them wherever you find them."[37]

It is important to understand that the radical Islamist desire to destroy the United States, as the leader of the democratic West, is not simply a political goal but also a metaphysical requirement for the transformation of reality. The United States must be destroyed because "America is evil in its essence (*Amreeka sharrun mutlaq*)," as pronounced by Sheikh Muhammad Hussein Fadlallah of Hezbollah.[38] "We are not fighting so that you will offer us something," warned Hussein Massawi, a former Hezbollah leader. "We are fighting to eliminate you."[39] "The real matter," announced Taliban leader Mullah Muhammad Omar, "is the extinction of America. And, God willing, it will fall to the ground."[40]

Within Islamism, this destruction is as metaphysically necessary as was the elimination of the bourgeoisie for the Marxists and inferior races for the Nazis for their respective millenarian projects. Like these twentieth-century totalitarians, radical Islamists use their view of reality to dehumanize large portions of mankind, justifying their slaughter—albeit in their case as "infidels," rather than as non-Aryans or bourgeoisie.

In this respect, radical Islamism is a form of neobarbarism. Civilization is defined by the act of recognizing another person as a human being. The definition of a barbarian is someone who cannot perform this act—often because he has either come from or chosen a universe of meaning that does not contain the term *human being*. It is hard to overstate the catastrophe resulting from this incapacity or refusal. If one is unable to recognize another person as a human being, then one does not know the difference between the human and the animal, or the human and the divine. Confusion over these matters leads to slavery, human sacrifice, cannibalism, genocide, and other horrors. Through Islamism, as through communism or Nazism, one loses one's ability to recognize another person as a human being. Like its totalitarian predecessors, Islamism is an engine of dehumanization—of turning other people into animals or less. In the name of this dark, neotribal god, one becomes a barbarian.

The Necessity of Force:
Terrorism as a Moral Obligation

Like both the communists and the Nazis, Islamists also see force as *necessary* to effect the transformation that they desire. Reason is impotent; therefore, force is the only instrument for fundamental change. A God without reason sets the theological foundations for violence. There are multiple examples of this doctrine of force. Bin Laden's spiritual mentor, Abdullah 'Azzam, said that "those who think that they can change reality, or change societies, without blood sacrifices and wounds . . . do not understand the essence of our religion." The price is high: "Glory does not build its lofty edifice except with skulls. Honour and respect cannot be established except on a foundation of cripples and corpses."[41] His cry was "jihad and the rifle alone: no negotiation, no conferences, and no dialogue."[42] Bin Laden's deputy, Ayman al-Zawahiri, announced, "Reform can only take place through Jihad for the sake of Allah, and any call for reform that is not through Jihad is doomed to death and failure. We must understand the nature of the battle and conflict."[43]

When a chastened former leader of Egyptian al-Jihad, Kamal el-Said Habib, says in way of criticism that "violence replaced politics as a means of interaction" in the behavior of Egyptian jihadists, he does so without seeming to realize that such violence is the *logical* working out in action of the premises on which jihadist "theology" is based.[44]

In a 1998 interview, Muhammad Khan—the amir of Lashkar-e Taiba, a group now notorious for sponsoring the terrorist attack in Mumbai, India—proclaimed this necessary connection with violence: "When change comes it will come when those opposing Islam will be crushed." "By force?" asked the interviewer. "Yes," responded the amir, "that is a must."[45] Indonesian Islamist Abu Bakar Bashir said, "The struggle for Islam can only come through crisis and confrontation. . . . Remember

that jihad is what brought Islam to power and built our community. There can be no Islam without jihad."[46]

On November 30, 2005, an al-Qaeda tape asked rhetorically, "How can we impose this religion? Can we do that
through peace? Can we do it through logic? Can we do it by
suggestions and ballots?" Then the voice answered: "The only
way we can do it is by the sword." Another al-Qaeda source,
showing al-Qaeda's lineage to the medieval antirationalists,
announces its call for violence in direct opposition to philosophy: "The confrontation that we are calling for with the apostate regimes does not know Socratic debates, Platonic ideals,
nor Aristotelian diplomacy. But it knows the dialogue of bullets,
the ideals of assassination, bombing, and destruction, and the
diplomacy of the cannon and machine-gun."[47]

This view is not exclusive to Sunnis. Ayatollah Khomeini
said: "Whatever good there is exists thanks to the sword and
in the shadow of the sword. People cannot be made obedient
except with the sword. The sword is the key to Paradise." In
a speech in December 1984, he spoke of the benefits of killing
infidels as a service to the infidels themselves. He said, "War is
a blessing for the world and for every nation. It is Allah himself who commands men to wage war and to kill."[48] And cleric
Morteza Muthhari said, "The factor of violence is necessary....
There is no inhibition against the use of violence."[49]

Radical Islamists translate their version of God's omnipotence into a politics of unlimited power. As God's instruments,
they are channels for this power.* The "vanguard" of God takes
the place of God somewhat as the vanguard of the proletariat
took the place of the proletariat in Marxism-Leninism, and
produces what then-Cardinal Joseph Ratzinger called, in reference to liberation theology, "a totalitarianism that practices
an atheistic sort of adoration ready to sacrifice all humanness

---

* There are obvious precedents in Islam to this notion. "I rule with the
omnipotence of God," announced Caliph Mu'awiya's adopted brother,
Ziyad, to the people when he was appointed governor in Basra.

to its false god."[50] In his 1998 *fatwa*, Osama bin Laden gave a good example of this transference of divine authority in his issuance of the ruling "to kill the Americans and their allies— civilians and military" by claiming it was "Allah's order to kill the Americans." Once the primacy of force is posited, terrorism becomes the next logical step to power, as it did in Nazism and Marxism-Leninism. This is what led Osama bin Laden to embrace the astonishing statement of his spiritual godfather, Abdullah 'Azzam, which Osama quoted in the November 2001 video, released after 9/11: "Terrorism is an obligation in Allah's religion."[51] This can be true—that violence in spreading faith is an *obligation*—only if God is without reason and, therefore, acting unreasonably is not against His nature.

'Azzam's announcement is news to most Muslims, who find terrorism morally repugnant and alien to Islam's core teachings, especially in regard to suicide killings of civilians. Islamism within Islam may be roughly analogous to the development of liberation theology within Christianity. Especially in Latin America, Catholicism was infected with Marxist ideology by way of Christianity's preferential option for the poor. According to liberation theology, it is not enough to help the poor through charity. One must root out the institutions that purportedly cause poverty. This includes property and other aspects of capitalism. Within this teaching, the Christian part was soon subsumed by the Marxist part and its promotion of the necessity of violence. Priests dropped their rosaries, picked up machine guns and grenades, and joined the revolution. In the ensuing struggle against this totalitarian infestation, the pope, John Paul II, won. In an exhortation that could have come from a liberation theologian, Muhammad Navab-Safavi called on his fellow Muslims: "Throw away your worry beads and buy a gun. For worry beads keep you silent, while guns silence the enemies of Islam."[52] Islam does not have a figure of authority corresponding to the pope who could definitively delegitimize Islamism, and it is uncertain, if there were such a figure, that he would do so, since Islamism has a claim to legitimacy despite its adulteration by Western ideology.

The problem today is that the side of reason in Islam lost, and therefore its natural antibodies to this totalitarian infection are weak. What we are witnessing today are the ultimate consequences of the rejection of human reason and the loss of causality as they are played out across the Muslim world in the dysfunctional culture engendered by them. It is not that the side of reason is not still there. As Fatima Mernissi says so poignantly, "The fact that the rationalist, humanistic tradition was rejected by despotic politicians does not mean that it doesn't exist. Having an arm amputated is not the same as being born with an arm missing. Studies of amputees show that the amputated member remains present in the person's mind. The more our rational faculty is suppressed, the more obsessed we are by it."[53]

There are some extraordinarily intelligent Muslim scholars who would like to see something like a neo-Mu'tazilite movement within Islam, a restoration of the primacy of reason so that they can reopen the doors to *ijtihad* and develop some kind of natural-law foundation for humane, political, constitutional rule. In fact, Indonesian scholar Harun Nasution (1919–1998) was willing to wear the neo-Mu'tazilite label openly, despite the imprecation of heresy that it carried. He explicitly called for the recognition of natural law and opposed Ash'arite occasionalism and determinism as inimical to social, economic, and political progress. He insisted on man's free will and accountability.[54] Reformist Tunisian-born thinker Latif Lakhdar calls for a revival of "Mu'atazila and philosophical thought that subjected the holy writings on which the religion is based to interpretation by the human mind."[55] He recommends that "open religious rationalism—subjecting the religious text to rational investigation and research—ought to become the core of the aspired religious education in the Arab-Islamic region, since it is absurd to believe the text and deny reality."[56]

In certain if not most places in the Islamic world, however, if one dares to suggest that the Qur'an is not coeternal
with Allah, one had better have protection. In Egypt, Dr. Nasr
Hamid Abu Zayd, an assistant professor of Arabic at the University of Cairo, provoked an uproar for suggesting that the
Qur'an was a partially human product because language is a
human convention. Appealing to the Mu'tazilites, he said, "The
Mu'tazilites drew from the Qur'anic text on the assumption
that it was a created action and not the eternal verbal utterance
of God. In other words, the relation between the signifier and
the signified exists only by human convention; there is nothing
divine in this relationship. They endeavoured to build a bridge
between the divine word and human reason. That is why they
maintained that the divine word was a fact which adjusted itself
to human language in order to ensure well-being for mankind.
They insisted that language was the product of man and that
the divine word respected the rules and forms of human language."[57] For this, he was brought to trial for apostasy. On June
14, 1995, the Appeals Court of Second Degree in Egypt ruled
that Dr. Abu Zayd was a *kafir* (unbeliever). The consequence of
this would have been a forced divorce from his wife, as Muslim women are not allowed to be married to non-Muslim men.
But Dr. Abu Zayd and his wife fled to Europe. Few voices were
raised in his defense.[58] Safely in exile, he recently stated that
"the Islamic reformation started as early as the 19th century
and, of course, it has even earlier roots as well. One important
school of Koranic scholarship, Mutazilism, held 1,000 years ago
that the Koran need not be interpreted literally, and even today
Iranian scholars are surprisingly open to critical scholarship
and interpretations."[59]

However, exile was also the fate of an Iranian, Abdolkarim
Soroush. Father Samir Khalil Samir related that "a young Iranian Muslim, with a degree in Islamic studies, told me the
other day: 'We can no longer think of the Qur'an as directly
dictated by God to Mohammad through the angel Gabriel. It

must be interpreted. Unfortunately, in today's Islam there is not much freedom: a few decades ago, one of our intellectuals, Abdolkarim Soroush was removed from university teaching for having taught such things. [Soroush was physically assaulted on several occasions.] In the end, to be able to live and express himself, he had to emigrate to Europe.'"[60] Many of the neo-Mu'tazilites, the ones who want to resuscitate the great tradition of Muslim rational theology and philosophy, are in the West as well.

Unfortunately, as Bassim Tibi has warned, "Those intellectually significant Muslims who . . . still hope to apply reason to Islamic reform, had better do so in their Western exile, be it Paris or London or Washington. Their ideas are discussed in Scandinavia, but not in the Islamic world."[61] Even in Europe, such Muslims have problems and have to confront the dangers of being labeled apostates. For several years in Germany, Tibi himself required armed bodyguards provided by the German state to protect him from assassination. Taj Hargey, a British imam, laments that "iconoclastic thinkers, liberals, and nonconformists who dare to challenge this self-assumed religious authority in Islam by presenting a rational or alternative interpretations of their faith are invariably branded as apostates, heretics, and non-believers."[62]

Chapter 9
THE CRISIS

The great crisis that has seized the Islamic world poses the question to Muslims: "Can we enter the modern world and also retain our faith?" Underlying this question is the widely held perception, stated by Chanddra Muzaffar, considered one of Malaysia's most respected Islamic philosophers, that "Islam and the post-Enlightenment secular West are diametrically opposed to one another. Muslims will then realize that unless they transform the secular world of the West, that vision of justice embodied in the Qur'an will never become a reality."[1] Transformation of the West is the objective; only the means of transformation are in dispute: peaceful or violent? One answer to the question above has been provided by the Islamists and Osama bin Laden. His answer is no; we cannot retain our faith in the modern world. Therefore, we must destroy modernity and reestablish the caliphate.

The answer of Islamism is grounded in a spiritual pathology based upon a theological deformation that has produced a dysfunctional culture. Therefore, the problem must be addressed at the level at which it exists. To say that the West needs to improve the economic conditions in the Middle East in order to drain the swamp of terrorism is, by itself, profoundly mistaken. Terrorists are produced by a totalitarian ideology justifying terrorism. That is its "root cause." If someone had suggested that in order to deal with Nazism one first had to overcome the problem of poverty in Germany, they would be laughed out of school. Yet this kind of thinking is taken seriously today.

The Middle East is poor because of a dysfunctional culture based upon a deformed theology, and unless it can be reformed at that level, economic engineering or the development of constitutional political order will not succeed. If one lives in a society that ascribes everything to first causes, one is not going to look around the world and try to figure out how it works or how to improve it. "In order to function," writes Pervez Hoodbhoy, "organized societies need modern people—people who can relate cause to effect."[2] As Fouad Ajami observed, the inability to relate cause to effect is pandemic in the Islamic world.

Is there a constituency within the Muslim world that can elaborate a theology that allows for the restoration of reason, a *rehellenization* of Islam with Allah as *ratio*? Can Islam undertake what Samir Khalil Samir calls "an Enlightenment, in other words, a revolution in thought that affirms the value of worldly reality in and of itself, detached from religion, though not in opposition to it"?[3] It is idle to pretend that it would take less than a sea change for this to happen. If it does not, it is hard to envisage upon what basis Muslims could modernize or upon what grounds a dialogue with Islam could take place. There are many Muslims (in Turkey and in the developing democracies of Indonesia and Malaysia, to say nothing of the democratic life followed by the huge Muslim population in India) who want to enter the modern world—with its modern science and modern political institutions—and also keep their faith. The past glories of Islamic civilization show that it was once able to progress. That progress was based upon a different set of ideas, antithetical to those of the Islamists, who would have been considered heretical then.

Fazlur Rahman contended that "the Qur'an itself not only has a great deal of definitive philosophic teaching, but also can be a powerful catalyst for the building up of a comprehensive world view consistent with that teaching. That has never been systematically attempted in Islamic history; it can and must be done."[4] It seems that Fazlur Rahman was calling for an effort in Islam somewhat analogous to what Thomas Aquinas undertook within Christianity. Aquinas developed what latent philosophic ideas existed in Christian scripture and reconciled them with reason. He showed that Greek *Logos* was really a preview of Christian *Logos*. Revelation and reason were ultimately grounded in the same source. The Thomist endeavor took place some thirteen centuries after Christ. Today, Islam stands at nearly the same chronological distance from its founding. Will those who follow Fazlur Rahman's thinking perceive the same need and undertake the task he outlined? There are notable Muslim thinkers who wish to do so and who are struggling to find the public space within which to make the effort.

Unfortunately, the ideas gaining traction today are not theirs. That is the crisis. The answer that is sweeping the Islamic world today does not come from people like them. It is from the al-Qaedists, neo-Kharijites, and Hanbalites. As described by analyst Tony Corn, "In the past 30 years, one particular brand—pan-Islamic Salafism—has been allowed to fill the vacuum left by the failure of pan-Arab Socialism and, in the process, to marginalize the more enlightened forms of Islam to the point where Salafism now occupies a quasi-hegemonic position in the Muslim world."[5] Hoodbhoy confirms this view: "Fundamentalist movements have come to dominate intellectual discourse in key Muslim countries and the Muslim modernist movement, which emphasized Islam's compatibility with science and rationalism, has lost its cultural and ideological hegemony. The modernist has been effectively banished from the political and cultural scene and the modern educational system, which was nascent 50 years ago, has visibly collapsed in key Islamic countries. Orthodoxy has arrogated to itself the task of guiding the destiny of Muslims. But their prescription for society is an invitation to catastrophe and possibly to a new Dark Age for Muslims."[6]

In a powerful description of the coming catastrophe, the contemporary Tunisian Muslim thinker Abdelwahab Meddeb, resident in Paris, says: "In this insane, absolute theocentrism, never before in the tradition of Islam so radically developed, the world is transformed into a cemetery. If Maududi reproached the West with the death of God, we can accuse him of having inaugurated the death of humanity. His outrageous system invents an unreal totalitarianism, which excites disciples and incites them to spread death and destruction over all continents. That is the kind of negation of life, the nihilism to which theoretical reasoning leads when it is not subject to the control of practical reasoning. . . . This radical and terrifying vision establishes a tabula rasa and transforms the world into a post nuclear place in which we find desolate landscapes wherever we look, on pages blackened by Sayyid Qutb."[7] Meddeb predicts that the fulfillment of Qutb's vision of "liberation" would "transform man into one of the living dead, on a scorched land."[8] But alas, Qutb is everywhere. And little is being done to counter this trend.

The transmogrification of Islam into Islamism is bad news not only for the West but also for the majority of Muslims who have no desire to live in totalitarian theocracies. "For the West it is but a physical threat in the form of terrorism," said Pakistani journalist Ayaz Amir. "For the world of Islam . . . to be trapped in bin Ladenism is to travel back in time to the dark ages of Muslim obscurantism. It means to be stuck in the mire which has held the Islamic world back."[9] In the case of most Muslims, their numbers may not matter, any more than they did for the hapless peoples of the Russian empire who suddenly found themselves ruled by a tiny, violent clique of Leninists in 1917. The problem for the side of reason, as expressed by an

Indonesian Islamist, is that "liberal Islam has no cadres."[10] There are ample cadres on the other side. The small, tightly organized, highly disciplined and well-funded groups of Islamists seek to emulate the Leninist success with similar tactics of propaganda and violence. The worse things get, especially in the Arab world, the more appealing the Islamist message becomes as an explanation for the predicament and a program of action to overcome it. For this reason, it is in the Islamists' self-interest that the situation gets worse. In fact, they can help ensure that it does.

It is not inevitable that the Islamists should succeed, except in the absence of any strategy to counter them. Muslim leaders like the former president of Indonesia, the late Abdurrahman Wahid, who was the spiritual head of the largest Muslim organization in the world, Nahdlatul Ulama, have called for a counterstrategy that would include offering "a compelling alternative vision of Islam, one that banishes the fanatical ideology of hatred to the darkness from which it emerged."[11] Up until his death in December 2009, Wahid tirelessly advocated a partnership with the non-Muslim world in a massively resourced effort to uphold human dignity, freedom of conscience, religious freedom, and the benefits of modernity before the juggernaut of Islamist ideology swamped the Muslim world. It was a compelling summons, but one that has yet to be answered.

In May 2008, I had the opportunity to talk with President Wahid. When I asked him about the significance of the suppression of the Mu'tazilites in the ninth century, he was somewhat elusive and would not directly respond, which is not surprising considering the regard in which Mu'tazilism is publicly held. However, he found another way to answer which said a great deal. President Wahid told me the story of his going into a mosque in Fez, Morocco. There, under a glass case, he saw a copy of Aristotle's *Nicomachean Ethics*. At the sight of it, he said, he burst into tears. Then he remarked: "If there had not been such a book, I would have been a fundamentalist." I asked

Wahid how it was that he knew Aristotle's *Nicomachean Ethics* in the first place. He told me that he had first read it at his father's boarding school in Indonesia. No doubt this was only one of a number of formative influences on Wahid, but an important—even decisive—one that could also be employed in this new "war of ideas" that is taking place within Islam.

There is, in fact, tremendous irony in this story when its lesson is applied to the U.S. response to radical Islamism, which can be encapsulated in the following vignette—a true story related to me by the American participant. A U.S. interrogator at Guantanamo, who has extensive knowledge of Islamic history and the Arabic language, told me about discussing Aristotle with a fairly high-profile Arab detainee during a conversation about the importance of critical thinking and its role in the works of some Muslim theologians. The detainee was keenly interested in this, and said that he had heard mention of Aristotle during his schooling but that, in his country, students do not have access to the texts of Aristotle. He asked if the interrogator would please provide him with some of the works of Aristotle in Arabic. However, when the interrogator tried to get the detainee library to order these works, the librarians—who were more focused on the Qur'an and light reading such as nature books with lots of pictures—could not see the relevance of Aristotle or believe that a detainee would be interested in him. (This interrogator pointed out to me that "the detainee was far more intellectually engaged than the library staff—no one should make the mistake of thinking these detainees are just violent thugs.") The library did not order any Aristotle, and yet another opportunity to address the problem at the level at which it exists was lost. This is a perfect illustration of how to lose a war of ideas because you do not even know what it is about.

The Choice

In conversation with a student in Rome, Pope Benedict XVI made a statement that neatly summarizes the core of what is at stake for both Islam and the West. I will omit only one word from it, indicated by empty brackets. He said: "There are only two options. Either one recognizes the priority of reason, of creative Reason that is at the beginning of all things and is the principle of all things—the priority of reason is also the priority of freedom—or one holds the priority of the irrational, inasmuch as everything that functions on our earth and in our lives would be only accidental, marginal, an irrational result—reason would be a product of irrationality. One cannot ultimately 'prove' either project, but the great option of [＿＿＿＿] is the option for rationality and for the priority of reason. This seems to me to be an excellent option, which shows us that behind everything is a great Intelligence to which we can entrust ourselves."[12]

Of course, the missing word in the bracket is *Christianity*. The question is whether the word *Islam* could be inserted in its stead and still have the statement read correctly. Does Sunni Islam still have the option open for the priority of reason? As we have seen, it most certainly attempted to exercise that option under the Mu'tazilites at a time generally acknowledged as being the apogee of Arab Islamic culture. One could have substituted the word *Islam* at that time, and the statement above would otherwise have stood unaltered as an expression of Mu'tazilite beliefs. We have also seen that there are Muslim thinkers today who are attempting something similar.

Of course, non-Muslims cannot make the choice for Muslims, but the advice of George Hourani comes close to what many Muslims, like Fazlur Rahman, have themselves said is needed: "If I had a choice of what intellectual path Muslims should follow—a choice which I do not have, looking at Islam from outside—I would start over again at the points where the early jurists and the Mu'tazilites left off, and work to develop a system of Islamic law which would openly make use of judgements of equity and public interest, and a system of ethical theology which would encourage judgements of right and wrong by the human mind, without having to look to scripture at every step. The Mu'tazilites were correct in their doctrine that we can make objective value judgements, even if their particular theory of ethics had weaknesses, which would have to be revised by modern ethical philosophers and theologians. So I think this is the best way for Muslims to revive Islam, and I wish them success in a formidable task."[13]

If Islam is to find its way out of its current dilemma with the choice Hourani recommends, it must somehow reconcile the unity of God (*tawhid*) with the unity of reason—reason in God, in His creation, and in man. If reason is absent from any one of the three, the relationship collapses into irrationality, and there would be no way to make "objective value judgements." If God is without reason, then so will be His creation—for from where else could its rationality come? If creation is bereft of reason's imprint, man's reason would be impotent because it would have nothing it could correspond to and with which it could interact. It would not even have anything to reflect upon through which to become aware of itself. All would be will, but it would be blind will, and any faith based upon it would be blind faith. Making either reason or revelation autonomous leads to a distortion of what each is. Reason raises questions that it cannot answer, and revelation's answers cannot be understood without reason. Divorcing reason from faith (the current crisis of the West) or faith from reason (the crisis of Islam) leads to catastrophe; they should be in partnership.[14]

As intimated above, what Thomas Aquinas did for Christianity, someone needs to do for Islam—if it can be done. This will depend on whether or not Ash'arite voluntarism and occasionalism are seen as integral to the Qur'an or as later accretions that can be disregarded. If for doctrinal or other reasons it cannot be done, if Sunni Islam continues to embrace the moral agnosticism of Ash'arism and the extreme fideism to which it leads, it will not be able to adapt itself to modernity, modern science, or democratic constitutional rule, and its future will be very bleak. The tempestuousness of our times, which many think augurs a resurgence of Islam, may in fact signal its further decline, which could be even more tempestuous. Dr. Muhammad al-Houni, a Libyan reformist living in Italy, comes to the following conclusion: "Arab societies have only one of two options: either to sever their ties with Western civilization and its cultural institutions and to continue to [do] themselves harm ... or to irrevocably sever their ties with the religious legacy of the Middle Ages, in order for their philosophy to be a philosophy of life and freedom, and not one of death and hatred."[15]

Or there is another way to put this choice with respect to a very different aspect of the Islamic legacy, expressed by Bassam Tibi: "If that Islamic medieval rationalism that recognized the universality of knowledge continues to be declared a heresy, and if authenticity is narrowed down to a polarization of the self and otherness, then Muslims of the twenty-first century will continue to be unsuccessful in embarking on modernity."[16]

The problem is that their prospective failure, as tragic as it will be for them, may enfold us all. As was seen in the blood-soaked history of the twentieth century, the "priority of the irrational"—even if embraced only by the radical few—can inexorably lead to limitless violence, because the primacy of the will, whether in God or man, knows no bounds. The recovery of reason, grounded in *Logos*, is the only sentinel of sanity. This is imperative for the East as well as the West. "Come now, let us reason together" (Isaiah 1:18).

Notes

Introduction: Intellectual Suicide

1. Dimitri Gutas, *Greek Thought, Arabic Culture* (New York: Routledge, 1998), 160.
2. Said to the author in 2005.
3. Fazlur Rahman, *Islam and Modernity* (Chicago: University of Chicago Press, 1982), 157–58.
4. Rashid Shaz, "Reinventing the Muslim Mind," at rashidshaz.com/articles/Reinventing_the_Muslim_Mind.htm.

Chapter 1: The Opening

1. Samir Khalil Samir, *111 Questions on Islam* (San Francisco: Ignatius Press, 2008), 65–66.
2. Pervez Hoodbhoy, *Islam and Science* (London: Zed Books, 1991), 104; Ibn Khaldun, *The Muqaddimah: An Introduction to History* (London: Routledge and Kegan Paul, 1978), 32–33.
3. United Nations Development Programme, Arab Human Development Report 2003 (New York: United Nations, 2003), 117.
4. Duncan B. Macdonald, *Development of Muslim Theology, Jurisprudence and Constitutional Theory* (Beirut Khayats; 1st edition January 1, 1965: paperback, Macdonald Press, March 15, 2007), ch. 3, at http://www.questia.com/library/book/development-of-muslim-theology-jurisprudence-and-constitutional-theory-by-duncan-b-macdonald.jsp.
5. Majid Fakhry, *A History of Islamic Philosophy* (New York: Columbia University Press, 1970 and 1983), 47.

6. Fazlur Rahman, *Islam* (Chicago: University of Chicago Press, 1979, 2002), 89.

7. Alfred Guillaume, *Islam* (London: Penguin, 1956), 131.

8. Muslim, *Kitab al-Qadar* Hadith 1848.

9. W. H. T. Gairdner, *God as Triune, Creator Incarnate, Atoner: A Reply to Muhammadan Objections and an Essay in Philosophic Apology* (Madras, Allahabad Calcutta, Rangoon, Colombo: The Christian Literature Society for India, 1916), 58 footnote, at www.muhammadanism.org, July 15, 2007. (Muslim, Imam, *Sahih Muslim: Being Traditions of the Sayings and Doings of the Prophet Muhammad as Narrated by His Companions* and compiled under the Title Al-Jami'-Us-Sahih, Translated by 'Abdul H. Siddiqi, Vol. IV, ch. MCVI, No. 6421, 1397–98.)

10. Fazlur Rahman, *Revival and Reform in Islam* (Oxford: Oneworld Publications, 2000), 153.

11. Ignaz Goldziher, *Introduction to Islamic Theology and Law* (Princeton: Princeton University Press, 1981), 84–85.

12. Macdonald, *Development of Muslim Theology, Jurisprudence and Constitutional Theory*, ch. 3, 5.

13. Richard C. Martin and Mark R. Woodward, *Defenders of Reason in Islam* (Oxford: Oneworld Publications, 2003), 91.

14. Ibid., 91.

15. Ibid., 189.

16. George Hourani, *Reason and Tradition in Islamic Ethics* (Cambridge: Cambridge Univeristy Press, 1985), 104.

17. Martin, *Defenders of Reason in Islam*, 189.

18. I. M. N. al-Jubouri, *History of Islamic Philosophy* (Hertford, England: Authors OnLine Ltd., 2004), 387.

19. Martin, *Defenders of Reason in Islam*, 103.

20. Ibid., 108.

21. Goldziher, *Introduction to Islamic Theology and Law*, 94.

22. Fakhry, *A History of Islamic Philosophy*, xvii.

23. Averroes, *Tahafut al-Tahafut* (*The Incoherence of the Incoherence*), 325, trans. Simon Van Den Bergh (London: E. J. W. Gibb Memorial Series, 2008), 325.

24. Martin, *Defenders of Reason in Islam*, 11.

25. Goldziher, *Introduction to Islamic Theology and Law*, 101.

26. James Schall, "Why the Bewilderment? Benedict XVI on Natural Law," *Ignatius Insight*, October 27, 2007, www.ignatiusinsight.com.

27. A. J. Wensinek, *The Muslim Creed* (Cambridge: Cambridge University Press, 1932), 62–63.

28. Martin, *Defenders of Reason in Islam*, 97.

29. "Causation in Islamic Thought," Philip P. Wiener, ed., *Dictionary of the*

History of Ideas (New York: Charles Scribner's Sons, 1973–74), Volume 1, 288, at http://etext.virginia.edu/cgi-local/DHI/dhi.cgi?id=dv1–39.

30. Martin, *Defenders of Reason in Islam*, 186.

31. Ibid., 96.

32. Ibid., 100.

33. Ibid., 97.

34. Ibid., 97.

35. Ibid., 93.

36. Fakhry, *A History of Islamic Philosophy*, 47.

37. Martin, *Defenders of Reason in Islam*, 92.

38. Ibid., 93.

39. De Lacy O'Leary, *Islamic Thought and its Place in History* (New Delhi: Goodword Books, 2001), 124. Also available as *Arabic Thought and its Place in History*, at www.sacred-texts.com.

40. Macdonald, *Development of Muslim Theology, Jurisprudence and Constitutional Theory*, 136.

41. M. Abdul Hye, "Ash'arism," in *A History of Muslim Philosophy*, M. M. Sharif, ed. (Pakistan Philosophical Congress), ch. 11, at http://www.muslimphilosophy.com/hmp/index.html.

42. Imad N. Shehadeh, "The Predicament of Islamic Monotheism," *Biblotheca Sacra* 161 (April–June 2004), 156.

43. Goldziher, *Introduction to Islamic Theology and Law*, 101.

44. Joseph Kenny, *Theological Themes Common to Islam and Christianity* (Lagos, Nigeria: Dominican Publications, 1997), ch. 5, 1.

45. Ibid., ch. 4, 2.

46. "Ash'ariyya and Mu'tazila," at www.muslimphilosophy.com/ip/rep/H052.htm), 4.

47. Thomas Aquinas, *Reasons for the Faith against Muslim Objections*, ch. 3, at http://www.catholicapologetics.info/apologetics/islam/rationes.htm.

48. Ibid.

49. Hoodbhoy, *Islam and Science*, 98.

50. Fakhry, *A History of Islamic Philosophy*, 14.

51. Hourani, *Reason and Tradition in Islamic Ethics*, 96.

52. Frances Luttikhuizen, "Early Eastern Christianity and Its Contribution to Science," *Christianity and Society*, Vol. XV, No. 1 (April 2005): 7.

53. Fakhry, *A History of Islamic Philosophy*, 71.

54. Gutas, *Greek Thought, Arabic Culture*, 158–59.

55. Joseph Kenny, *Philosophy of the Muslim World* (Washington, DC: The Council for Research in Values and Philosophy, 2003), 154.

56. Averroes, *The Book of the Decisive Treatise*, trans. Charles E. Butterworth (Provo, UT: Brigham Young University, 2001), section 10. Also cited by Ter-

ence J. Kleven, "'For Truth Does Not Oppose Truth': The Argument of Divine Law and Philosophy in Averroes' *The Book of the Decisive Treatise* (*Kitab Fasl al-Maqal*)," unpublished paper, 9.

57. Averroes, *Faith and Reason in Islam: Averroes' Exposition of Religious Arguments*, trans. by Ibrahim Najjar (Oxford: Oneworld Publications, 2001), 16–17. See also, Averroes, *On the Harmony of Religions and Philosophy*: "Now, it being established that the Law makes the observation and consideration of creation by reason obligatory—and consideration is nothing but to make explicit the implicit—this can only be done through reason. Thus we must look into creation with the reason." Posted at http://www.fordham.edu/halsall/source/1190averroes.html.

58. W. Montgomery Watt, *Muslim Intellectual: A Study of Al-Ghazali* (Edinburgh: Edinburgh University Press, 1963), 21.

Chapter 2: The Overthrow of the Mu'tazilites

1. Abuz-Zubair, *Imam Ahmad ibn Hanbal: Life & Madhab*, at http://www.islamicawakening.com/viewarticle.php?articleID=1193&.

2. Kenny, *Theological Themes Common to Islam and Christianity*, ch. 5, 1.

3. Joseph Kenny, *Philosophy of the Muslim World* at http://www.diafrica.org/kenny/phil/default.htm, 6.

4. Hoodbhoy, *Islam and Science*, 111.

5. Gutas, *Greek Thought, Arabic Culture*, 161–162.

6. Hoodbhoy, *Islam and Science*, 101.

7. Gutas, *Greek Thought, Arabic Culture*, 163.

8. G. W. Kayani, "The Political Factors That Brought the Asharite School to a Majority," May 2005, at www.hawza.org.uk.

9. Albert Hourani, *A History of the Arab Peoples* (New York: Warner Books, 1992), 182.

10. Hourani, *Reason and Tradition in Islamic Ethics*, 57.

11. Hoodbhoy, *Islam and Science*, 100.

12. Ibid.

13. Martin, *Defenders of Reason in Islam*, 42.

14. Raphael Patai, *The Arab Mind* (New York: Hatherleigh Press, 2002), 395.

15. Stanley L. Jaki, "The Physics of Impetus and the Impetus of the Qur'an," *Modern Age* (Spring, 1985), 159.

16. Floy E. Doull, "Peace with Islam," *Animus* (December 2004), 10, at http://www2.swgc.mun.ca/animus/Articles/Volume%209/doull.pdf.

17. W. Montgomery Watt, *Islamic Philosophy and Theology* (Edinburgh: University Press Edinburgh, 1962), 76.

18. Rahman, *Islam*, 123.

19. Edward Mortimer, *Faith and Power: The Politics of Islam* (New York: Random House/Vintage Books, 1982): 74.

20. Hye, "Ash'arism," *A History of Muslim Philosophy*, ch. 11.

21. Hadith quoted at http://www.muslimwiki.com/mw/index.php/Bida'ah.

22. Ibn Hanbal.

23. A. Zumarlee, ed., *The Foundations of the Sunna* (April 1991), 169. Quoted by Stephen Ulph, "The Fabric of Qur'anic Scripture," unpublished paper, 3.

24. Hoodbhoy, *Islam and Science*, 99.

25. Raymond Ibrahim, *The Al-Qaeda Reader* (New York: Broadway Books, 2007), 8.

26. Kenny, *Theological Themes Common to Islam and Christianity*, ch. 4, 8.

27. Hoodbhoy, *Islam and Science*, 99.

28. Posted at allaahuakbar.net, 2008.

29. Macdonald, *Development of Muslim Theology, Jurisprudence and Constitutional Theory*, 14.

30. Hourani, *Reason and Tradition in Islamic Ethics*, 10.

31. Muhammad Arkoun, *Islam: To Reform or To Subvert?* (London: Saqi Books, 2006), 161.

32. W. H. T. Gairdner, *The Rebuke of Islam* (London: United Council for Missionary Education,1920), also posted at www.muhammadanism.org, March 6, 2003.

33. Hye, "Ash'arism," 4.

34. Watt, *Islamic Philosophy and Theology*, 65.

35. Macdonald, *Development of Muslim Theology, Jurisprudence and Constitutional Theory*, Chapter 3, 9.

36. Ibid.

37. Averroes, *Tahafut al-Tahufat* (*The Incoherence of the Incoherence*), 522.

38. Macdonald, *Development of Muslim Theology, Jurisprudence and Constitutional Theory*, 7.

39. T. J. De Boer, *The History of Philosophy in Islam* (New York: Dover Publications, 1967), 163.

40. Rahman, *Revival and Reform in Islam*, 119.

41. Hye, "Ash'arism," 20.

42. Fadlou Shehadi, *Ghazali's Unique Unknowable God* (Leiden, Netherlands: E. J. Brill, 1964), 83.

43. Rahman, *Islam*, 62.

44. Ibid., 107.

45. Shehadeh, "The Predicament of Islamic Monotheism," 155.

46. Ibid., 149.

47. From Simon Van Den Bergh's introduction to Averroes's *The Incoher-*

ence of the Incoherence, "I may remark here that it seems to me probable that Nicholas of Autrecourt, 'the medieval Hume,' was influenced by Ghazali's Ash'arite theories. He denies in the same way as Ghazali the logical connexion between cause and effect: *ex eo quod aliqua res est cognita esse, non potest evidenter evidentia reducta in primum principium vel in certitudinem primi principii inferri, quod alia res sit* (cf. Lappe, *Nicolaus von Autrecourt*, Beitr. z. Gesch. d. Phil. d. M. B.vi, H.2, 11); he gives the same example of ignis and stupa, he seems to hold also the Ash'arite thesis of God as the sole cause of all action (cf. op. cit., 24), and he quotes in one place Ghazali's Metaphysics (cf. N. of Autrecourt, *Exigit ordo executionis*, in *Mediaeval Studies*, vol. i, ed. by J. Reginald O'Donnell, Toronto, 1931, 208)." Posted at: http://www.wikilivres. info/wiki/The_Incoherence_of_the_Incoherence/Introduction.

48. Benedict XVI, : "Creation Is a Revelation of God's Presence," *National Catholic Register* (November 20, 2005).

49. Cardinal Joseph Ratzinger, "The Permanent Significance of the Christian Faith," Subiaco, Italy, April 1, 2005, at http://www.catholic.org/featured/headline.php?ID=2424.

50. See Jaki's extraordinary monograph, *Jesus, Islam, Science* (Pickney, MI: Real View Books, 2001).

Chapter 3: The Metaphysics of the Will

1. Lucretius, *De Rerum Natura*, v. 76–81.

2. Malise Ruthven, *Islam in the World* (New York: Oxford University Press, 1984), 195.

3. Hoodbhoy, *Islam and Science*, 120.

4. Doull, "Peace with Islam," 11.

5. Macdonald, *Development of Muslim Theology, Jurisprudence and Constitutional Theory*.

6. Majid Fakhry, *Classical Arguments for the Existence of God*, at http://www. muslimphilosophy.com/ip/pg1.htm.

7. Louis Gardet, *Ilm al-Kalam*, 10, at www.muslimphilosophy.com/ei/kalam. htm.

8. R. J. McCarthy, "Abu Bakr al-Baqillani," at http://www.muslimphilosophy.com/ei2/baqillani.htm.

9. Al-Ghazali, *The Incoherence of the Philosophers*, trans. Michael E. Marmura (Provo, UT: Brigham University Press, 1997), 170.

10. Ibid.

11. Thomas Aquinas, *Summa Contra Gentiles*, Book 3, ch. 97, at http://www. op-stjoseph.org/Students/study/thomas/ContraGentiles3b.htm#97.

12. Al-Ghazali, *The Incoherence of the Philosophers*, 174.

13. Ibid.

14. Ibid.

15. Duncan Macdonald, *Aspects of Islam* (New York: Macmillan Company, 1911), 142. Posted at www.muhammadanism.org, July 26, 2003.

16. Averroes, *Faith and Reason in Islam*, 87.

17. Ahmad ibn Naqib al-Misri, *Reliance of the Traveller: A Classic Manual of Sacred Islamic Law* (*'Umdat al-Salik*), edited and translated by Nuh Ha Mim Keller, revised edition (Beltsville, MD: Amana Publications, 1997).

18. Guillaume, *Islam*, 141. See also Joseph Kenny, *Philosophy of the Muslim World*, 61.

19. As stated to the author in Washington, DC, 2005.

20. Hoodbhoy, *Islam and Science*, 54.

21. Ibid., 55.

22. Ibid., 47.

23. Averroes, *Tahafut al-Tahufat* (*The Incoherence of the Incoherence*), 522.

24. Majid Fakhry, *Rationality in Islamic Philosophy*, 508.

25. Averroes, *The Incoherence of the Incoherence*, 317.

26. Ibid., 325.

27. Hourani, *Reason and Tradition in Islamic Ethics*, 17.

28. Rahman, *Islam*, 61.

29. Ibid., 106.

30. Ibid.

31. Hourani, *Reason and Tradition in Islamic Ethics*, 133.

32. Rahman, Islam, 106.

33. Rémi Brague, *The Law of God* (Chicago: University of Chicago Press, 2007), 166.

34. Plato, *The Euthyphro*

35. *Kitāb al-Ibāna 'an Usul al-Diyāna*, trans. W. Klein (New Haven, 1940), 47–49. www.sacred-texts.com.

36. Hourani, *Reason and Tradition in Islamic Ethics*, 125.

37. John A. Williams, ed., *Islam: An Anthology of Some Key Texts Across the Entire Spectrum of Islamic Tradition* (Forgotten Books, 1962), 193.

38. Hourani, *Reason and Tradition in Islamic Ethics*, 17.

39. Doull, "Peace with Islam," 15.

40. Algis Valiunas, "Encountering Islam," *Claremont Review of Books,* Spring 2007, 32.

41. Hourani, *Reason and Tradition in Islamic Ethics*, 133.

42. Laurent Murawiec, *The Mind of Jihad* (Cambridge: Cambridge University Press, 2008), 155.

43. Regensburg: University Address cited at http://www.ewtn.com/library/papaldoc/b16bavaria11.htm.

44. Hourani, *Reason and Tradition in Islamic Ethics*, 170.

45. Al-Misri, *Reliance of the Traveller.*

46. Joseph Kenny, *Islamic Monotheism: Principles and Consequence,* 8.

47. Ed Husain, *The Islamist* (London: Penguin Books, 2007), 42.

48. Murawiec, *The Mind of Jihad*, 156.

49. Lawrence Wright, "The Rebellion Within," *New Yorker,* June 2, 2008.

50. Rahman, *Revival and Reform in Islam*, 61.

51. Brague, *The Law of God*, 160.

52. Bassam Tibi, *Islam's Predicament with Modernity* (New York: Routledge: 2009), 244.

53. Ibid., 254.

54. Samir Khalil Samir, "Imams' Ignorance Holds Back Cultural Development of Those Who Want to Live According to Islam," *Asia News* (September 6, 2006), at: http://www.asianews.it/index.php?l=en&art=7143&dos=73&size=A.

55. Rémi Brague, "Are Non-Theocratic Regimes Possible?" *Intercollegiate Review* (Spring, 2006), 11.

56. Goldziher, *Introduction to Islamic Theology and Law*, 16.

57. Hourani, *Reason and Tradition in Islamic Ethics*, 33.

58. Ibid., 140 and 156.

59. Ibid., 156.

60. Al-Ghazali, *The Incoherence of the Philosophers.*

61. Hourani, *Reason and Tradition in Islamic Ethics*, 144.

62. Gairdner, *The Rebuke of Islam*, 58.

63. Ibid. Quotation from *Al Hadis, Mishkat-ul-Masabih*, trans. al-Haj Maulana Fazlul Karim (New Delhi, India, Islamic Book Service, 1998), Vol. 3, ch. xxxii, 454w, 117–18.

64. Sir William Muir, *Corân* (London: Society for Promoting Christian Knowledge, 1854), 55–56, at www.muhammadanism.org, September, 2006.

65. Hourani, *Reason and Tradition in Islamic Ethics*, 173 (*Fisal*, 3:98 and 105).

66. Ibid., 174 (*Fisal*, 3:92).

67. Shehadeh, "The Predicament of Islamic Monotheism," 149.

68. Jaki, *Science and Creation*, 214; Maimonides, *Guide for the Perplexed*, Part 1, ch. 73, 128.

69. Doull, "Peace with Islam," 11.

70. Ibid. (Hegel, "Arabic Philosophy" in *Lectures on the History of Philosophy* (ed. Brown), 38–39.)

71. Oswald Spengler, *The Decline of the West*, trans. Arthur Helps (Oxford: Oxford University Press, 1991).

72. Shehadeh, "The Predicament of Islamic Monotheism," 149.

73. Fakhry, *Rationality in Islamic Philosophy*, 207–8.

74. Duncan Macdonald, *Aspects of Islam*, 136–138.

75. Duncan Macdonald, *Development of Muslim Theology, Jurisprudence and Constitutional Theory.*

76. Al-Shahrastani.

77. Rahman, *Revival and Reform in Islam*, 59.

78. Williams, *Islam*, 192.

79. Averroes, *Faith and Reason in Islam*, 107.

80. Eric L. Ormsby, ed., *Theodicy in Islamic Thought* (Princeton: Princeton University Press, 1984), 40–41.

81. Len Goodman, "Humanism and Islamic Ethics," *Logos*, 1.2 (Spring, 2002), 16.

82. Hourani, *Reason and Tradition in Islamic Ethics*, 12.

83. Rahman, *Revival and Reform in Islam*, 59.

84. Hourani, *Reason and Tradition in Islamic Ethics*, 122.

85. Al-Ghazali, *The Incoherence of the Philosophers*, 177.

86. Plato, *Cratylus.*

87. Rahman, *Islam*, 97.

88. Macdonald, *Development of Muslim Theology, Jurisprudence and Constituional Theory*, 203.

Chapter 4: The Triumph of Ash'arism

1. Watt, *Islamic Philosophy and Theology*, 49.

2. Ibid.

3. Sheikh Abu-Uthman Faisal bin Qazar al-Jassim, *The 'Ash'aris: In the Scales of Ahl us-Sunnah*, 11, at http://www.salafimanhaj.com/pdf/SalafiManhaj_AshariCreed.pdf.

4. M. Saeed Sheikh, *Islamic Philosophy*, 104.

5. Al-Ghazali, *Deliverance from Error*, 3, at http://www.fordham.edu/halsall/basis/1100ghazali-truth.html, from *The Sacred Books and Early Literature of the East*, Charles F. Horne, ed. (New York: Parke, Austin, & Lipscomb, 1917), Vol. VI: *Medieval Arabia*, 99–133. This was a reprint of *The Confessions of al-Ghazali*, trans. Claud Field (London: J. Murray, 1909).

6. Ibid., 9.

7. Ibid., 11.

8. Al-Ghazali, *The Incoherence of the Incoherence.* (Pagination in the printed version only.)

9. Ibid.

10. Al-Ghazali, *Deliverance from Error*, 3.

11. Ibid.

12. Ibid., 4.

13. Ibid.

14. Ibid.

15. Ibid., 4, 5.

16. Ibid., 5.

17. Ibid.

18. Ibid.

19. Ibid.

20. Ibid., 7.

21. Al-Ghazali, *The Incoherence of the Philosophers*.

22. Kenny, *Theological Themes Common to Islam and Christianity*, chap. 11, 4.

23. Al-Ghazali, *Deliverance from Error*, 14.

24. Ibid., 15.

25. Ibid., 16.

26. Ibid., 21.

27. Ibid.

28. Macdonald, *Aspects of Islam*, 201.

29. Rahman, *Revival and Reform in Islam*, 112.

30. Fakhry, *A History of Islamic Philosophy*, 243.

31. M. Saeed Sheikh, "Al-Ghazali," *A History of Muslim Philosophy*, at http://ghazali.org/articles/hmp-4–30.htm#INF.

32. Rahman, *Islam*, 137.

33. Ibid., 142.

34. Goldziher, *Introduction to Islamic Theology and Law*, 151.

35. Ibid., 153.

36. Rahman, *Revival and Reform in Islam*, 88.

37. Eric L. Ormsby, "The Taste of Truth," in *God and Creation: An Ecumenical Symposium*, eds., David B. Burrell and Bernard McGinn (South Bend, IN: University of Notre Dame, 1990), 151, at http://www.ghazali.org/articles/e01.pdf.

38. Al-Ghazali, *Deliverance from Error*, 61, at http://ghazali.org/articles/hmp-4–30.htm#_ftnref107.

39. Ibid., 18, at http://www.fordham.edu/halsall/basis/1100ghazali-truth.html.

40. Ibid.

41. Samir, *111 Questions on Islam*, 210.

42. O'Leary, *Islamic Thought and its Place in History*, 221–22.

43. Macdonald, *Development of Muslim Theology*, ch. 3, 8.

44. Rahman, *Revival and Reform in Islam*, 118–19.

45. Fakhry, *A History of Islamic Philosophy*, 249.

46. Paul Valery, *Mauvaises Pensées et Autres* (1942), *Encarta Book of Quotations* (2000), 951.

47. Macdonald, *Development of Muslim Theology*, ch. 3, 8.

48. W. H. T. Gairdner, *The Muslim Idea of God* (Madras Allahabad Rangoon Colombo, 1925), 13, at muhammadanism.org, August 11, 2003.

49. W. H. T. Gairdner, *God as Triune, Creator, Incarnate, Atoner,* 34–35. Posted at: muhammadanism.org, July 16, 2007.

50. Hans Jonas, *Gnostic Religion: The Message of the Alien God and the Beginnings of Christianity* (Boston: Beacon Press, 1963), 34–35.

51. Al-Ghazali, *The Niche for Lights,* trans. W. H. T. Gairdner (first published as Monograph Vol. XIX by the Royal Asiatic Society, London, 1924)— scanned at sacred-texts.com, October 2001.

52. Ibid., 52.

53. Ibid.

54. Rahman, *Islam,* 144.

55. Goldziher, *Introduction to Islamic Theology and Law,* 153.

56. Rahman, *Revival and Reform in Islam,* 118.

57. Hourani, *Reason and Tradition in Islamic Ethics,* 165–66.

58. Samir, *111 Questions on Islam,* 180.

59. "Ibn Miskawayh,'" in ch. 8, *History of Islamic Philosophy,* Seyyed Hossein Nasr and Leaman Oliver, eds. (New York: Routledge, 2001), 1211.

60. Kaufmann Kohler and Isaac Broyde, "Arabic Philosophy—Its Influence on Judaism," at http://www.jewishencyclopedia.com/view jsp?artid= 1688&letter=A.

61. Brague, *The Law of God,* 166.

62. Tawfik Hamid, "The Development of a Jihadist's Mind," *Current Trends* (April 6, 2007), at www.CurrentTrends.org.

63. George Weigel, *Faith, Reason, and the War against Jihadism* (New York: Doubleday, 2007), 50.

Chapter 5: The Unfortunate Victory of al-Ghazali and the Dehellenization of Islam

1. Hye, "Ash'arism," ch. 11, at http://www.muslimphilosophy.com/hmp/index.html.

2. Seyyed Hossein Nasr, *Islamic Life and Thought* (Albany, NY: State University Press, 1981), 72.

3. Rahman, *Islam,* 117.

4. Cited at http://www.ghazali.org/articles/hmp-4-30.htm, footnote 21.

5. Macdonald, *Development of Muslim Theology, Jurisprudence and Constitutional Thought,* 7.

6. Macdonald, *Aspects of Islam,* 148–149.

7. Averroes, *The Book of the Decisive Treatise,* section 10. Also cited by Kleven, "For Truth Does Not Oppose Truth," 9.

8. Hourani, *Reason and Tradition in Islamic Ethics*, 275.

9. Kenny, *Philosophy of the Muslim World*, 145.

10. Joel Kraemer, "Humanism in the Renaissance of Islam," *Journal of the American Oriental Society*, 104.1 (1984): 143.

11. Ibid., see footnote 37.

12. Hoodbhoy, *Islam and Science*, 120.

13. Rahman, *Revival and Reform in Islam*, 60.

14. G. F. Haddad, "Al Fakhr al-Razi," at http://www.sunnah.org/history/Scholars/al_fakhr_al_razi.htm.

15. Hoodbhoy, *Islam and Science*, 103.

16. Fakhry, *A History of Islamic Philosophy*, 323.

17. Serajul Haque, "Ibn Taimiyah," in Sharif, *A History of Muslim Philosophy*, ch. 41, 799, at http://www.muslimphilosophy.com/hmp/index.html.

18. Rahman, *Islam*, 108.

19. Ibid., 187.

20. MEMRI, at http://memri.org/bin/articles.cgi?Page=archives&Area=sd&ID=SP206708.

21. Ibrahim al-Buleihi, *Ukkaz*, April 23, 2009, at http://www.elaph.com/Web/NewsPapers/2009/4/433121.htm.

22. Bassam Tibi, *The Challenge of Fundamentalism* (Berkeley: University of California Press, 1998), 71.

23. Ibid.

24. Tarek Heggy, at, www.alwaref.org/en/islamic-culture/157-rise-militant-islam, May 6, 2009.

25. Rahman, *Islam*, 110.

Chapter 6: Decline and Consequences

1. Tarek Heggy, "The Prisons of the Arab Mind," posted at http://www.jamaliya.com/new/show.php?sub=5483, August 14, 2009.

2. Rahman, *Islam*, 123.

3. Martin, *Defenders of Reason in Islam*, 192.

4. Hassan Hanafi, "The Middle East, in Whose World?" unedited paper as given at the Oslo conference "The Middle East in a Globalized World," August 13–16, 1998, at http://www.hf.uib.no/smi/pao/hanafi.html.

5. Rahman, *Islam*, 99.

6. Hourani, *Reason and Tradition in Islamic Ethics*, 123.

7. Patai, *The Arab Mind*, 172.

8. Martin Kramer, "Politics and the Prophet," *The New Republic*, at http://www.geocities.com/martinkramerorg/PoliticsandProphet.htm.

9. *2010 Freedom House Survey* at: http://www.freedomhouse.org/uploads/

fiw10/FIW_2010_Overview_Essay.pdf.

10. Quoted by Martin Kramer, "Democracy Promotion in the Middle East: Time for a Plan B," December 5, 2006, at the Washington Institute for Near East Policy, at, www.washingtoninstitute.org/templateC07.php?CID=315.

11. Tibi, *The Challenge of Fundamentalism*, 138.

12. David Pryce-Jones, *The Closed Circle* (New York: Harper Perennial, 1991), 18.

13. Michael Hirsh, "Misreading Islam," *Washington Monthly*, November 19, 2004.

14. MEMRI, at http://memri.org/bin/articles.cgi?Page=archives&Area=sd&ID=SP112106.

15. MEMRI, at http://www.memri.org/bin/articles.cgi?Page=countries&Area=northafrica&ID=SP181008.

16. Abdolkarim Soroush, on receipt of the Erasmus Prize in 2004, posted at http://www.drsoroush.com/PDF/E-CMB-20041113-%20Rationalist_Traditions_in_Islam-Soroush_in_Heidelberg.pdf.

17. Transcript of TV interview with Dr. Soroush by Dariush Sajjadi, broadcast on Homa TV on March 9, 2006, at http://www.drsoroush.com/English/Interviews/E-INT-HomaTV.html.

18. *Qur'an* (Riyadh: Abulqasim Publishing House, 1997), 346.

19. Ruthven, *Islam in the World*, 13.

20. Arun Shourie, "To Paradise—Via the Jehad in Kashmir!" at http://arunshourie.voiceofdharma.com/print/19980820.htm.

21. UNDP, Arab Human Development Report 2003 (New York: United Nations, 2003), 152.

22. UNDP, Arab Human Development Report 2009 (New York: United Nations, 2009), 5.

23. *The Cairo Declaration on Human Rights in Islam*, at http://www.religlaw.org/interdocs/docs/cairohrislam1990.htm.

24. Laurent Murawiec, *Princes of Darkness* (Lanham, MD: Rowman & Littlefield, 2005), 56.

25. "Libyan Intellectual Dr. Muhammad al-Houni: The Arabs Must Choose Between Western Civilization and the Legacy of the Middle Ages," Middle East Media Research Institute *Inquiry and Analysis* No. 240, September 12, 2005, at http://www.memri.org/bin/articles.cgi?Area=ia&ID=IA24005&Page=archives.

26. Abu Hamza, "Are They the People of the Book? Questions and Answers," *Al-Jihaad*, no. 2, at http://www.shareeah.com/Eng/aj/aj2.html.

27. MEMRI, at http://memri.org/bin/articles.cgi?Page=archives&Area=sd&ID=SP146007#_ednref2.

28. MEMRI, at http://www.memri.org/bin/articles.cgi?Page=countries&Area=northafrica&ID=SP181008.

29. Ali Allawi, *The Crisis of Islamic Civilization* (New Haven: Yale University Press, 2009), 11.

30. Lawrence Freedman, *The Transformation of Strategic Affairs* (New York: Routledge for the International Institute for Strategic Studies, 2006), 23.

31. Patai, *The Arab Mind*, 22.

32. Fatima Mernissi, *Islam and Democracy* (Cambridge, MA: Perseus Books, 1992), 34–37.

33. Hourani, *Reason and Tradition in Islamic Ethics*, 275.

34. Samir Khalil Samir, "Islam Needs Renewal from Within, Not Withdrawal into Itself, to Overcome its Crisis," *Asia News*, March 8, 2007, 5, at http://www.asianews.it/index.php?l =en&art=7164&dos&size=A.

35. Hirsh, "Misreading Islam."

36. Muhammad Khair, "Hegel and Islam," *The Philosopher* Vol. LXXXX, No. 2, at http://www.the-philosopher.co.uk/hegel&islam.htm.

37. MEMRI, at http://www.memritv.org/clip/en/1700.htm.

38. Patai, *The Arab Mind*, 51.

39. Dennis Overbye, "How Islam Won, and Lost, the Lead in Science," *New York Times,* October 10, 2001, at http://www.nytimes.com/2001/10/30/science/social/30ISLA.html?pagewanted=4.

40. "A Comprehensive Interview with Syrian Philosopher Sadik Jalal al-'Azm," Middle East Media Research Institute *Special Dispatch* No. 1913, May 1, 2008, at http://www.memri.org/bin/articles.cgi?Page=archives&Area=sd&ID=SP191308.

41. Husain, *The Islamist*, 101.

42. Alia Ibrahim, "A Divine Seal of Approval," *Washington Post*, November 19, 2006.

43. Pervez Hoodbhoy, "Between Imperialism and Islamism," *Himal Southasian* (October–November 2007).

44. MEMRI, at http://www.memri.org/bin/articles.cgi?Page=countries&Area=northafrica&ID=SP181008.

45. Stephen Schwartz, "Allah and the Tsunami," *Front Page Magazine,* January 13, 2005, at http://www.frontpagemag.com/readArticle.aspx?ARTID=9941.

46. "Senior Kuwaiti Official: 'Katrina Is a Wind of Torment and Evil from Allah Sent to This American Empire,'" Middle East Media Research Institute *Special Dispatch* No. 977, September 2, 2005, at http://memri.org/bin/articles.cgi?Page=archives&Area=sd&ID=SP97705.

47. Pervez Hoodbhoy, "Science and the Islamic World: The Quest for Rapprochement" in *Physics Today* (August, 2007).

48. Ibid.

49. UNDP, Arab Human Development Report 2003, op. cit., 61.

50. Yaroslav Trofimov, "Crisis Rocks Mideast Power Balance," *Wall Street Journal,* June 24, 2009, A8.

51. Sadanand Dhume, *My Friend the Fanatic* (New York: Skyhorse Publishing, 2009), 270.

52. MEMRI, at http://www.memri.org/bin/latestnews cgi?ID=SD252909.

53. Shankar Vedantam, "Persistence of Myths Could Alter Public Policy Approach," *Washington Post*, September 3, 2007 at http://www.washington-post.com/wp-dyn/content/article/2007/09/03/AR200709000933-pf.html

54. Olivier Guitta, "The Islamization of Morocco," in *The Weekly Standard*, Volume 12, Issue 3, October 2, 2006.

55. Video and text available at http://www.memri.org/report/en/0/0/0/0/0/0/3168.htm. Accessed December 15, 2009.

56. For a list of videos and news stories proclaiming various September 11 conspiracy theories, please visit http://www.memri.org/report/en/0/0/0/0/0/0/1491.htm. Accessed December 15, 2009.

57. Video and text available at http://www.memri.org/report/en/0/0/0/0/0/0/3291.htm. Accessed December 15, 2009.

58. Text available at http://www.memri.org/report/en/0/0/0/0/0/0/3184.htm. Accessed December 15, 2009.

59. Full text available at http://www.memri.org/report/en/0/0/0/0/0/0/2953.htm. Accessed December 15, 2009.

60. Text available at http://www.memri.org/report/en/0/0/0/0/0/0/2888.htm. Accessed December 15, 2009.

61. Text available at http://www.memri.org/report/en/0/0/0/0/0/0/2723.htm. Accessed December 15, 2009.

62. Full text available at http://www.memri.org/report/en/0/0/0/0/0/0/2030.htm. Accessed December 15, 2009.

63. http://memri.netstrategies.com/report/en/2974.htm.

64. Text available at http://www.memri.org/report/en/0/0/0/0/0/0/1620.htm. Accessed December 15, 2009.

65. http://www.memritv.org/clip/en/1850.htm and http://www.memritv.org/clip_transcript/en/1850.htm.

66. Text available at http://www.memri.org/report/en/0/0/0/0/0/0/1685.htm. Accessed December 15, 2009.

67. Video is available at http://www.memritv.org/clip/en/1104.htm. Accessed December 15, 2009.

68. http://www.memritv.org/Transcript.asp?P1=695.

69. There are many video clips available at http://memritv.org. You will be required to sign up for the service, but you do not have to pay a fee. You can also find hundreds of special dispatches or news stories here: http://www.memri.org/more_reports/en/latest/6.htm.

Chapter 7: The Wreckage: Muslim Testimonials

1. Mansoor Moaddel and Kamran Talattof, eds., *Modernist and Fundamentalist Debates in Islam: A Reader* (New York: Palgrave Macmillan, 2002), 27.

2. MEMRI, at http://memri.org/bin/articles.cgi?Page=archives&Area=sd &ID=SP139306.

3. MEMRI, at http://memri.org/bin/articles.cgi?Page=archives&Area=ia &ID=IA31507.

4. Sadik Jalal al-'Azm, MEMRI, at http://www.memri.org/bin/articles.cgi? Page=archives&Area=sd&ID=SP191308.

5. Rashid Shaz, "Tension in the Muslim Mind," posted at rashidshaz.com/ articles/Reinventing_the_Muslim_Mind.htm.

6. Tibi, *The Challenge of Fundamentalism*, 105.

7. Ibid., 106.

8. UNDP Arab Human Development Report 2003, 114, at http://hdr.undp. org/en/reports/regionalreports/arabstates/arab_states_2003_en.pdf.

9. Ibid., 118.

10. Hoodbhoy, "Science and the Islamic World," 49.

11. Ibid., 71.

12. Ibid., 49.

13. Kenny, *Philosophy of the Muslim World*, 6.

14. UNDP Arab Human Development Report 2002, 85.

15. Ibid., 4.

16. Ibid., 3.

17. Ibid., 65.

18. John B. Taylor, "The Private Sector's Role in Promoting Economic Growth in the Broader Middle East and North Africa" (US Treasury Department Press Release: Davos), January 28, 2005, JS-2216.

19. *Arab Human Knowledge Report 2009*, (UNDP and the Muhammad bin Rashid Al Maktoum Foundation: Dubai, 2009), 99.

20. Ibid., 27.

21. UNDP, Arab Human Development Report 2003, 77.

22. Ibid.

23. Ibid., 67.

24. Ibid., 138.

25. Ibid., 138.

26. MEMRI, at http://memri.org/bin/articles.cgi?Page=archives&Area=s d&ID=SP191308.

27. Sheikh Muhammad bin Rashid al Maktoum, "Education vs. Extremism," *Wall Street Journal*, June 3, 2009, A15.

28. Allawi, *The Crisis of Islamic Civilization*, 233.

29. Bat Yeor, *The Decline of Eastern Christianity under Islam* (Madison, NJ: Fairleigh Dickinson University Press, 1996), 296.

30. Ahmad Kazmi, quoted in Heidi Kingstone, "Foreign Bodies," *Jerusalem Report*, October 30, 2006, 24.

31. "Back in 1975, the director of Dar al Ifta' in Beirut, the highest Sunni authority in the country, wrote in the daily *as Safir* that 'Muslims should only be ruled by Muslims.'" From Walid Phares, *The War of Ideas* (New York: Palgrave Macmillan, 2007), 78.

32. Hoodbhoy, *Islam and Science*, 60.

33. Ibid., 61.

34. Pryce-Jones, *The Closed Circle*, 88.

35. Martin, *Defenders of Reason in Islam*, 130.

36. Ibid., 131.

37. Rahman, *Islam and Modernity*, 64.

38. Martin, *Defenders of Reason in Islam*, 132.

39. Ruthven, *Islam in the World*, 303.

40. Albert Hourani, *Arabic Thought in the Liberal Age 1798-1939* (London: Oxford University Press, 1962), 140–41.

41. Ibid.

42. Mortimer, *Faith and Power: The Politics of Islam*, 239.

43. Martin, *Defenders of Reason in Islam*, 136.

44. Hoodbhoy, *Islam and Science*, 56.

45. Ibid.

46. Rahman, *Islam*, 218.

47. Hoodbhoy, *Islam and Science*, 59.

48. See al-Afghani's scathing "Commentary on the Commentator," a denunciation of Ahmed Khan for weakening the faith of Muslims, from *An Islamic Response to Imperialism; Political and Religious Writings of Sayyid Jamal ad-Din "al-Afghani,"* edited and translated by Nikki R. Keddie (Berkeley: University of California Press, 1968), 123–29.

49. Tibi, *Islam's Predicament with Modernity*, 261.

50. Pryce-Jones, *The Closed Circle*, 87.

Chapter 8: The Sources of Islamism

1. Fawaz A. Gerges, *Journey of the Jihadist* (New York: Harcourt Books, 2007), 169.

2. Hilaire Belloc, *The Great Heresies* (Rockford, IL: Tan Books and Publishers, 1991), 73.

3. Ibid., 77.

4. Paul Berman, *Terror and Liberalism* (New York: Norton, 2004), 86.

5. Paul Eidelberg, *Beyond Détente* (La Salle, IL: Sherwood Sugden, 1977), 65.

6. Bernard Lewis, *The Middle East* (New York: Touchstone, 1995), 371.

7. Pryce-Jones, *The Closed Circle*, 194.

8. Sayeed Abdul A'la Maududi, *Jihad in Islam* (Lahore, Pakistan: 7th Edition, December 2001), 8.

9. Ibid., 9.

10. John C. Zimmerman, "Sayyid Qutb's Influence on the 11 September Attacks," *Terrorism and Political Violence*, Vol. 16, No. 2 (Summer 2004) 233.

11. Murawiec, *The Mind of Jihad*.

12. Zimmerman, "Sayyid Qutb's Influence on the 11 September Attacks," 223.

13. Sayyid Qutb, *Milestones* (Cedar Rapids, IA: The Mother of Mosque Foundation), 56.

14. Jessica Stern, *Terror in the Name of God: Why Religious Militants Kill* (New York: Harper Perennial, 2004), 281.

15. Peter Wonacott and Geeta Anand, "Sole Captured Suspect Offers Grim Insights into Massacre," *The Wall Street Journal*, December 4, 2008, at http://online.wsj.com/article/SB122834446748477265.html.

16. MEMRI, at http://memri.org/bin/articles.cgi?Page=archives&Area=iia&ID=IA31507.

17. Zimmerman, "Sayyid Qutb's Influence on the 11 September Attacks," 223.

18. Mawlana Maududi, *Jihad in Islam*, at http://www.islamistwatch.org/texts/maududi/maududi.html.

19. Sayyid Qutb, *Social Justice in Islam*, revised edition, translated by John B. Hardie, revised and introduced by Hamid Algar (Oneonta, NY: Islamic Publications International, 2000), 26.

20. Qutb, *Milestones*, 91. (A slightly different translation from an unpublished paper by Stephen Ulph is used here rather than the one cited because of its added clarity.)

21. Ibid.

22. Qutb, *Milestones*, 131.

23. Sayyid Qutb, *Islam and Universal Peace* (Plainfield, IN: American Trust Publications, 1993), 27.

24. Malise Ruthven, *A Fury for God* (London: Granata Books, 2002), 71.

25. Sheikh Abul Ala Maududi, *Islamic Law and Constitution* (Chicago: Kazi Publications, Inc., 1955), 262.

26. Emmanuel Sivan, *Radical Islam: Medieval Theology and Modern Politics* (New Haven: Yale University Press, 1990), 73.

27. Sayyid Qutb, *Milestones*, trans. S. Badrul Hasan (Karachi, Pakistan: International Islamic Publishers, 1981), 112.

28. Murawiec, *The Mind of Jihad*, 36.

29. V. I. Lenin, "Defeat of One's Own Government in Imperialist War," 1915, *Selected Works* (New York: International Publishers, 1945), vol. 5, 147.

30. Raymond Ibrahim, "Osama bin Laden as Robin Hood?" *American Thinker*, September 11, 2008, at http://www.americanthinker.com/2008/09/osama_bin_laden_as_robin_hood.html.

31. Sarah Kershaw, "The Terrorist Mind: An Update," *New York Times*, January 10, 2010, WK1.

32. Yussuf al-Ayyeri, *The Future of Iraq and the Arabian Peninsula After the Fall of Baghdad* (New York and London: Centre for Islamic Research and Studies, 2003). See also Amir Taheri, "Al-Qaeda's Agenda in Iraq," *New York Post*, online edition, September 4, 2003, at http://www.magitsurplus.com/PDF%20Files/Soapbox/AQ_agenda.pdf.

33. Qutb, *Milestones*.

34. Steven Brooke, "The Preacher and the Jihadi," *Current Trends in Islamist Ideology*, Vol. 3, (Center for Islam, Democracy, and the Future of the Muslim World), 2.

35. MEMRI, at http://memri.org/bin/articles.cgi?Page=archives&Area=sd&ID=SP128506.

36. "'Why We Fight America': Al-Qa'ida Spokesman Explains September 11 and Declares Intentions to Kill 4 Million Americans with Weapons of Mass Destruction," Middle East Media Research Institute *Special Dispatch* No. 388, June 12, 2002, at http://www.memri.org/bin/articles.cgi?ID=sp38802.

37. Andrew C. McCarthy, "Free Speech for Terrorists?" *Commentary*, March 2005, 1.

38. Sheikh Muhammad Hussein Fadlallah at http://phaed02000.com/Terrorism.html. See also Walid Phares, *Future Jihad*.

39. Mark Steyn, "Jihad Goes Mainstream," *National Review*, August 30, 2009, at http://www.steynonline.com/content/view/2389/111/.

40. BBC News, "Interview with Mullah Omar," November 15, 2001, at http://news.bbc.co.uk/2/hi/south_asia/1657368.stm.

41. Ruthven, *A Fury for God*, 104.

42. Abdullah Azzam, *Join the Caravan* (Azzam Publications, 2001) 9.

43. "Al-Qaeda Deputy Ayman al-Zawahiri Claims Responsibility for the London Bombings, Discusses Elections in Afghanistan, and Declares: 'Reform Can Only Take Place Through Jihad,'" Middle East Media Research Institute *Special Dispatch* no. 989, September 20, 2005, at http://memri.org/bin/articles.cgi?Page=subjects&Area=jihad&ID=SP98905.

44. Gerges, *Journey of the Jihadist*, 112.

45. Interview with Muhammad Khan, *Pakistan*, January 1998.

46. MEMRI, at http://memri.org/bin/articles.cgi?Page=archives&Area=s d&ID=SP128506.

47. *Military Studies in the Jihad Against the Tyrants/The Al-Qaeda Training Manual*, Jerrold M. Post, ed., preface by Ambassador Paul Bremer (Maxwell Air Force Base, AL: USAF Counterproliferation Center, 2004), 13.

48. Roger Scruton, *The West and the Rest* (Wilmington, DE: ISI Books, 2002), 119.

49. Murawiec, *The Mind of Jihad*, 46.

50. Joseph Ratzinger, *Milestones: Memoirs 1927–1977* (San Francisco: Ignatius Press, 1998), 137.

51. Ruthven, *A Fury for God*, 209.

52. Murawiec, *The Mind of Jihad*, 42.

53. Mernissi, *Islam and Democracy*, 27.

54. Martin, *Defenders of Reason in Islam*, 158.

55. MEMRI, at http://memri.org/bin/articles.cgi?Page=archives&Area=ia &ID=IA22205.

56. Latif Lakhdar, "Moving from Salafi to Rationalist Education," *Middle East Review of International Affairs*, Vol. 9, No. 1 (March 2005), 30.

57. Ruthven, *Islam in the World*, 380.

58. Martin, *Defenders of Reason in Islam*, 216.

59. Nicholas D. Kristof, "Islam, Virgins and Grapes," *New York Times*, April 22, 2009, A27.

60. Samir Khalil Samir, "Church-Islam Dialogue," *Asia News*, January 17, 2007, 3, at http://www.asianews.it/view4print.php?1=en&art+8242.

61. Tibi, *The Challenge of Fundamentalism*, 31.

62. David J. Rusin, "Why Islamists Accuse Moderate Muslims of Apostasy," *Islamist Watch*, September 30, 2009.

Chapter 9: The Crisis

1. Mehran Kamrava, ed., *The New Voices of Islam* (Los Angeles: University of California Press, 2006), 224.

2. Hoodbhoy, *Islam and Science*, 136.

3. Samir Khalil Samir, "Islamic Terrorism: A Result of What Is Being Taught at Madrassas," *Asia News*, March 8, 2007, 4, at http://www.asianews.it/index.php?=en&aart=4071.

4. Rahman, *Islam*, 256.

5. Tony Corn, "World War IV as Fourth-Generation Warfare," *Policy Review*, January 2006, II.

6. Hoodbhoy, *Islam and Science*, 135.

7. Abdelwahab Meddeb, *The Malady of Islam* (New York: Basic Books, 2003), 104.

8. Ibid., 105.

9. Thomas K. Grosse, "The War Within Islam," *U.S. News and World Report*, March 12, 2009.

10. Dhume, *My Friend the Fanatic*, 124.

11. Abdurrahman Wahid, "Right Islam vs. Wrong Islam," *Wall Street Journal*, December 30, 2005, A16, at http://www.opinionjournal.com/extra/?id=110007743.

12. Sandro Magister, "Faith by Numbers: When Ratzinger Puts on Galileo's Robes," *Express Online*, January 9, 2009, at www.chiesa.expressonline.it.

13. Hourani, *Reason and Tradition in Islamic Ethics*, 276.

14. I am indebted to Father James Schall for this formulation.

15. MEMRI, at http://memri.org/bin/articles.cgi?Page=archives&Area=ia&ID=IA24005.

16. Tibi, *Islam's Predicament with Modernity*, 262.

Further Reading

Averroes. *The Book of the Decisive Treatise*, translated by Charles E. Butterworth (Provo, UT: Brigham Young University, 2001).

Averroes. *Faith and Reason in Islam: Averroes' Exposition of Religious Arguments*, translated by Ibrahim Najjar (Oxford: Oneworld Publications, 2001.

Averroes. *The Incoherence of the Incoherence*, translated by Simon Van Den Bergh, (London, E. J. W. Gibb Memorial Series, 2008).

Cox, Caroline and John Marks. *The West, Islam and Islamism*, (Civitas, London: Civitas, 2006).

Fakhry, Majid. *A History of Islamic Philosophy* (New York: Columbia University Press, 1970 and 1983).

Al-Ghazali. *The Incoherence of the Philosophers*, translated by Michael E. Marmura (Provo, UT: Brigham University Press, 1997).

Goldziher, Ignaz. *Introduction to Islamic Theology and Law* (Princeton: Princeton University Press, 1981).

Hoodbhoy, Pervez. Islam and Science (London: Zed Books, 1991).

Hourani, Albert. *A History of the Arab Peoples* (New York: Warner Books, 1992).

Hourani, George. *Reason and Tradition in Islamic Ethics* (Cambridge: Cambridge University Press, 1985).

Ibrahim, Raymond. *The Al-Qaeda Reader* (New York: Broadway Books, 2007).

Jaki, Stanley. *Jesus, Islam, Science* (Pickney, MI: Real View Books, 2001).

Jaki, Stanley. *Science and Creation,* (Edinburgh: Scottish Academic Press, 1986).

Kenny, Joseph. *Theological Themes Common to Islam and Christianity* (Lagos, Nigeria: Dominican Publications, 1997).

Macdonald, Duncan B. *Aspects of Islam* (New York: Macmillan Company, 1911).

Macdonald, Duncan B. *Development of Muslim Theology, Jurisprudence and Constitutional Theory* (Beirut Khayats; 1st edition, January, 1, 1965: paperback, Macdonald Press, March 15, 2007).

Meddeb, Abdelwahab. *The Malady of Islam* (New York: Basic Books, 2003).

Middle East Media Research Institute (MEMRI). at http://memri.org

Mernissi, Fatima. *Islam and Democracy* (Cambridge, MA: Perseus Books, 1992).

Murawiec, Laurent. *The Mind of Jihad* (Cambridge: Cambridge University Press, 2008).

Patai, Raphael. *The Arab Mind* (New York: Hatherleigh Press, 2002).

Martin, Richard C. and Mark R. Woodward. *Defenders of Reason in Islam* (Oxford: Oneworld Publications, 1997).

Rahman, Fazlur. *Islam* (Chicago: University of Chicago Press, 1979, 2002).

Rahman, Fazlur. *Islam and Modernity* (Chicago: University of Chicago Press, 1982).

Rahman, Fazlur. *Revival and Reform in Islam* (Oxford: Oneworld Publications, 2000).

Ruthven, Malise. *A Fury for God* (London: Granta Books, 2002).

Ruthven, Malise. *Islam in the World* (New York: Oxford University Press, 1984).

Samir Khalil Samir. *111 Questions on Islam* (San Francisco: Ignatius Press, 2008).

Schall, James. *The Regensburg Lecture* (South Bend, IN: St. Augustine's Press, 2007).

Scruton, Roger. *The West and the Rest* (Wilmington, DE: ISI Books, 2002).

Shehadeh, Imad N. "The Predicament of Islamic Monotheism," *Biblotheca Sacra* 161(April–June 2004).

Sivan, Emmanuel. *Radical Islam: Medieval Theology and Modern Politics*, (New Haven: Yale University Press, 1990).

Sookhdeo, Patrick. *Global Jihad* (McLean, VA: Isaac Publishing, 2007).

Tibi, Bassam. *The Challenge of Fundamentalism* (Berkeley: University of California Press, 1998).

Tibi, Bassam. *Islam's Predicament with Modernity* (New York: Routledge, 2009).

Acknowledgments

I first embarked on the subject of this book in a lecture in Slovenia and then a briefing paper for the Centre for Research into Post-Communist Economies (London). I am particularly indebted to its president, Ljubo Sirc, and its executive director, Lisl Biggs-Davison, for their encouragement and support.

I am especially grateful for the generous support of the Earhart Foundation; its president, Ingrid A. Gregg; and its board of directors in granting me a research fellowship for this book.

Many years ago, my interest in the subject of Islam was sparked by the writings of, and my discussions with, the late Father Stanley Jaki, physicist and theologian, especially by his book *Science and Creation*, in which he gave convincing answers as to why, after making certain advances, science was stillborn in the Islamic world.

I have particularly benefited from interchanges with my colleagues when working in the Near East/South Asia section of International Security Affairs in the Office of the Secretary of Defense. The same is true of my teaching time at the National Defense University, where conversations with Dr. Thomas Blau, Dr. Joe DeSutter, David Belt, and others were very fruitful, as most particularly were the exchanges with my Muslim students from the Middle East and South Asia.

Regarding issues of general philosophical and theological import, as well as matters directly related to Islam, I have benefited for many years from the wisdom, in both conversation and reading, of Father James Schall at Georgetown University.

I am also indebted to my friend Angelo Codevilla (for this and many other things), Richard Bastien, Stephen Ulph, and Roger Scruton for having read the manuscript and given their sage advice, and to Patrick Poole and Jennifer Bryson for guiding me to some invaluable materials. For their help, I owe special thanks to Yigal Carmon, Steven Stalinksy, Menahem Milson, and Daniel Lav from the Middle East Media Research Institute, and to Patrick Sookhdeo from the Westminster Institute.

I owe special thanks to Jed Donahue, Christian Tappe, Chris Michalski, and Jennifer Fox at ISI Books for their invaluable help in bringing this work to fruition.

My wife, Blanca, is my best editor. I alone, of course, am responsible for any errors contained in this work. I also thank my children, Michael, Catherine, Matthew, and Teresa, for their patience. They are well-informed on the frustrations of attempting to write a book about ninth-century Muslim theology.

Index